BODY LANGUAGE PSYCHOLOGY AND PERSUASION TECHNIQUES

The Ultimate Guide to all the Secrets to Understand and Influence People Through Body Language. Discover the Power of Gestures for Your Daily Life

STEVE BROOKS

THIS BOOK INCLUDES

BOOK 1:

BODY LANGUAGE PSYCHOLOGY
THE ULTIMATE GUIDE TO ANALYZE AND UNDERSTAND
PEOPLE THANKS TO BEHAVIORAL PSYCHOLOGY. LEARN
HOW TO READ BODY LANGUAGE AND DISCOVER ALL ITS
SECRETS

BOOK 2:

PERSUASION TECHNIQUES
NLP FOR BEGINNERS. CONTROL PEOPLE'S MINDS AND
INFLUENCE THEM THROUGH DARK PSYCHOLOGY,
EMOTIONAL MANIPULATION, AND PERSUASION WITH A
FOCUS ON HYPNOTHERAPY AND MIND GAMES

BODY LANGUAGE PSYCHOLOGY

Table of Contents

Introduction 12

Chapter 1: Nonverbal Communication 14

Chapter 2: How To Improve Nonverbal Communication 20

Chapter 3: What Is Body Language? 28

Chapter 4: The Origin Of Body Language 33

Chapter 5: The Study Of Body Language.................................... 38

Chapter 6: The Psychology Behind Body Language 44

Chapter 7: Neuro-Linguistic Programming And Non-Verbal
Communication 50

Chapter 8: Behaviorism.. 56

Chapter 9: Learning And Types Conditioning 60

Chapter 10: Emotional Psychology 66

Chapter 11: Mind Control 72

Chapter 12: Body Language And Personality 78

Chapter 13: Personality Type 84

Chapter 14: Analyzing People Through Body Language............. 92

Chapter 15: Understanding The Self–What Does My Behavior
Display? 96

Chapter 16: Mirroring 100

Chapter 17: How To Read People's Body Language 106

Chapter 18: Basic Techniques To Easily Improve Your Body Language 112

Chapter 19: Body Language Applications 116

Chapter 20: How To Control Your Body Language 124

Chapter 21: Interpretation Of Some Of The Most Common Gesture When Greeting With Hands 130

Chapter 22: Lie Detection And Deception 136

Chapter 23: How To Spot The Liars 142

Chapter 24: How Brainwashing Works 148

Chapter 25: Body Posture 154

Chapter 26: Interpret Body Language And Decipher Different Gestures 160

Chapter 27: Body Language Codes 166

Chapter 28: Facial Expressions 172

Chapter 29: Microexpression 178

Chapter 30: Micro-Expressions And Body Language Signs 184

Conclusion 188

PERSUASION TECHNIQUES

Table of Contents

Introduction 194

Chapter 1: What Is Dark Psychology? 196

Chapter 2: Dark Traits Psychology 202

Chapter 3: How To Use Dark Psychology In Your Life 208

Chapter 4: Differences Between Persuasion And Manipulation 212

Chapter 5: What Is The Persuasion.. 216

Chapter 6: History Of Persuasion 222

Chapter 7: Principles Of Persuasion... 226

Chapter 8: Subliminal Persuasion 232

Chapter 9: Persuasion Techniques 238

Chapter 10: Dark Persuasion And Personality............................ 244

Chapter 11: What Is Manipulation?... 250

Chapter 12: Manipulation Techniques....................................... 256

Chapter 13: What Is Emotional Manipulation? 262

Chapter 14: Psychological Manipulation Techniques 268

Chapter 15: Dark Manipulation 276

Chapter 16: The Qualities Of A Manipulative Person 280

Chapter 17: Types Of Manipulation... 286

Chapter 18: Manipulation Techniques, Manipulation Tactics And Schemes 290

Chapter 19: Body Language And How It Works With Manipulation **296**

Chapter 20: Neuro-Linguistic Programming And Manipulation **300**

Chapter 21: Verbal And Non-Verbal Communication **306**

Chapter 22: Hypnosis **312**

Chapter 23: Brainwashing **318**

Chapter 24: Deception **322**

Chapter 25: Reverse Psychology... **328**

Chapter 26: Mind Control And Mind Games **334**

Chapter 27: Character Traits Of Manipulators **340**

Chapter 28: The Signs Of A Manipulative Person And How To Spot Them. **346**

Chapter 29: Favorite Victims Of Manipulation **350**

Chapter 30: How To Protect Yourself Against Emotional Predator **354**

Conclusion **360**

BODY LANGUAGE PSYCHOLOGY

the ultimate guide to analyze and understand people thanks to Behavioral psychology. learn how to read body language and discover all its secrets

STEVE BROOKS

Introduction

Our body language is the way we speak with our outside world—and the more significant part of us don't understand, we are doing it! Body language phenomenally affects the center of who you are as an individual. It impacts our posture and physiological wellbeing, yet it can likewise change our psychological viewpoint, our impression of the world and others' perception of us.

We utilize our body language to communicate, our musings, thoughts, feelings; we synchronize body developments to the words that we express. We impart purposefully through activities like shrugging our shoulders or applauding just as through inadvertent correspondence like twisting in on ourselves or guiding our feet an alternate way toward the individual we are discussing with. Before spoken language was made, our body language was the primary technique for correspondence. Our body is our major method to speak with life!

Our body language is the way that we interface with our outside world, yet it is likewise a way that we associate with ourselves. How would you treat yourself? Do you slouch over when you walk, or do you walk tall and satisfied? It is true to say that you are thankful for each development that your body makes for you?

Most likely not; we regularly underestimate our body; we frequently decide to condemn it. Body language can impact our physical body and posture. However, it can likewise change how we are feeling. Having a great attitude can affect misery and causes us to keep up more elevated levels of confidence and energy when we are confronted with pressure.

An up and coming field of psychology, known as installed comprehension, asserts that the association between our body and our general surroundings doesn't merely impact us. However, we are personally woven into the way that we think. Studies in this field show that the individuals who are sitting in a hard seat are less inclined to bargain than those sitting in a delicate chair, and those holding warm beverages saw others as more mindful and liberal than those holding cold drinks. This examination shows that body language is a two-way road prompting both the outside and inward world.

Body language likely isn't the first sport you'd think to look when you are experiencing a low state of mind, however investigating our body language can reveal to us how we are truly feeling. Our body language has an immediate connection to our temperament, similarly that our mindset influences our posture.

Simple ways you can fix your posture to adjust your state of mind:

- Smile when you are having a terrible day!
- Unfold your arms when you feel anxious and permit yourself to be available to circumstances
- Turning the palms of your hands forward when you walk will urge the shoulders to unwind back as opposed to moving advances
- Power present before pressure instigating situations like prospective employee meet-ups

Body language signs when someone hides something from you

Untrustworthiness. It happens in many connections–and a great deal of the time, it accomplishes more mischief than anything. It's once in a while ever astute to keep insider facts from your accomplice in a relationship. You never need to keep your accomplice in obscurity about a lot of things in your lives together. That is simply out and out insolent. It shows that you don't regard your accomplice enough to recognize that they are deserving of reality. You are saying that they aren't sufficient to be determined what's genuine–and that is, in every case, terrible in a relationship. You generally need to confess all to your accomplice, particularly about vital issues encompassing your relationship.

CHAPTER 1:

Nonverbal Communication

Essentially, Body Language is transmitted through gestures and postures. The studies about body language analyze emotions reached by movement, such as facial expression, movement of hands, legs, feet, eyes and the whole body. These studies, combined or separately, can predict the mood or intentions from an individual and features of the personality, such as security, shyness, violence, possessiveness, competitiveness, etc. We can say, then, postures express attitudes and feelings about people.

Body Language real value can be found in the summation of all levels of communication from oral and visual language and imagination.

Genetic Roots and Culture

Dehumanization has begun with our growing dependency on mobile phones. But the real obstacle in this situation is the posture we assume when we interact in this way. Almost imperceptibly, we keep the head down, eyes in the mobile's screen while both hands keep it near our chest.

What is the body doing by adopting this posture? A kind of inaccessible closed field and we don't allow anything or anyone to enter. And when we say anything, we are talking about attitudes, opinions, ideas, feelings... in short, any approach hinting some reaction in us, rational or emotional.

And we think we are comfortable this way. Even when we put down the phone, our head tends to keep leaning to the front (and down) in a permanent "keep out" gesture. We live rapidly and this posture demonstrates it; we want to arrive at our destination faster, even when we are not going to any particular place.

In this accelerated world it would be very convenient to use a nonverbal communication form; with a look or a gesture we could transmit an idea, a thought, even an answer. The desire of connection among human beings is not new. From the Paleolithic era, human beings let register of messages in the walls of caves the made their homes. Stories in those messages were transmitted by using draws and symbols.

Can the Body's Posture Be Assumed as A Nonverbal Communication Form?

Answer is an emphatic yes. What the experts have named body language. Body Language is the most antique way of communication among human beings, before the written and spoken language. It is the vehicle to express sensations, feelings, emotions and thoughts. This way, the body becomes an irreplaceable instrument of human expression which allows to be in contact with the environment and the others.

The verbal communication we, human beings, communicate, consists of words. Nonverbal communication consists of posture and semantic prosody (the intonation we give to the words, inflection, tone and emphasis in the voice). This exposes us frequently.

We want to impress, show confidence, conquer, convince, persuade and to achieve that, we measure what we say and the way we express ourselves thoroughly, but sometimes the body moves by itself transmitting just the opposite.

Because "reading" the others' gestures give us plenty of information about what the other person is feeling truly.

Face and body movements give data about personality and emotional condition in the individual: the face, for instance, can express joy, fear, amazement, sadness, etc. Body's posture can project one's attitude when interacting with others: tension, interest, boredom.

What is the first thing we think when someone speaks about body language?

Some instantly say "if you cross your arms over your chest you are closed" (I don't know what they mean, really) or "If you touch your nose your lying" "if you drag your feet, you are feeling dispirited" "if someone make a face then is sad or thoughtful" and they think they have an idea.

Most of Body Language books feed this trend, since they are focused on satisfying the necessity in our brain's left hemisphere, where A means A and there is no way it could mean B.

But this approach is childishly simple, because obviously, something so complex like kinesics cannot be labeled in the same way as words (even these latter are confusing enough). Then, how can we understand Body Language if we don't have a "Table" which indicates every gesture's meaning?

At this point, left cerebral hemisphere comes to action. Right hemisphere develops and processes information in a different way. It is an integrating hemisphere specialized in sensations, feelings and special skills (visuals, with sound) as music and nonverbal arts. Right hemisphere is the key to decode such tangled gestures because it always has been there to do it (even when we didn't notice it).

The key is, this approximation is a little more integral. Right hemisphere determines the general meaning in the whole "body phrase" from a person and then look for little keys to confirm its hypothesis.

That's how we read a text, for instance. We didn't stop to think in the meaning of every word separately. Instead, we absorb every phrase like a whole and, in some cases, we can understand a paragraph with just one look.

Keeping this reality in mind, we cannot think that by learning a list of signs we are able to "read" people. We need to focus on feelings and emotions one person can transmit us while we are talking, when we observe that person, walking or sitting.

We must be careful, since rational mind is so attached to logics, therefore, it will do everything it can to interfere and let clear logics is more certain that intuition. But, as every mental faculty, intuition is, literally, a muscle. If you dedicate yourself to flex it every day, silencing the logical reasoning in some cases and allowing this faculty (which all we have) to expand, it will be more and more easy "to read" gestures resounding with what we are feeling. It will be coherent between what we see and what our emotions can capture.

Capacity to keep the whole attention in what the other person is saying and the position this person takes while talking is a habit which will be very useful not only when comes to learn body language, but for your life. We can save uncountable misunderstandings and arguments in our daily life, just by paying attention what other people is saying and how are they saying it.

Body language is studied by kinesics, which analyze movements of every part of the body. This movements can be conscious or unconscious. Therefore, body position and gesticulation, the group of movements we make with our arms, hands and head, are included.

Body movements are considered a multi message system. Although there are movements which clearly reveal an attitude, an emotion or an intention, it is very difficult to stablish a dictionary of gestures with exact correspondence of its specific social exclusive meaning. They acquire a significance by being executed under a determined context or circumstance.

In one person's movements everything is an influence: Culture, personality, genre, environment. And not always we know all that background, not always we have it on hand to predict how the person would react in front a determined stimulation.

That's why the more we know one person, the more knowledge about all his or her behavior's patterns we have and we can identify easily sudden changes in this individual's behavior, to recognize signs which give us leads about the individual's mood, capacity to tell the truth or not, if upset or joyful.

Fundamental Characteristics of Body Language

We, human beings have unlimited number of gestures we are able to do, almost imperceptibly. Gestures support what we're talking at the time, and also, what we are not saying.

Gestures says a lot. According with a study, verbal communication represents 35% of someone's total communication and the other 65% belongs to nonverbal communication or body language.

When we introduce ourselves or receive that first impression, when we met someone for the first time, more than 95% of qualification we are doing is completely visual, it's based in what we are seeing at the moment.

That communicative expression is the most important in communication, gestures are the support of what we are saying. With gestures, we give emphasis on the words we are saying, with them we express feelings and emotions.

When we blink, when we tilt our head, when we are gesturing with our hands. At every moment, body language is expressing what we are saying.

Body Language in An Individual Can Be Innate, Learned and Imitative

As any aspect of our psyche, body language is different in each person, so it is impossible to generalize about it. Here we have the famous dilemma that humans have asked about practically any aspect of their behavior: is it innate or is it socially acquired?

This question is interesting, because in the case of a universal phenomenon being innate, scientific research around the subject of body language can be generalized. Well, the University of British Columbia has answered this question. A team from this university investigated a group of athletes who had been born with total blindness. People who had never seen language from anyone else. So, they were not going to be able to produce it by imitation, but spontaneously.

This team chose athletes from all over the world and from different cultures and observed their body language. What they discovered was these athletes all shared the same body language at the moment they won any competition: they raised their arms towards the sky and opened their mouths, this being the universal gesture of pride and victory in body language.

They also displayed the same body language when they lost: eyes to the ground and hunched back; exactly the same body language observed in athletes with visual capacity. This research helped to scientifically support the fact that body language is a universal phenomenon, it is something innate so it can be studied as universal. There are certain specific elements that are cultural and are different from one culture to another, indeed, but those elements are really the least interesting, because they only are useful to identify very specific intentions in very specific contexts. Body language is innate and universal, and is rooted in evolutionary processes, that is the best part about it.

Among gestures we can consider innate: smiling, since nobody teach us how to smile; babies smiles are innate gestures in all human beings.

Imitative: When someone from Western go to Japan, for instance, bends as a greeting, because in Japan, that is a cultural custom, it is a signal for respect and tourists in that country tend to copy that greeting.

Body Language Learned: Most of gestures we make are learned. The famous peace symbol, with two semi-open fingers making a V, is a learned gesture.

Thumbs up, as a signal everything is okay, is learned too.

CHAPTER 2:

How to Improve Nonverbal Communication

S trong social capacities can help you in all aspects of your life. While verbal and created social capacities are critical, research shows that nonverbal practices make up a tremendous degree of our step by step social communication.

If you want to understand how to improve nonverbal communication, consider the information provided in the graph below on how to select the most appropriate way of reading people in order to improve your skills;

By what means may you improve your nonverbal social capacities? The tips below can empower you to make sense of how to scrutinize the nonverbal indication of different people and improve your very own ability to communicate reasonably.

Pay Attention to Your Tone of Voice When Talking

Your way of talking can pass on a plenitude of information, running from enthusiasm to absence of commitment to shock. Start perceiving how your way of talking impacts how others respond to you and have a go at using your tone to complement contemplations that you have to pass on.

For instance, if you have to exhibit veritable excitement for something, express your energy by using an invigorated way of talking. Such banner does not simply pass on your feelings about a subject; they can in like manner help produce energy for the all-inclusive community checking out you talk.

Concentrate on Nonverbal Signals with Strong Nonverbal Social Capacities

People can confer information from various perspectives, so center around things like eye to eye association, movements, present, body advancements, and way of talking. These signs can pass on critical information that is not explained. By giving closer thought to other people's certain practices, you will improve your own one of a kind ability to pass on nonverbally.

Posture Inquiries About Nonverbal Signals

c. A shrewd idea is to repeat back your interpretation of what has been said and demand clarification. An instance of this might be, "So what you are expressing is…"

Every so often, basically, presenting such request can credit a great deal of clearness to a condition. For example, an individual may produce certain nonverbal sign since he has something else at the cutting edge of his contemplations. By curious further into his message and point, you may give indications of progress thought of what he is genuinely endeavoring to state.

Search for In-steady Behaviors

In case someone's words do not organize their nonverbal practices, you should give careful thought. For example, someone may uncover to you they are energetic while glaring and looking at the ground.

Research has shown that when words disregard to facilitate with a nonverbal sign, people will, as a rule, ignore what has been said and base rather on understood enunciations of perspectives, thoughts, and sentiments. So, when someone says a specific something, anyway his or her nonverbal communication seems to prescribe something else, it might be important to give extra thought to those subtle nonverbal signs.

Pay Attention to Your Expressions

A couple of individuals essentially seem to have an ability of using nonverbal communication sufficiently and precisely translating sign from others. These people are much of the time depicted as having the alternative to read people.

In fact, you can gather this capacity by giving mindful thought to nonverbal direct and practicing different sorts of nonverbal communication with others. By observing nonverbal direct and practicing your very own aptitudes, you can essentially improve your communication limits.

Nonverbal social capacities are fundamental and can make it more straightforward to pass on your point and to examine what others are endeavoring to tell you. A couple of individuals seem to drop by these capacities regularly, yet anyone can improve their nonverbal aptitudes with preparing.

Use Gestures to Ensure Communication is More Significant

Remember that verbal and nonverbal communication coordinate to pass on a message. You can improve your communication by using nonverbal communication that reinforces and supports what you are expressing. This can be especially useful when making presentations or when tending to a gigantic social occasion of people.

For example, on the off chance that you will probably appear to be certain and masterminded during a presentation, you should focus on sending a nonverbal sign that certifies that others believe you to be sure and skilled. Standing unequivocally in one spot, shoulder back, and your weight balanced on the two feet is an exceptional strategy to strike a definite stance.

Observe Signals as a Group

Another huge bit of good nonverbal social capacities incorporates having the choice to receive a continuously sweeping system to what an individual is granting. A single sign can mean any number of things, or maybe nothing using any and all means. The best approach to absolutely scrutinizing nonverbal direct is to scan for social events of sign that brace a common point. If you place an over the top measure of complement on just one sign out of many, you may achieve an inaccurate assurance about what an individual is endeavoring to state.

Pay Attention to the Context

When you are talking with others, for the most part, consider the situation and the setting wherein the communication occurs. A couple of conditions require progressively formal practices that might be interpreted in all regards differently in some other setting.

Consider whether nonverbal practices are fitting for a particular circumstance. In case you are endeavoring to improve your own nonverbal communication, center around ways to deal with making your sign match the level of show required by the situation.

For example, the nonverbal communication you use at work are likely out and out not the same as the sort of sign you would send on an agreeable Friday night out with mates. Attempt to facilitate your nonverbal sign to the situation to ensure that you are passing on the message you genuinely need to send.

Realize That Signals Can be Misunderstood

According to around, a certain handshake exhibits a strong character while a weak handshake is taken as nonattendance of guts. This model blueprints a noteworthy point about the probability of misreading the nonverbal sign. A limp handshake may truly exhibit something other than what's expected absolutely, for instance, joint aggravation.

Constantly make a point to scan for social events of lead. A person's general way is certainly more telling than a lone sign found in detachment.

Use Excellent Eye Contact

Extraordinary eye to eye association is another fundamental nonverbal communication capacity. Exactly when people disregard to take a gander at others without wincing, it can seem like they are maintaining a strategic distance from or endeavoring to cover something. On the other hand, an abundance of eye to eye association can have all the earmarks of being wild or undermining.

While eye to eye association is a huge bit of communication, recall that incredible eye to eye association does not mean looking consistently at somebody. In what manner may you determine what measure of eye to eye association is correct?

Some communication pros recommend intervals of eye to eye association suffering four to five seconds. Feasible eye to eye association should feel typical and pleasant for both you and the individual you are chatting with.

Nonverbal communication is critical in the workplace since it impacts the working environment. In a couple of respects, we can grant to such a degree, if not more, nonverbally than we do with our communicated words. What you give nonverbally can reveal how you feel. If your nonverbal exchanges aptitudes are poor, you may bestow opposition and making your associates ungainly or undermining your message with signs about lacking conviction. To improve your nonverbal capacities, you ought to at first perceive the zones where you need improvement.

Your Posture Must Be Right

Look at your position. Drooping exhibits that you are not roused by what an individual is expressing. Your body improvement is moreover noteworthy.

For example, swinging your leg forward and in reverse, while sitting on a social occasion or drumming your fingers on the table tells others you are on edge, depleted and uninterested. Sit up straight and face others when talking.

Consider Your Voice

Your way of talking and the sounds you make can pass on your thoughts to others without your despite talking. In case you get heading from a chief and speedily grunt, you are exhibiting your executive that you do not agree with what he said. Your tone or sounds can prompt people in regards to your anger, disappointment or joke. Refuse to groan needlessly or to talk in a high-pitched voice. Talk quietly and gently.

Personal Space Should Be Maintained

Concentrate on your closeness to other individuals. Different social orders see the region in various ways, so pay notice if the individual you are talking with is cumbersome. This could suggest that you are standing too close, and should make some partition among you. The proportion of physical space given can pass on various sentiments.

For example, a person who is continuing compellingly is likely remaining close to the next person. Be aware of the individual space of others.

Keep up Eye Contact

Develop eye to eye association when tending to other people. When you look, it shows the other party that you are enthused about what he is expressing. If you should give a presentation at work, set up eye to eye association with the gathering of observers. It uncovers to them that you are sure about what you are showing.

Looking outfits others with the comfort expected to talk with you thus. Be cautious, in any case, not to change your undertakings at eye to eye association into a persistent look; balance is the key.

Facial Expressions are Important

Your outward appearances pass on your sentiments. Outward appearances are typical across the board, which means they pass on a comparative message all around. A glaring individual is typically bothered. Offer a smile when bantering with someone, as long as it is not ill-advised to the situation.

This tells people that you are playful or feeling extraordinary. It in like manner makes a domain with warmth and kind aura, empowering others to feel better.

Your face can demonstrate a store of emotions. Right when a smile is not called for, think about your air and react as necessities are. A look of sincerity when your work is being assessed or an attentive response to someone's appearance of difficulties can go far to passing on your dedication with the condition.

A significant much can be said without words in a very close discourse. Oftentimes, our nonverbal communication, our outward appearances, body act and our eye to eye association talks generally seriously. These nonverbal prompts accept a tremendous activity in how our words and desires are deciphered. Extraordinary nonverbal aptitudes can help exhibit your assistance by conveying you truly care and are truly hearing what someone needs to state.

CHAPTER 3:

What Is Body Language?

Sometimes we might only think of body language as the signals and movements that we're trying to send using our arms and our face. Having furrowed eyebrows or a frown are easy signs of body language. There's so much more that's deeper than this that we have to start to understand so we can get a better realization of what people are trying to say. Humans are the only animals who use words to communicate with each other. Though other animals might use sounds such as growls, hisses, whines, and other noises to communicate; often, a lot of this is just reactionary. Most of the communication that is done on an animal level is through their bodies. Let's take a look at every facet of body language so that you can best understand the full spectrum of communication between individuals.

Factors That Affect Body Language

At the core of all communication, there is a truth that we all know amongst ourselves. If you have a best friend that smells bad, of course, everybody kind of knows that the truth is she feels terrible. However, one person might tell her that she stinks and she needs to take more showers. Another person might try to say it more delicately, by asking them if they need any help with their hygiene, or they might mention how they are concerned that they aren't taking good enough care of themselves. Then there might be another friend who doesn't say anything at all. Instead, she puts together an elaborate gift package where she gives her soaps, lotions, perfumes, and other things that smell good. All three of these situations are communication.

What we have to remember more importantly about language is that it is not just words that leave your mouth. It is everything from the top of your head to the tip of your tongue. Most individuals who believe that they have excellent communication skills are only talking about the words that they share. We have to consider all other aspects of our language and how it might be affecting people to truly understand what excellent communication is and what it might look like. We are going to take you through every facet of language and communication that you will need to understand to have success.

We don't just communicate with the people that we like; we often communicate with people that we aren't so fond of as well. The better that you can learn all aspects of communication, the easier your life will be. Even if you are somebody who doesn't have a broad vocabulary, has trouble coming up with unique or creative words, or also as a person that stumbles or stutters, you can still have adequate and healthy communication.

It's all about tone, body language, what you're wearing, what you look like, physical objects, symbols, and other things that can all play into how we communicate with one another. Language is not just linguistics. That's what we need to understand. Your body can tell you so much more than anything else. Think of a simple phrase such as "I'm fine."

These are two simple words stuck together that we say all the time. Anybody that asks us how we're doing, we always simply tell them, "I'm fine," "I'm good," or "I'm okay." These are simple phrases, but they can mean so many different things depending on every other factor. Imagine that somebody is sick, blowing their nose and coughing constantly. If they say "I'm fine," that's a clear indicator that they're not okay. If somebody's just lost a loved one, and they seem to be smiling a little bit, maybe with a positive and happier energy, and they say "I'm fine," then we know that that is about how they might be coping with the situation.

They're not exceptional, but you can still be content and a little bit more okay now than when they first found out about the death as they soon start to deal with the grieving process. Somebody else might say "I'm fine," with a delighted and cheery tone, letting you know that they are beautiful. They really just mean precisely what they're saying. Then there are others who frequently use sarcasm. Perhaps they just slipped and fell on the sidewalk in the middle of a substantial icy block. They might put their thumbs up and say "I'm fine," with a sarcastic tone even though they clearly aren't.

While words are essential in communication, you have to remember how body language will play in. We can have full-on conversations with people without muttering more than just a couple of words based on body language alone. How many times have you been out to lunch or dinner with three or four people, and then there's one person that happens to say something embarrassing or silly? You might shoot a look at the other people around you, and everybody knows that what they said was awkward, but nobody is going to call them out for that. There are so many factors that will affect body language and how you communicate with other people. By the end of this reading, you're going to feel extremely comfortable picking up and understanding what somebody else's body language is trying to tell you (Cherry, 2019).

Why We Use Body Language

There are a ton of different reasons that we use body language. First and foremost, what you have to understand is that the only way that we can verbally communicate with other people is based on words that we know.

The words that we know are words that we have been taught and that we've picked up throughout our lives. Think back to when you were a child and still learning certain words. There are probably times that you correctly remember learning what a new word is. Even as an adult, you might stumble upon certain words that you don't quite know what you have to Google Search when reading something to help you better understand what the person is trying to say.

The thing about words is that they are based upon the culture in which we were raised. People from different cultures use different words. Various words have different meanings, as well.

For example, think of a word only like 'chips.' Chips in the US typically means sliced potatoes that are fried and crispy. Chips in the UK more frequently refer to what is referred to in the US as French fries. These would be softer potatoes.

It's not a word that really causes many misunderstandings between people because you can easily describe what you're trying to say afterward. For example, if you are from the UK and you come to the US and order chips, then you could explain to the waitress that you will want soft, long, skinny potatoes not sliced, fried, and crispy potatoes.

Even when we do run into words that we don't quite understand or that we might use differently, you can still use other words to explain that difference. However, there are many feelings, thoughts, and actions that we have in particular in which we can't always wholly describe.

How many times have you just had a thought or feeling, but you had no way of describing it. It wasn't even that you couldn't put it into terms for somebody else to understand. It was merely that you didn't even know how to describe that feeling to yourself.

The only way that we can interpret certain things is through our verbal language. This is why we have to recognize the body language of other individuals so that we can better understand the words that they're trying to say.

We also need to use body language because it can be the way that we give messages that we either don't want to say out loud or that we don't understand ourselves. How many times have you been uncomfortable in a situation that you were too afraid to say something about?

Perhaps a friend was talking about going on a vacation. You don't want to have to break it to her that you can't really afford the holiday and that you don't really even want to go there. Even if you could, maybe she's talking about going on a trip to Florida and discusses how it's going to be a certain amount of money, and she wants to do certain activities. In your mind, you have no desire to go to Florida because that's where you're from, and you've gone on vacation there a few times anyway. You don't have the money, and even if you did have the money, you'd rather spend it on holiday to somewhere you've never been, maybe New York City or Los Angeles.

She seemed incredibly excited about it, and you don't want to hurt her feelings. So instead of telling her, "Hey, I don't want to go on this vacation," you come up with other excuses or reasons to try and make it seem as though this isn't a great idea. You could even use body language. Maybe you pull out your phone and look at it, appearing distracted. You continue acting as though you're not interested in the conversation. Perhaps you start fidgeting with your hands, touch your face, push your hair behind your ear, have a shaky voice, look around, or using a variety of other body language signals to try to let her know that you're not really interested in this conversation.

We need to use body language to help us tell others the things that we can't say ourselves. Alternatively, we need to understand body language so that we can pick up on these different kinds of social cues. Younger children and even some older adults with dementia or other mental ailments can make it difficult for certain people to pick up on body language.

Those with Asperger's syndrome or autism might struggle to pick up on specific social cues as well. This is because a lot of our body language develops throughout society. We learn different methods of communicating based on how we were raised. While some things come naturally, such as covering your eyes or your mouth if you were shocked or upset; other things are taught to us, like how we might hold our arms or the way that we sit across from somebody. There are a ton of different factors that will affect body language, and we'll try to discuss as many as we can. What we have to remember, more importantly, is why we use these; because we are trying to share messages between each other, that can't always be communicated verbally.

CHAPTER 4:

The Origin of Body Language

If you've ever been to another country, you're sure to realize that some of the body languages that you use at home are going to be translated differently than it would at home. This's because there're cultural differences that're present between America & the country you're visiting & each group of people is going to see things in a slightly different way.

The differences that show up in various cultures are also going to be present in many different circumstances. This might simply include interactions that occur between different genders, the interactions that occur between those of the same gender, the conversational distance that you should've with people & how much physical touch should be allowed in the conversation. For example, there're some cultures that feel that physical touch is expressive & they use it a lot in their country. You'll be able to find this in places such as Italy where a kiss on each cheek & a big hug is considered acceptable & even common when it comes to greetings. On the other hand, when you're in Japan you'll find that a proper greeting is going to include a respectful bow & there'll be no touch at all.

Comfort distances & personal space are often influenced by the culture that you live in or are visiting. For example, those who're from South America will see that their comfort distances & personal space tends to be a lot smaller than those you expect to find in other cultures. People from these countries will stand close to each other when they're talking; it doesn't really matter whether they know each other that well or not. On the other hand, people in the United States also value a larger personal space & they're not that comfortable when others are standing close to them, especially when the other person isn't known to them.

These kinds of cultural differences that're found in body language are often going to be the most pronounced when it comes to gender interactions. A lot of cultures still see the man as the dominant gender & assume the male to be of higher status than the female. Often, the body language that's used in these interactions will be reflected from this viewpoint. You may find in some cultures that women are required to avert their eyes when they're in the presence of a man, or they might be required to walk a few steps behind any male they're with. On the other hand, in western cultures you'll find that gender expectations have changed & this allows men & women to share a more equal status when it comes to acceptable body language.

You may wonder why these differences in cultural body language are going to be so important. These differences are a direct result of how the culture thinks & acts & so you'll be able to learn a lot about that culture by the body language exhibited. If you're planning on going to visit an unfamiliar country, whether for pleasure or business, it's often good to have an understanding of the body language that they value. Displaying the wrong kind of body language could land you in a lot of trouble with people who're unfamiliar with this style of behavior. For example, if you're on a trip for business & you use the wrong kind of body language, you can send out messages that're going to hurt the deal that you're trying to make really fast. In the world of travelling for pleasure, the wrong kind of body language is going to lead to hostile & sometimes dangerous situations.

A good example of this's in the Middle East. In this scenario, a male businessperson is going to have much more leeway in the manner that he conducts business there as well as where he's able to walk. There's also more access to local business opportunities at many different levels. This's in comparison to women, most of whom aren't able to do business in this area due to the cultural aversion to interacting with women which's often too much to overcome so most businesses will avoid that happening.

If you're planning on going on a vacation to a different culture, it might be a good idea to pay some attention to the body language that's expected in that area in order to understand what's going on better & help you to avoid any problems that may arise. For instance, if you happen to get lost in Japan, you're more likely to receive some help from a citizen there if you're able to show some respectful body language & then follow the local customs such as avoiding touch & perhaps respecting that you bow when you ask for help. If you're rude or don't follow customs, it might be difficult to get the kind of help that you need.

There're a lot of different things that you can consider when you're looking at body language in the United States compared to other countries. Some of these would include:

- **Eye contact** – In the U.S. & Canada intermittent eye contact is very important in order to show that you're interested & paying attention to the other person. On the other hand, in a lot of the cultures of the Middle East, intense eye contact that's shared between those of the same gender is a symbol of sincerity & trust while eye contact that occurs between those of opposite genders, especially when it comes Muslim cultures, anything that's longer than a brief eye contact is going to be seen as inappropriate. In addition, Latin American, African & Asian cultures are going to see extended eye contact as a challenge & the Japanese see even a little bit of eye contact as something that's uncomfortable. In some other cultures, it's expected that a woman looks down when she's talking to a man.

- **Handshakes** – In Western cultures it's acceptable to shake hands as a form of greeting another person when you're meeting up. In other cultures, there're quite a few differences that might surprise you. For example, a lot of northern European cultures will also use a firm one pump handshake as a greeting while parts of South America, Central America & Southern Europe will use a longer handshake that's considered warmer; this means that they'll take the left hand & use it to clasp the hand, elbow, & sometimes the lapel of the other person. You should be careful with the handshake in Turkey, this kind of thing is often considered aggressive & rude. In some African countries, a limp form of handshake is the norm. In Islamic countries, a man will also never shake the hand of a woman who's not a part of his family.

- **Greetings** – In America, there're many different types of standard greetings that can be used, & many people have learned these greetings since their childhood. But these kinds of greetings aren't going to be found everywhere that you look & sometimes you might confuse another culture by using them abroad. For example, if you're in Japan, you'll be expected to bow to those you're greeting while in Italy you'd give people kisses on the cheek.

- **Personal Space** – This was mentioned briefly above, but each culture is also going to have a different meaning for personal space. In America, personal space is valued & most people don't want to have others too close to them, especially if they've just met. In China, those who're doing business together wouldn't find it acceptable to have any personal space at all. Strangers are going to touch often when they're in crowded meetings.

- **Touching** – Touching is another thing that's going to vary depending on the country you're in. While touching is fine in America, there're many cultures that would've rules on how this should take place. In countries which are Islamic, a man is only allowed ever to touch his wife. In England, Scandinavia & Japan, touching isn't that frequent. Latino cultures go the opposite way in that touching is often encouraged. Often, it's best to follow the lead when visiting other countries. Let the other people guide you a bit & soon you'll be able to determine what behavior is appropriate. There're certain countries that don't encourage the touching of the heads of children, for example, so steer clear of this unless you're sure this's acceptable.

- **Personal hygiene & dress** – About the only thing that's common between cultures is that brushing teeth is usually normal practice. Otherwise, there're a lot of differences that you'll find as you travel. In come cultures, women aren't expected to shave. Some cultures are never going to wear deodorant & might not reserve as much time for bathing. You must make sure that when you're going to another country that you aren't offending anyone or that you're easily offended.

- **Gestures** – The gestures that you make with your hands are also going to mean different things in various parts of the world. You may find that avoiding these gestures is the best bet when you're in another country. If you were to use a rude hand gesture toward someone in one country, they may not realize what you're doing & won't get offended because it has no meaning in their country. In some cultures, the middle finger is going to be used as the pointer finger so they'll really not understand what you're trying to do. The thumbs up signal is often different as well. Other signs that you should actually watch out for would include the OK sign & placing your hands on your hips. If you aren't sure that they'll be recognized as polite, then it's best to avoid gestures that may cause offense.

The thing to remember about this's that when it comes to the differences in body language culturally, it's important to have a little bit of knowledge ahead of time. This will allow you to understand what's expected of you so that you can enjoy your experience in the new country without actually causing any issues with the citizens who live there.

CHAPTER 5:

The Study of Body language

If you want to make sure you know what a person feels just by looking at her face, maybe it's time to understand a little more about body reading, which is nothing more than to realize that gestures and positions also have a lot to say—much more than you can imagine. To give you an idea, 55% of the information a person relays when communicating comes from body language. This body reading thing is so curious that it is interesting to highlight some of the many types of research already done addressing the theme:

Did you know, for example, that psychopaths can detect vulnerability only by analyzing the way a person walks?

Another study suggests that it is possible to understand what a politician thinks about a particular subject solely based on his hands. Possible?

How to "Read" Someone

Typically, you are wondering how one person interprets the other through body language. You must be aware of the unconscious signals issued by your interlocutor, without them knowing that they are being analyzed. The three key points of body language are:

- Speech and Behavior: To tell if a person feels emotionally attuned to you, notice if they use the same words as you; they speak in a tone and at a speed similar to the ones you use to talk; if they are sitting in the same position as you. If the conversation continues at a pace that makes it sound like a "follow the master" game, the emotional connection between both of you is adequately established;

- Levels of agitation and activity: If the person does not move, he or she has little interest in what you have to say however if they run out after the meeting, it indicates that they are excited. Several surveys have already confirmed that when a woman swings her feet while on a romantic date, she probably likes the man she is with.
- Emphasis and timing: The term "timing" means that the person is speaking or doing the right thing at the right time. If in addition to having a schedule for the relevant comments, the person emphasizes specific points, it means that they are focused and controlled. On the other hand, a person that does not show security in what he speaks, due to lack of timing and emphasis, is easily manipulated.

Still, on the quest for excellence in body language, you need to pay close attention to the interlocutor. In that sense, there are biases that you must analyze to improve your ability to perceive:

- Think of the context: Would people in this situation act in the same way that the person who is talking to you is acting?
- Look for joint, non-isolated actions: Do not focus on just one detail or gesture. Always observe the entire body.

Compare: How Does This Person Act Normally?

Know that your prejudices can deceive you. To understand the other, you need to understand yourself: see if you are not drawing conclusions because you like or because you do not like the person.

The way the human body communicates is often the subject of research, and scientists have come up with some rather curious specific conclusions about body language:

Crossed legs are a bad sign during negotiations. It sounds bizarre, but business meetings end better when no one is cross-legged. Just to give you an idea, the analysis of 2,000 meetings showed that none of them ended well when at least one person was cross-legged.

Want to know if someone is lying or betraying your trust? Notice that during a conversation the person has these four attitudes: he leans on his hand, he leans on his face, he crosses his arms and he maintains a posture that is tilted somewhere, not erect. These isolated signs do not amount to much, but when presented together, they probably indicate lies and/or betrayal;

On the other hand, research has already proven that trustworthy people are emotionally expressive. Trust someone pleasing to all people, and not just to a specific group.

Concerning the Hands: Gestures Made with the Palms Down Indicate Power and the Opposite Is Submission.

Men and women use different body languages at the time of seduction. Women start smiling, raising their eyebrows, lowering their eyelids quickly, and then look away. Next, almost without exception, they place their hands close to their mouths and smile or lick their lips.

Men, on the other hand, inflame the chest, jut their chin, arch their backs, make gestures with their hands and arms and make movements that can demonstrate confidence and call attention to their power.

The fact is that if you want to read the body language, you need to avoid falling into some common traps; after all, crossed arms do not always mean lack of interest. Here are a few common mistakes made by people trying to gauge how others communicate by gesture:

- You cannot ignore the context: The idea that someone is with crossed arms does not mean that he or she is not interested. It could be that they are in an icy environment or if the chair in which he or she is sitting does not have an armrest.
- Notice the entire picture: Some people become obsessed with the idea of body reading and end up focusing only on one point of analysis, when, in fact, the ideal scenario would

be to observe the entire situation: if the person is sweating, how is the breath, if they touch their face and so on;

- Realize standard behaviors: If a person is always bouncing, you do not need to analyze it. Now if the person is always bouncing and, from one moment to another, the behavior changes, then you need to pay attention;

- Stay tuned for these details: just know that if you already like or dislike a person, it will affect the judgment you make of them. If the person compliments you or if you find her attractive, maybe your judgments about them are favorable, even if you do not realize it–things of the human unconscious.

So, did you already know that body language may end up revealing some information that we do not make clear through words?

Body Language and Non-Verbal Communication

Body language tells who we are, how we feel or what our tastes are. In the interaction, the nonverbal behavior also informs our degree of understanding and level of agreement, and can even deny what we are saying at that moment.

Unfortunately, in real life it does not happen as on the screen of our browser: no alert message reminds us that cookies will take advantage of any oversight to deliver valuable information about us, something that will inevitably affect the way we relate to others. And even if we were warned, we would probably act as we do when surfing the web: we would ignore cookies and continue looking for the next website. Big mistake!

Speaking is much more than gathering words in a more or less fortunate way; listening is much more than hearing, and communicating is much more than sending and receiving data packets. To communicate is to share rational and emotional information, agreeing with the other person on its meaning and value. And that is not fully achieved without the intervention of nonverbal behavior.

Speaking and body language accompanies us long before we become humans, is strongly linked to the emotional, intuitive and instinctive part of our brain, and develops mainly on the unconscious plane.

Perhaps our species is not more than 200,000 years old, but the origin of our body language dates back to the appearance of the first mammals, about 300 million years ago. The age difference is abysmal. And although the arrogance of our brand-new neo-cortex invites us to think that nonverbal behavior is the most primitive part of communication, in reality, it is that which accumulates the most evolutionary experience and, in all probability, the most influential in our behavior.

Who Are the Best Non-Verbal Communicators?

Precisely for this reason, the best non-verbal communicators are those who are aware of their body language, people capable of monitoring their behavior and of calibrating the effect it produces on others. There is no exact profile scientifically established, although they are usually observers, with a broad perspective, and open to new experiences and realities. Traits such as emotional stability and empathy also help.

It may be easier to recognize them in the world of art and communication, but they are equally common in all professions. Some studies show that the most influential and persuasive people have a great awareness of their own and other people's body language, regardless of the professional field in which they have triumphed. It is a fundamental condition for success.

Becoming a good nonverbal communicator requires, therefore, developing self-awareness of body behavior, in the same way, that elite athletes perfect the condition of their muscles. The good news is that both skills can be developed with training. In addition, we can do it on our own, and at any time and circumstance.

It's a matter of concentration and to focus attention on the main channels of body language, seeking its congruence and synchronicity with words.

CHAPTER 6:

The Psychology Behind Body Language

R egardless of how great you get at perusing non-verbal communication; you may never feel that you have idealized it since this is such an immense subject. Nonetheless, there are a couple of essentials that will consistently enable you to get a reasonable thought of what is happening. This as a matter of first importance, is the ability that you'll have to create, which is a sharp perception. You need to begin searching for the indications. However, this must be done normally and pair with your verbal correspondence, except if you need to crack the other individual out totally. The indications are:

- Inconsistencies – is the body language in a state of harmony with the verbal language? Is the individual saying "yes" while the body is stating "no"? Non-verbal correspondence assembled–one single motion may not so much mean excessively. Try not to peruse a lot there. Or maybe, focus on bunches of gathering signals that are sent–like the tone of the voice, outward appearance, eye development, hands developments, and so on. What do they say together?

- Check out your hunches–most people "know" what the other says. You will have that premonition that this individual isn't coming clean, or isn't intrigued or that he is engrossed with something different–don't disregard your hunch because the individual is stating the inverse too articulately. Know and be increasingly cautious when their hunch is sending you cautioning signals. Watch intently for body language that does not coordinate the words.

- Eye contact–is the eye-to-eye connection without flaw? Or then again, is it subtle or excessively exceptional?

- Facial appearance–is the face responsive? Is it a cover of a lack of interest? Is it hard and unforgiving? Is it vivified with intrigue? Does it coordinate the words?

- The tone of the voice–there are 1001 different ways to state "come here" or "bless your heart." Attempt it. Let's assume it with shock, outrage, pity, enthusiasm, bliss, etc. The manner of speaking can disclose your bounty. Do you discover warmth there or frigidity? Is it stressed? Is it sure or bashful? Is it trying or empowering? Here and there, a simple "how would you do" could establish the tone of the dialog.

- The posture of the body and motions–investigate how the individual is holding his body. Is it firm and antagonistic? Is it "I'm into you" type? Is it slumped and sad? Is it tense–are shoulders unbending and raised? Is the chest area turned one side while feet are another? Are the hands motions inside the body edge or move much outward?

- Touch–is there contact? If there is, is it proper? Is the individual attacking your well-being zone? Is the contact commanding or agreeable? Does it make you feel better, disturb you, or it fills you with fear?

- The intensity of the character–is the individual excessively sensational? Excessively calm? Excessively cold? Excessively risky? Excessively level?

- Timing and pace of the discussion/exchange–is the verbal communication too quick that it looks restless? Or, on the other hand, too moderate that it looks uninterested? Do the non-verbal sign stay aware of the words–or is the mouth saying something and the body language is saying something different. All these are signals that will disclose to you what the other individual is thinking and intending to do. The capacity to peruse it precisely would enable you to acquire the activity and intercede in such a way that you get the activity you need from the individual you are conversing with. At last, it is tied in with getting your direction.

- Outward appearance–In many cases, what you think and feel is reflected in your face. A few people ace the craftsmanship to keep a clear face, yet that would be temporarily similar to when seeming a meeting or betting–

and this would be to anticipate the other individual read what the genuine sentiments are.

Six fundamental appearances are basic to the human species and can be perused the same everywhere throughout the world:

- Anger. You will know from the substance of the individual that he is irate. There is a scowl; eyelids become limited, lips are tight and frequently in a straight line, and nostrils flare.

- Appall. The nose wrinkles in a disgusting manner, and the face folds—eyebrows descend, and cheek muscles are pulled up.

- Fear. The outward appearance for dread is all-inclusive. Eyes augment, the mouth opens in a wheezing signal, cheek muscles get tense, and eyebrows shoot up wrinkling the brow.

- Satisfaction. Smiling is the first and most basic outward appearance that says, "I'm upbeat." The face is loose, inviting, and warm. Wrinkles are framed at the side of the eyes—snicker lines.

- Trouble. You will find that within corners of the eyebrow go marginally up, lips corners descend (tragic smiley or emoji) at some point they quiver declaring tears. Tears are additionally an indication of misery (likewise of extreme satisfaction).

- Shock. Jaw drops, eyebrows shoot up, and eyes enlarge. Wrinkles would be shaped in the brow, and the mouth would be open.

Furthermore, some all-inclusive and simple to read articulations are a lot more mix and changes. The eyes are the most "loquacious" in outward appearances. Other than demonstrating these essential articulations/feelings, there are:

- Uncomfortable–sideway looking, subtle looking, dashing eye-to-eye connection, looking down, looking everywhere throughout the room, or towards the entryway may pass on this. An excessive amount of flickering likewise can be taken as an indication of anxiety.

- Lying–subtle looks, failure to keep up watchful gaze contact, taking a gander at hands, could be signs that the individual isn't coming clean.

- Giving space–is utilized in jam-packed spots where eye-to-eye connection could wind up overpowering. You would encounter this look in lifts, trams, railroad stations, air terminals, and so on where you are in a group; however, I would prefer not to interface not enable anybody to contact you.

- Deference–in numerous societies, someone "looking straight without flinching" is viewed as a proud and testing specialist. Thus, the lower rank would bring down their eyes when tending to somebody of higher position. In some cultures, ladies are relied upon to look down as an affirmation of unobtrusiveness. Ladies who look up would be deciphered as "lose character" or "requesting sex" in specific parts of the world.

- Dominance–you'd have known about the articulation, "gazing him down." This is the point at which the eyes are exhausting and courageous, compelling the other individual to break contact first. This is the commanding look and is utilized typically by one who either accepts he is higher in rank or needs to threaten others into accepting that. For instance, how an individual conveys his body says a ton regarding what the individual feels. A shy individual will conduct himself uniquely in contrast to how a certain and confident individual does.

- Nervous, hesitant, low confidence–the body is slumping, bears down in a practically recoiling stance, head twisted forward, eyes looking down or shooting quickly around, legs either crossed firmly or with feet extremely near one another, arms covering the defenseless zone of the body (neck, tummy catch level and crotch). It says, "Let me out of here. I'm not comfortable here."

- Dominant, brimming with certainty, pioneer–body upstanding, jaw pushed forward, head tilted upwards, incredible step, feet at shoulder's width or marginally more, hands along the edge and outward, chest swollen, shoulders squared, hands moving inside the body width with exact developments, eyes full contact, checking you.

- Arrogant, grandiose, loaded with himself–body taking more space than required, head tilted in reverse, eyes testing, feet wide separated, hands signal noisy, energetic and wide, crotch uncovered improperly, eyes pushing you into the ground.

- Arm Position - How you hold your arms opposite your body will likewise enlighten a great deal regarding what you feel and think. Individuals will, in general, make self-defensive motions when they are not happy with what they see, hear, or feel. Whenever agreeable and pleasant, they enable themselves to be uncovered and open.

- Uncomfortable, untrusting, shut–the arms and hands will attempt to cover the powerless parts of the body. You will discover the arms contacting the neck divide, round the belly button, or in the lap covering the crotch territory. You may likewise discover the arms crossed before the chest.

- Trusting, intrigued, open–the arms of the individual who is intrigued, open, and trusting would have the arms from the powerless zones of the body. The hands would either be hanging freely along the edge of the body or utilized for expressive motioning.

Space Zones— Space isn't non-verbal communication; however, it is a significant factor. The space one makes around him can demonstrate reasonably precisely how they are feeling. There are four sorts of zones, for example, the open zone, the social zone, the individual zone, and the cozy zone.

- The Public Zone–around 12 feet from some other individual. This is commonly the separation one puts among himself and an open speaker. This is non-threatening and non-attacking. It is additionally a zone where there is almost no dedication between the speaker and the audience.

- The Social Zone–this is a separation of 4-12 feet and would characterize the space put among us and the individual whom we know, however, not actually. The clerk, the copier machine administrator, etc. In this zone are individuals who you don't permit to get to your private emotions; in any case, in this zone, there is a level of amicability and solace.
- The Personal zone–this covers a separation on 1½ - 4 feet around us. This is where we permit individuals when connecting in open places, for example, eateries, workplace, parties, and so forth
- The Intimate Zone–this is around 18 creeps to contacting separation, and in this circle/zone, we permit just those whom we trust totally. When you discover outsiders in this space, it makes you awkward. This is the reason for swarmed of small places, for example, lifts, trains, and so on, individuals keep away from eye-to-eye connection.

As should be obvious, the intricacy of body language can fill volumes. In any case, we are not here to peruse volumes of scholarly stuff on what body language shows. We can leave that for researchers and scholars. What we have to know is how to utilize it in our everyday lives to improve our connections at work and at home.

CHAPTER 7:

Neuro-Linguistic Programming and Non-verbal Communication

During the 1970s, a new social and cultural movement was established, in which the virtues of self-improvement and the development of one's full human potential were cited as a sort of Holy Grail of higher education. These movements were associated with so-called New Age Spirituality, which challenged traditional beliefs of established Western religious and social conventions.

For example, success in one's personal and professional life have traditionally been regarded as the result of external recognition of one's efforts. Whether God rewards someone's virtuous conduct, or whether society's institutions recognize the value of someone's professional contributions, the key to success in personal and professional life have generally followed from people's ability to conduct themselves according to the established standards and traditions of the larger societies and belief systems in which they live.

New Age Spirituality and the Human Potential Movement attempted to establish an alternate route to success. These new schools of thought used scientific advances in linguistics, political science, technology, sociology, psychology, and medicine to argue that people no longer needed to depend on external recognition for success in any area of their lives. Instead, the general theory was that all people are born with an innate ability to succeed in any area of life, and that the key to unlocking success lies in an individual's ability to harness the power of positive psychology, thereby empowering them to achieve success at anything simply by virtue of perfecting their own unique human psychological and intellectual characteristics.

The school of NLP emerged during this time. The Esalen Center in Northern California was a famous liberal think tank through which the founders of NLP generated hundreds of thousands of dollars in book sales and therapy and training workshops. The NLP foundation has produced several books, which sold hundreds of thousands of copies. Although it eventually became notorious for its pseudo-scientific methods and theories based on little, if any, actual scientific proof or evidence, self-help has become a multi-billion-dollar global industry, and NLP and the many self-improvement businesses and training programs it inspired are still very much a part of the professional and political landscape.

What Is NLP?

Neuro-linguistic programming is a system of education and training based on an understanding of developmental, behavioral, and cognitive psychology. Education and training in NLP focuses on three aspects of human psychology: the neurological system, which regulates the physical functioning of the human body; language function, which determines how we interact with other people; and "programming," a term used to describe the beliefs, knowledge, and experiences we accumulate over time that together inform our worldview and determine how we behave.

NLP was originally founded in the 1970s by John Grinder and Richard Bandler. The theories behind their work are based in both the scientific study of linguistics, sociology, and political science, as well as New Age mysticism and the self-improvement movement that also began in the 1970s. Specifically, their claim that the "map is not the territory," as a way of describing the disconnection between our subjective perception of the world and reality itself are taken directly from the work of Alfred Korzybski, who founded the school of general semantics in 1933.

In addition, they reference Gregory Bateson's work detailing the conflict between flaws in societal and governmental systems and how they can cause problems in human communication and government. Finally, the work of Noam Chomsky, whose theories of transformational and universal grammar linked the important influence language function has in areas as seemingly unrelated as world government and politics, is one of the primary theories used to support claims that NLP therapy can transform the lives of its followers. NLP is also influenced by many non-scientific movements, including the mystical writings of Carlos Castenada. Many sociologists have categorized NLP not only as a pseudo-science, but also as a quasi-religion that belongs to the large sphere of New Age and/or Human Potential movements. Some have criticized NLP as a form of folk magic that borrows the language and theories of science and medicine to validate practices that are completely non-scientific. Carlos Castaneda wrote a series of novels in the 1970s portraying the power of shamanism among the indigenous tribes of North America, and many of the NLP modeling techniques borrow directly from Castaneda's novels, including "double induction" and "stopping the world." NLP behavior modification techniques based in modeling and the use of NLP language coaching use mimetics similar to the rituals of many New Age syncretic religions.

There is a basic philosophical assumption underlying all of the human potential and self-improvement programs that originated during the time NLP was developed. Objectivism is a philosophy based on the understanding that reality is a fundamental, physical fact—the material world that surrounds is objective reality, and we can come to an understanding of this reality through our senses. More importantly, objectivism insists that reality is the same for everyone because it is objective.

Though individual perceptions may differ, the objective reality does not.

The philosophies upon which NLP is based take a radically different approach and may be regarded as subjectivism. T

he basic theory is that each of us is incapable of knowing reality, because we all perceive the world subjectively, filtered by what we have learned from previous experiences and cultural and traditional learning. In addition, the part of the world we live in is governed by laws and customs we have come to know as "true." But these laws and customs differ from one geographical location to the next, and from one demographic group to the next. Thus, for each of us, the world is limited because we can only perceive it from a limited and subjective perspective.

According to the founders of NLP, your thoughts, feelings, and beliefs are not things that actually exist; they are things that you have learned to do.

Because we have spent so many years of our lives learning how to do these things from the people around us, our neurological systems, at some point, accept them as reality.

We stop questioning whether other facts or perspectives exist, or, using the language of NLP, whether there are other facts and perspectives that would help us to do other things. In the language of NLP, this is known as an internal "map of the world" that we learn through sensory experience.

We learn to communicate using both verbal and non-verbal language. The words we use, the metaphors we are most comfortable with, the analogies that are most common in our speech, our vocabulary, our level of discipline in using correct grammar or pronunciation, the amount of slang we use, whether our language is casual or formal, the ideas we talk about, the accent we are most likely to use when speaking—all of these linguistic abilities follow directly from our map of the world.

Although this dual form of communication is very complex and powerful, our ability to communicate is limited by this subjective experience of reality.

Together, these two elements, our neurological maps, which in turn form our patterns of linguistic expression, represent our "programming," hence, neuro-linguistic programming.

Below is a diagram illustrating the theory behind NLP:

NLP Model of Therapeutic Change

Present State

1. Model of the World

Meta Model	Establishing Rapport
Personal History	Set Goals
Beliefs	WFOC
Criteria	Presuppositions
Thoughts/Strategies	Meta Programs
Behaviors	Calibrating Physiology

Old Model of the World

2. Loosen the Model
Meta Model
Milton Model
Sleight of Mouth Patterns
Logical Levels of Therapy

3. Change Work
Anchoring
Submodalities/ Swish Patterns
Parts Integration/ Core Transformation
Strategy Installation/ Changes
Time Line Processes
Hypnosis
Reframing

4. Clean Up
Check Ecology
Parts Integration
Criteria Alignment

New Model of the World

5. Future Pace
Generalize Changes
Put in Future
Convincer Strategy

Desired State

CHAPTER 8:

Behaviorism

Behaviorists believe that our experiences turn us into who we are, and that what we learn and observe of the outer world is almost enough to completely shape us. They focus on action and its quantifiable measurement. What stimuli did we notice yesterday, and how have those stimuli influenced our behavior today? What consequences, in terms of rewards and punishments, can most quickly teach us to choose to act certain ways in the future? Behaviorism at its most pure says that we are virtually a blank slate at birth, ready to be molded by our environments for better and for worse, and not fundamentally different from each other in terms of temperaments, subjective emotional experiences, or personalities. Behaviorists view the connections between our environmental influences and our life choices as being prime in their importance, superseding things like genetic predispositions or cognitive interpretations. Behaviorists often study animals and draw connections to humans, as they view the mechanisms of motivation for action as fundamentally similar across species. Early in the 20th century, the behaviorists single-handedly shifted the focus of psychology from being concerned solely with the internal workings of the mind and emotions into a larger focus that included how we make our way, externally, through the world. That broadened focus remains today, and though behavioral psychology is now often combined with findings from cognitive psychology for a fuller picture, especially in terms of treatment for psychological challenges, the influence of its earliest theories remains strong and quite present in day-to-day life.

The Theory of Learning in Psychology

Edward Thorndike's law of effect was his biggest idea. It is behaviorism in a nutshell. It states that a behavior that evokes a pleasurable response is more likely to be repeated than a behavior that evokes an unpleasant one. This became a fundamental tenet of later conditioning theories.

Thorndike eventually refined this idea even further, saying that rewards work much more effectively to strengthen learned responses than punishments do to deter undesired responses.

Thorndike also put forth the law of use and the law of disuse. The former says that the more frequently a stimulus and a response are connected, the more ingrained the resulting association will become. And the latter is its counterpart—the longer a stimulus and a response have been disconnected, the less ingrained the connection will become.

Thorndike built on Pavlov's theories of classical conditioning by delving further into the concept of learning; in fact, we can consider him the first educational psychologist. Like the behaviorist pioneers before him, Thorndike was an empiricist, interested above all in measuring and quantifying his findings.

Thorndike called his overarching theory connectionism. This term refers to the application of conditioning principles to learning; the name came from the idea that learning is always the result of the connection between a stimulus and a response.

Thorndike also did work that altered the way reading and spelling were taught. He analyzed the frequency of words found in various children's works, and from them he compiled dictionaries specifically for children. His rationale was that language learning would be improved through greater focus on common words than on less common ones. That no one before Thorndike had tried such a rational, practical approach may seem surprising in retrospect, but it took Thorndike's interest in the intersection of data and education to bring that change about.

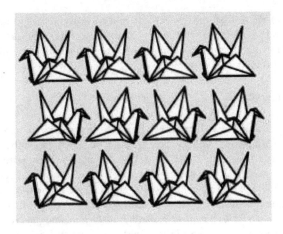

Thorndike created scales to assess students' growth across various areas, from arithmetic to handwriting, and these led to his development of several intelligence tests. And he advanced the idea that intelligence has different aspects—that a person can be strong in one area but not in another, or that someone can understand advanced calculus but not have the spatial wherewithal to figure out which way to turn in order to get back on the freeway.

Also credited to Thorndike's research is the concept of trial and error, which he developed by studying cats and their process of learning how to escape from an enclosure, called a puzzle box, by pressing a foot pedal. As the cats tried to escape, they made errors, but they made fewer and fewer errors as the experiment went on. Thorndike's key finding was that multiple trials and multiple errors are necessary components of the learning process.

Tasks in which participants exhibit the pattern of a learning curve are those in which participants display gradual growth and decreased mistakes, but mistakes are not eliminated all at once. If sudden insight were to eliminate all errors, then the typical learning curve would show a steep spike in competence, but in fact the typical learning curve shows sloping upward progress. This is why, in our modern-day use of the phrase learning curve, we are getting it 100 percent wrong. A steep learning curve, which many people associate with something that will be hard at first to learn, actually indicates quick and easy improvement in performance. It's important to remember that the curve represents improvement in performance, not the difficulty of the task.

Behaviorism

When you think of behaviorism, you may picture rats in mazes, or even the notorious Skinner box. If so, you're on the right track. Behaviorists believe that how we act is almost exclusively influenced by how we are conditioned; in other words, our behavior is overwhelmingly a response to the stimuli we encounter in our environment. Adherents of this school would also say that every experience we have, by either rewarding us or punishing us, serves to reinforce a certain behavior in the future. And sometimes the reward, or especially the punishment, comes about so automatically that we don't even realize it or can't control it. For example, imagine how you flinch when you see someone bring a pin near a balloon. You've been startled by that loud popping noise in the past, and your body has taught you to brace for it. Behaviorism also brought forth a new emphasis on quantitative measurement. Unlike some of the more subjective schools of thought that came before, behaviorism has been far more interested in quantifying than in conceptualizing. A typical behaviorist experiment has a lot in common with an experiment in physics or chemistry—it focuses on observable actions and reactions, and it looks to measure them in mathematical and systematic ways. For a behaviorist, the path to understanding is not introspection or interpretation. Behaviorism, to its credit, helped usher psychology into the world of the hard sciences and empirical validation

CHAPTER 9:

Learning and Types Conditioning

Our nervous system is also involved in the learning process. But how is it defined, and what are other concepts? Learning, by definition, is an adaptive function by which our nervous system alters concerning stimuli in the environment, thereby bringing a change in our behavioral responses and allowing us to function in our environment.

Initially, the process is established in the nervous system in a bit to respond to environmental stimuli. As a result, neural pathways can be strengthened, activated, even pruned, and all these can bring about a change in our behavioral responses.

When it comes to reflexes and instincts, they are innate behaviors. That is, they occur naturally and wouldn't demand to learn. However, learning, in turn, is an alteration in behavior that results from experience. In the field of behavioral psychology, it involves mainly on measurable behaviors that are learned; instead, if working hard to understand internal states like emotions and attitudes. But in learning, there are three fundamental aspects, they are classical conditioning, operant conditioning, and observational learning. The first two, classical and operant conditioning, forms if associative learning, their associations are developed between events that happen together. Whereas the third one, observational learning, is learning by observing others. Let's get into details about the three types of learning.

Classical Conditioning

Classical conditioning is defined as the process whereby we learn to relate stimuli and events that regularly happen together. As a result, we then learn to anticipate what will happen next. Take, for example;

some experts have trained animals like to associate the sound of an object to the presence of food. For instance, Ivan was able to condition his dog to identify the relationship between the sounds of a bell with the presence of the meal. This was achieved because each time; the dog hears the sound of the bell, what comes to mind is that it's time for lunch. So, in a sense, that scene makes the dog anticipate the meal.

Operant Conditioning

This is defined as the learning process in which behaviors are reinforced or punished, thereby strengthening a response. So, any act that is backed up with pleasant consequences is more likely to be repeated, whereas actions that are followed by unpleasant experiences are less likely to be repeated. So, it merely means that either punishments or rewards can impact behavior.

Observational Learning

This type of learning occurs when a person observes the behavior of others and imitate those behaviors. For example, it is common for children to learn or imitate adults, so if there is a right attitude that you needed to emulate, applying observational learning is the best way to achieve it. It is being used both in the therapeutic and advertising industry. In the commercial industry, they often feature attractive models. Thus, they apply the principles of associative learning.

Attention

In the world of cognitive psychology, attention is a concept that is being studied, and it refers to how we actively process particular information in our environment. Most times, many sensations are going on around us; they demand attention. Unfortunately, our attentional resources aren't limitless; it has boundaries. Therefore, we need to find out how we can experience all these sensations and still lay focus on just one particular thing, and how can we employ the scarce resources at our disposal to make sense of the world around us.

As defined by psychologist experts, attention is defined as taking possessing by the mind, in bright and vivid form out of what may appear to be numerous simultaneously possible objects or lines of thought. Or it could be defined as the withdrawal of some things to deal or pay closer attention to others.

Attention isn't about focusing attention on one particular thing; it also includes ignoring a great deal of fighting for information and stimuli. Attention makes it possible to tune out information, perception, sensation that aren't in correlation with the moment and then focus energy in the information that is vital.

Additionally, the attentional system offers the ability to focus on something specific in our environment while we send our incoherent details. In some situations, our attention might be centered on a particular thing which will cause us to ignore other things. That is, when we lay focus on something in the environment, we at times miss the several things that are right in front of us. And that is why most times in a room, you will be so engrossed that you won't notice that someone is approaching you or has walked inside the toilet.

But to understand more in-depth how attention works, and how it influences your perception, you have in mind these few points out that are highlighted.

Attention is Limited.

 Researchers have found that what influences our ability to stay on a given task include how interested we are in the stimulus and the number of distractions that surround us. Attention is limited when it comes to capacity and duration. So, multitasking doesn't work well, because our attention is limited.

Attention is Selective.

Since it is understood that attention is limited. We need to be selective about what we decide to focus on. We need to be selective in what we attend to. This stage is so fast that we hardly remember that we've neglected what happens in our environment.

Attention is a Fundamental Part of The Cognitive System.

Attention is even present at birth. This occurs when orienting reflexes help to determine which events in our environment need to be attended to. And right from that stage, the orienting reflex continues to be of immeasurable benefits to us throughout our life span.

Understanding this fact about attention enrich our productivity, it stops us from spending more energy on multitasking, instead of focusing on one thing at a time, which will enhance positive thinking and lead to success eventually.

Intelligence

Intelligence is an aspect that is often talk about in psychology, yet, there isn't one specific standard to define what intelligence is. Some have maintained that intelligence is single, others say that it is a general ability, while some still insist that intelligence covers a wide range of aptitudes, talents, and skills. Regardless of the opinions that are being held today, there is consensus agreement about intelligence. They are:

1. Learning. The ability to acquire, retain, and apply knowledge–these are vital parts of learning.
2. Identify Problems. To put knowledge to use, the likely problems have to be identified and be cared for.
3. Solve Problem. The output of learning is taking the knowledge and use it to solve the recognized problem.

Intelligence includes various mental abilities like planning, reasoning, logic, and problem-solving.

Also, isn't something we can hear or see or even taste? But we can peer into the result of intelligence. However, a big question that comes up is: is there a way to increase one's intelligence? Fortunately, the answer is yes. Psychologists who figured cognitive training and pharmacological intervention, so the approach to aid the improvement of the brain.

There are incredible ways to improve one's intelligence;

1. **Regular Exercise.** If you want to improve your intelligence, you have to exercise your brain and body. Like a muscle that requires training, your brain does need too. When you use, you are energizing your body, and this can lead to a wave of energy to your brain. Exercise aids you in concentrating better and making learning more accessible. Therefore, the more you use your brain positively, the more skilled and a great thinker you become. Your ability to focus will be enhanced when you exercise your brain.

2. **Meditation.** What meditation accomplishes is neuroplasticity. As soon as this is launched, the brain can make physiological changes for the better. Additionally, meditation enhances gray and white brain matter. Their functions differ. For example, gray matter is responsible for processing information, while white matter enhances communication skills.

3. **Watch Less or no Television.** I know this might be a sad fact, but more relaxed you admit, the better. When you watch television, you think less, and thus you aren't putting your mental power into use. So, if you crave for relaxation, read a book or play a crossword puzzle game.

4. **Reading Challenging Selections**. Reading improves one's ability to understand and encourage critical thinking. Thus, select more books among the ones that offer aptitude. Examples of these books include newspapers, classic novel, multi-content periodicals and when you come in contact with new words, check them up in your dictionary or ask an expert who knows and can explain explicitly about the topic.

5. **Rest Well**. Psychologists hold the widespread belief that ensuring adequate sleep will enhance smartness. It helps one feel revitalized if one gets to bed early and have quality 8 hours rest, waking up will be immersed with productivity and use your brain to the optimal level.

6. **Write**. You need not be an expert, pick up something you have either seen or read. Doing this will enhance visual simulation and kinesthetic. Also, practice writing with your non-dominant hand to improve both side simulation.

7. **Play Video Games**. Invest quality times to play new games. Seek for Ines that gives you the ability that will enforce quick thinking abilities. Just like scientists recommend, game Tetras.
8. **Invest in Cryptology.** Logic puzzle enhances brain intelligence and functioning. The puzzle entails a message written in codes for solving. When continuously played, you will strengthen your simulation ability and relaxing.

State of Consciousness

The separate awareness of your unique sensations, environment, feelings, memories, and thoughts are what consciousness is all about. Consciousness in an individual is always changing. Take, for instance, it is very likely that when you were reading this book, you were focused, but at a point, your consciousness shifted to something you had earlier done with a coworker. It might not stop there, but move to change dramatically from one moment to the next one, but all in all, your experience of it seems effortless.

As you may have realized, it is not all forms of awareness that are similar. Thus, there are several states of human consciousness as well as a variety of things that are capable of impacting states of awareness.

Has it ever occurred to you that every morning, you always feel energetic, question hypnosis, and even try explaining your dreams? All these are several concepts of how consciousness works. All these briefly mentioned are related to human consciousness, which can be influenced in several ways.

Body Clocks

Many start their day with full energy, but by midday, it's down. For some, they try to be energetic in the morning with no result, but amazingly, they pick up in the evening. This daily fluctuation of energy levels is identified as circadian rhythm or body's clock. They have a significant impact on consciousness and other psychological states.

CHAPTER 10:

Emotional Psychology

Our emotions appear to be in control of our daily lives. The decisions we make are based on whether we are sad, happy, angry, frustrated, or bored. The hobbies and activities we choose to partake in are incited by our emotions. Moving through our daily lives, we get to experience a variety of emotions.

What are emotions? Emotions are complex psychological states that encompass three different components: a subjective experience, a behavioral or expressive response, and a physiological response. Adding to the definition of emotions, researchers have been able to identify and classify emotions into types.

However, these descriptions and insights appear to be changing over time.

Emotion is a subjective state of being, which we often describe as feelings. Emotion and mood are sometimes used interchangeably, but psychologists have pointed out that these words mean two different things. Basically, the word emotion denotes a subjective affective state which is relatively intense and occurs in response to what we experience. Emotions are experienced intentionally and consciously. On the other hand, mood refers to a less intense, prolonged, affective state which doesn't occur in response to what we experience

Our emotions are essential to our ability to adapt to life's challenges. When we have a good feeling, we are able to shrug off even the biggest of tasks, but when we feel troubled or worried, we tend to see an enjoyable task as too burdensome and view it with a sense of doom and gloom. Our emotions can even go beyond and affect our relationships with other people. For example, if a friend is telling you a sad story and expects you to respond looking sad or concerned, but you choose to look unconcerned and snicker instead, you will only appear rude and insensitive. Likewise, if you are frowning when a friend is telling you of a very funny joke, you will also appear offensive and uninterested.

Going off the handle just because of a minor annoyance can make you appear unbalanced or too hyper.

If you give an undue happy reaction to information tagged as good news, people will start to question your stability and maturity. If it was a baby, they are totally allowed to wail with rage and shriek with pleasure at any time, but as an adult, people expect you to rein in the outward expression of your feelings.

Our emotions play an important role in our ability to succeed or fail in the challenges thrown at us. Just think about the famous people whose careers have taken a step back because of the way their feelings were expressed. For example, during the primary run-up to the 2004 United States presidential election, the candidacy of Howard Dean ended overnight after his "YAAAAHHH" moment became an internet frenzy.

Prior to that, Edmund Muskie made the same political blunder during the 1972 primary season. Muskie shed tears after he won the New Hampshire primary. However, he claimed the tears were snowflakes that were shimmering in the morning light. In the same light, Hillary Clinton wasn't seen as a sympathetic fellow until she had her eyes wet when answering a voter's question. Of course, some pundits used that act against her and questioned her sincerity. You might be asking what these examples have to do with the role of emotions in our lives.

The above examples show us that the outward display of our inner feelings has the power to influence how we are treated by others. Meanwhile, these emotional displays are greatly dependent on our cultural norms. To be recognized as a well-adapted member of society, it is important that we adhere to the norms or risk ridicule or condemnation from other people.

According to the findings of psychologist Paul Ekman in 1972, there are six basic emotions that are recognized widely. These are happiness, sadness, fear, anger, surprise, and disgust. The way in which people express these emotions differs quite radically based on the norms of everyone's culture. In 1999, Ekman expanded his list of basic emotions and included a number of others, including excitement, embarrassment, contempt, pride, shame, amusement, and satisfaction.

Prominent psychologist Robert Plutchik also introduced an emotion classification he called the "wheel of emotions." This model of emotion classification shows how different emotion types can be combined or mixed together just like a color wheel where primary colors are mixed to make other colors.

Emotional manipulation can be absolutely devastating to people. Remember, emotions are massively motivating, and if you manage to manipulate one's emotions properly, you can encourage the individual to cater to your every whim. In doing so, you will be able to get exactly what you want. Of course, these techniques can also be incredibly harmful to the individual they are attempting to control simply because they are putting such a strain on the victim's mental state at the moment.

Understanding Emotions for Manipulation

When using emotional manipulation tactics, the most popular ones play off of one of four emotions: anger, fear, guilt, and sadness. In playing off of these emotions, you are more likely to get the desired results, especially if you understand the implications of each of those emotions. By developing a solid understanding of what each of these emotions entails, you are able to better control people simply by knowing which emotions to trigger.

Anger

Anger can be incredibly motivating. You can use it to direct blame onto someone else or encourage a degrading of a relationship between two people if you are able to trigger it. Remember, anger typically implies a degradation of some important boundary that was violated, and if you understand and recognize the importance of anger, you can wield it to your advantage.

For example, imagine that your victim has a friend that is nosy and seems to be on to the fact that you are manipulating her best friend. You cannot just tell your victim to stop talking to this individual as they are best friends and have been for the better part of a decade. What you can do instead, however, is direct anger toward the best friend to erode at the relationship. You could tell your victim that her friend did or said something harmful about the victim or about yourself in hopes of your victim coming to your defense. Your victim gets angry and directs that anger at the best friend, who, of course, grows defensive, and the entire situation blows up, causing a big argument while you are seen as an innocent bystander to the situation.

Fear

Fear motivates people because it tells them that they are in danger, somehow. This can be incredibly useful to utilize toward people, particularly in situations in which you are responsible for selling something. For example, imagine that you are a real estate agent. You directly get a cut of the value of the house as a commission for facilitating the sale. If your clients have been looking at a house that, admittedly, does fit their needs, but is in a less-than-stellar neighborhood in town and therefore is cheaper than many other similar houses elsewhere, you may mention to the individual that crime has been getting out of control in the area, or that you have heard stories of shootings or finding needles nearby. The entire purpose is to appeal to the fact that the individuals will likely become afraid at the idea of finding needles on their front lawn, and because of that, they are likely to look elsewhere. After all, no one wants to live somewhere they are afraid to call home.

Guilt

Guilt frequently encourages people to meet certain obligations. By appealing to guilt, you are able to tell someone that they have failed in achieving the completion of a specific need, and by accusing the individual of doing so, you are able to convince the other person to give in. For example, if your partner is supposed to take you out to dinner that night at a restaurant that you have had reservations at for the last month but has been seeming hesitant after an unexpected car accident, and deductible wiped out his savings, you may lay on the guilt, reminding him that he promised in an attempt to get him to follow through, though you know that it is not the right thing to do in the circumstances, and may actually put him in a really bad financial spot.

Sadness

Remember, sadness implied that there was a loss or pain somewhere and is meant to remind the individual not to repeat whatever had just happened. It is entirely meant to be discouraging, and it is incredibly powerful. People feel sadness when something significant has happened, but it may also be felt empathetically as well. This is how many charities seek out donations—they show pictures of sad, starving children or animals recovering from surgery needed after they were abused or neglected. In showing these sad images with sad music playing, with a quick message about how you can save the animals or children with a meager daily contribution, these charities are able to encourage people to donate massive amounts of money simply because the people are more willing to do whatever it will take to escape the massive amount of sadness they are feeling as a result of the ad.

Aggression

Sometimes, the easiest way to convince the other person to do what it is that you want or need is through more coercive means. You need to scare the victim in order to get obedience through fear, or at least, you assume you need to. When you want to convince people to be obedient, you may see value in utilizing intimidation or subtle threats. You know that they lead to discomfort in the victim, and that is exactly why you do so. You know that the discomfort will lead to the other person caving and not bothering to push the point further.

Utilizing your aggression or anger can take several different forms. You can threaten action or imply threats, such as saying that your partner will not like you if you are pushed, or you may even decide to do things that border on illegal but never quite cross the line into assault and battery, such as punching holes in the wall or attempting to otherwise make your partner fear your reaction.

You may even resort to tantrums in general, screaming and crying when you do not get your way, knowing that the other person is not likely to challenge you if you put on this largely angry show. Of course, you will likely have to slowly escalate this as the victim becomes accustomed to your behaviors over time.

CHAPTER 11:

Mind Control

Mind control sounds like a devious plot in a movie, but you have most likely experienced it many times a day for many years and never noticed it. Mind control, or the idea of thought-reform, is a controversial theory and practice, but one that does not necessarily mean tricking and scheming. As a matter of fact, mind control can be as simple as subliminal suggestion used to steer one in the direction you want rather than the direction they were going autonomously.

There are many schools of thought in regards to mind control, but, let's look at a common example of mind control to start. Color, smell, sight, sound, and taste are used on the consumer by every company selling a product to advance their customers and sales. When you enter your local grocery store, often there are fresh cut flowers at the entrance. Now, how often have you bought those flowers? Chances are, never, if maybe a time or two because you forgot a special occasion. Grocers use the presence of these flowers as a means of manipulating the subconscious of their customers. Fresh cut flowers are, well, fresh. Ripe. Pleasant. They subliminally convey the thought of freshness, and your local grocery store wants you to be thinking about all the fresh produce they have waiting for you. More often, these grocers make more on the sale of their fresh produce over name brand canned and frozen produce, and if you buy the produce, they have available, more of your dollars go in their pocket as opposed to mass production companies.

Every day, you are exposed to one form of mind control or another. Product placement on television and in movies. The music you hear in a store or even an elevator. Friends that are so convincing, you can't help but agree, or you find yourself always saying yes to them.

Re-education is a very optimal, but controversial tool in mind control. The ability to re-educate another person's previous thought process or beliefs is possible, but can take time. At the heart of re-education sits repetition. I repeat, repetition. By repeating the same belief, idea, or thought to another person, repeatedly, you are impressing upon them the change from their own ideas towards your own. And this repetition leads to immersion in the idea or action you want them to follow. Being immersed in an idea, the idea in question always being repeated, the idea or goal always being spoken of, leads to the individual re-examining their previous feelings about the issue. Re-examining one's feelings often leads to them coming to a new conclusion. Your conclusion. You have just exerted a form of mind control on another individual, and now they agree with you.

Priming an individual is another effective way to get what you want. Some who see this activity negatively may refer to in as indoctrination, but the goal is not to necessarily start a cult. You are just trying to get others to agree with you, and are trying to use all the available tools you possess to your advantage. Priming involves softening a person towards you and your ideas, easing them into the thought that you know what is best. Softening can include hours of conversation, empathizing with them and showing them that you care or love them. You care about what happens, you understand them. Once you have a foundation of trust through understanding and priming, soft persuasion towards the new idea, belief, or action can be introduced. It is imperative that you have formed a mutual bond or respect with the person who you want to influence. And it is a given that change takes time.

A few techniques to help you on your path to persuasion using coercion may involve thinking for others, being specific in your logic and requests, creating a real sense of urgency, and stressing the importance of your goal or idea. When presenting someone with a change in long held ideas or requests, thinking for them takes the pressure of deciding off them. People often have enough on their mental plates as it is, you shouldn't be asking them to take on more, especially when you can do the heavy lifting for them. Explain exactly why they should see things your way, offering as many examples as possible as to the correctness to your idea, proof that what you want is not only right, but it is proven to be effective or accurate. Once you have specifically lined out why they should agree with you, tell them what is next and why things need to be done your way. Be friendly but as firm and confident in your pitch to them as you need be, and often discouraging questions until you are finished explaining your stance helps steer others in your direction. They often forget their questions or objections as they listen to you explain what you want, why, and what you think needs to happen next to achieve the goal. It is all about the goal.

While on the topic of your goals and what you want to achieve, it is imperative to stress the importance of what you want to achieve. If others are consistently being spoken with on how important the idea or goal is, and specifics on why it is so important, eventually they start to see your idea as more than just something you want, but an issue of utmost importance. Your thought or goal becomes something more, and it should be more to you too. It should be a movement. A goal doesn't have to be a social ideal to be a movement, you just need others to feel its importance as much as you do. Everybody wishes to be on the right side of history, no matter how big or small the issue is. And all it takes is someone to see your want as a matter that needs to be addressed or adjusted, and where there is one person who agrees with you, there are two, and more soon to follow.

So, your idea, goal, or thought is now more than just something you want. Other people want it too. And it is not just important, it is imperative. And it needs to happen now. Creating a sense of urgency is another effective form of utilizing mind control techniques to your benefit. Making urgent statements, or claiming that this situation is time sensitive will create an emotional response in those you wish to influence or persuade. A specific deadline needs to be in place, but the idea that this can't wait long needs to be an underlying sentiment. The quicker you get other people on board, the more important you convince them your want is, the more urgent they believe things are, the less resistance you will run into. Repeating equals results. The more information backing your idea or goal people are given, the more likely they will let you think for them and just go with the flow. The more urgent the matter is, the less time people have to ask discouraging questions or second guess their shift in ideas.

Being consistent is the core aspect of implementing mind control techniques to get what you want. Consistently repeating what you want, and be consistent when rejecting old ideas or goals. Be consistent when speaking about what needs to happen, when and why. These factors should be underlined, in bold print, repeated regularly, and the time sensitivity needs to be stressed.

There is nothing wrong with being a little pushy to get what you want out of your life. Another great technique when using mind control is to ask small things of others, or asking for small changes in another's ideas, and then expanding from there. Let's use a raise from your employer as an example. If you want a decent increase in pay, don't ask for your top dollar pay increase. Ask for a small increase in pay based on your performance and loyalty. Your boss will agree (considering you are worthy of the raise to begin with) and think that they got off cheap keeping you happy. After you have reached the first step in reaching your ultimate pay goal, ask for more work. Let your employer know you are more than happy taking on more responsibility. You can possibly save them money if you are doing more work than before, they may not have to hire another employee to work weekends if you are willing to come in for a few hours on a Saturday. Now, you have a pay increase, but you have more responsibility. It only seems fair that you are paid a little more now that you are a more valuable resource for your employer to utilize. It's better they give you another slight pay increase to cover your knowledge and expertise in the workplace than bother trying to hire another employee to replace you. You see how simple it can be? Now, that isn't saying that you have a boss or employer this would work on, but if you are implementing the other tools you have in your fast-growing arsenal, you are now a very well-liked employee and co-worker who knows how to influence and persuade others to see things the way you do. Your employer may dislike the idea of paying you even more than before, but sometimes it's not just your work ethic that matters, sometimes it's what you bring to the table for everyone you encounter.

It is not easy to say no to someone who you feel a debt to. The final technique of mood control we should consider is generosity. You should always strive to give more than you take from others. When you give more of your time, your effort, your attention, to others, they appreciate it. They remember it. And, when the moment comes that you want something in return, it is much harder to say no, or disagree, or refuse to cooperate with another who has freely offered up so much to them. Even in circumstances or changes others may not want to agree or get on board with, if they know that you have been offered the same courtesy by you previously, they find it hard to go against you. It falls back to persuasion, influence, and reciprocation. Most often, those that you have committed your time and attention to will return the favor. Even if you are met with resistance by someone who you have given to, a gentle reminder of what you have done for them is often all that is needed to get them on board with what you want. Sometimes it isn't the loudest voice in the room that matters, but the most consistent and softest from the individual who has done the most to help others. That soft but firm voice can be yours; you only need to take your opportunities as they present themselves.

CHAPTER 12:

Body Language and Personality

Having to gain the art of understanding people's nonverbal communication is a hard thing. You may be wondering how the heck can you focus on learning other people's cues while you do not know yourself fully. Well, the book must help you demystify the art of understanding the body language for different people.

All of us are subconscious experts in interpreting the thoughts of other individuals towards us. In the woolly mammoth age, we developed these abilities since our life depended on them, and the unconscious mind would work more efficiently than the conscious mind. But when we make this unconscious understanding conscious, it does not have a good result. We can respond with lightning speed to dodge a fist that some whiny brat throws in our way, or to jump out from the way of an approaching car, practically before we can think about it explicitly.

Allied and Opposed

How would you tell whether somebody is your ally or not? The fundamental nonverbal communication to search for to decide if individuals are united to you or restricted is generally speaking physical position and their direction. This makes for engaging people viewing. When you're on to this part of conduct, you'll see that it is easy to get.

Simply, individuals who are in understanding will in general mirror each other's conduct. One will lead, and the other will pursue. This is particularly simple to tell when there are three individuals present, and you need to make sense of who's your ally and who isn't. Search for the person who has a similar essential body direction as you. For a test, move and check whether the other individual sticks to this same pattern in the following thirty seconds.

Strong and Subservient

In space and height, the story of power in a room is written. Scan the alpha. If possible, he or she would be the greatest person in the room. That's why kings and queens have had daises thrones since they started ruling others.

Powerful individuals are also taking up so much space: splaying out their legs or arms, or hogging more space in the room. That's why influential people get larger apartments than fewer men, and that's why taller people in their careers are significantly more likely to rise faster than short people.

Powerful individuals use a host of bolder indicators of their dominance to indulge in shorter breaks, from upsetting smaller individuals to talking more. We make more or less eye contact on the basis of their choice. In fact, they monitor the communication of the second speaker's ballet with the eye and the outside contact.

Committed and Uncommitted

Commitment is the moment you close the offer, the contract ink, get the job, get the 'go forward.' It's a key moment, and it's important to be able to see it so that at the pivotal moment you aren't doing the wrong thing. People learn to you when they are serious. They are transparent, submissive at times, always genuine, and generally well connected.

It starts with your eyes: they're completely open and you're focused. Likewise, the face is open. It will be very close to yours more than anything. It's all about completing the sale to close the distance. That's why your hand is regularly shaken by car sales representatives. The torso, if not engaged, is accessible and nearer to you. From the arms and hands, feet and legs, there is no oppositional chatter. If appropriate in the situations, the person or persons may well mimic you. The act of communication is often indicated by a change of nonverbal communication, which suggests a decision has been made.

Open and Closed

The very first way to determine the motives of others is the most important: their level of transparency. It is the most important since interaction will start if people are honest with one another. Nothing good can happen if they aren't. You ought to be prepared to scale individuals more along the lines quite easily in an almost automated way with just a little training. But don't ask for an immediate reading what people these days call thin-slicing. In reality, it takes a little time for each new individual you meet to measure the performance of conduct. The idea isn't to be capable of carrying out this role immediately but to be able to size up somebody with high efficiency in terms of whether this person is open to you within a few minutes.

Arms and Legs Crossed Suggest Opposition to Your Ideas

Legs and arms crossed are obstructions that indicate that the other individual is not receptive to what you tell. You find that, even if they tend to engage in the good conversation and smile, most of the time the real truth is revealed through body language. A case is studied by authors who were doing negotiations for their new book on reading body language. They held many meetings and later revealed that among all the meetings, not one resulted in an agreement whenever one of the parties crossed their legs and feet when negotiating. Mentally, legs crossed and arms mean an individual is being mentally, emotionally, or physically stopped from what's before them. It's not deliberate so it's so surprising.

Copying Your Body Language

Have any of you ever met somebody and found that they do the same if you cross or uncross your legs and feet? Or maybe when you're thinking, they lean their heads the very same position as yours? In reality, that's a good indication. If we experience a bond with another person, mirroring body language comes in unintentionally.

It's an indication that the discussion is moving well enough and your message is being received by another group. Such information can be particularly helpful when bargaining, as it tells you what the other party feels about the contract.

The Story is Told by Posture

Have you ever seen someone come into a room, and you immediately knew that they are in control? This influence is primarily about the language of the body, and often involves an upright stance, movements with the palms facing forward, and generally open and expressive gestures. The brain is programmed to balance energy with the number of people taking up space. It's a position of authority to stand straight with your shoulders back; it seems to maximize the amount of storage you fill. On the other hand, slouching is the product of the collapse of your shape; it seems to take up less space and less energy for activities. Maintaining good posture commands respect and fosters commitment, regardless of being in a leadership position or not.

The Eyes are Crinkled by Genuine Smiles

The mouth can deceive whenever it applies to laugh, however, the eyes can never lie. Genuine smiles touch the ears and crinkle the skin in front of them to build the feet of the crow. Individuals sometimes smile to conceal what they might feel and think, so watch for crinkles at the edges of their eyes the next time you want to know if somebody's smile is real. If they're not there, something covers the smile.

Discomfort in Raised Eyebrows

Three fundamental feelings cause your eyebrows to go up shock, stress, and the feeling of fear. Have a go at causing a stir when you're having a casual easygoing discussion with a companion. It's difficult to do, would it say it isn't? If someone who is conversing with you happens to have raised eyebrows, yet the subject of the discussion isn't one that would consistently cause shock, stress, or dread, there is something different going on.

Misrepresented Nodes Signal Nervousness About Acceptance

At the point when you're telling somebody something and they keep nodding too much, this implies they are stressed over what you consider them or that you question their capacity to adhere to your guidelines.

A Held Jaw Signals Pressure

A gripped jaw, a fixed neck, or wrinkled temples are altogether indications of stress. Despite what the individual is stating, these are indications of significant inconvenience. The discussion may be diving into something they're on edge about or their psyche maybe somewhere else and they're concentrating on what's worrying them. The key is to look for that befuddle between what the individual says and what their strained nonverbal communication is letting you know.

.

CHAPTER 13:

Personality Type

Realizing that areas of your personalities are engaged at different levels daily at work, home and play—is one thing, and understanding how to use that knowledge is another. But it is very vital. When you can identify personality types, it can assist you to exert your influence, enhance relationships, communicate effectively, and accomplish success in whatever desire is in play. Personality type is defined as the psychological categorization of the various kinds of individuals. Personality types are sometimes separated from personality traits; the latter embodies a less categorization of behavioral tendencies. Personality types are also said to engage qualitative differences among people, while traits might be construed as quantitative differences.

ISTJ Personality–The Inspector

At your first impression, ISTJs are so intimidating. ISTJs are seen as formal, proper, and serious. ISTJs like old-school traits and traditions that uphold cultural responsibility, honor, patience, and hard work. ISTJs are upright, calm, and quiet.

I–Introvert: Self-sufficient, quiet, and reserved. Their energy is drained by them socializing. So they tend to be comfortable when they are alone. They process their thoughts internally. They need time to be alone for them to recharge.

S–Sensing: They are aware of, trust facts, details, specifics, present realities, and past experiences. ISTJs are often pragmatic, observant, and realistic. They live in the now-and-here.

T–Thinking: ISTJs make decisions mainly based on logic rather than their emotional feels. They are governed by their head and not their heart. They are very concerned with truths or facts than protecting other people's emotions.

J–Judging: They are disciplined, organized, and strategic. ISTJs are very responsible, and they stick to the schedules. They like to prepare and plan ahead.

ISTJs Traits

- They love to memorize facts and details

- ISTJs are people who are well respected in society

- They are calm and clear-headed during tense events

- They are committed and serious when it comes to relationships

- They are highly intelligent and have excellent planning skills

- ISTJs are mentally and physically organized

- They believe in traditions, and they tend to follow them to the latter.

INFJ Personality–The Counselor

These are idealists and visionaries who produce brilliant ideas and creative imaginations. INFJs have a totally different and very profound aspect of viewing the universe. Counselors tend to have a depth and substance in the manner they think, they never take anything at a surface level or accept things the way they are. Many people may perceive this kind of people as weird because they view life differently.

I–Introvert: Self-sufficient, quiet, and reserved. Their energy is drained by them socializing. So they tend to be comfortable when they are alone. They process their thoughts internally. They need time to be alone to recharge.

N–Intuitive: Introspective, imaginative, and creative. They are perfect at analyzing complex topics. They mainly focus on the future rather than the present. They trust their gut instincts.

F–Feeling: INFJs tend to make use of their subjective criteria, values, and feeling when they are making decisions. They are mostly ruled by their hearts and not the head. They are very tactful, empathetic, and diplomatic. INFJs are mostly motivated by appreciation, and they prefer to avoid conflicts and arguments with others.

J–Judging: They are disciplined, organized, and strategic. INFJs are very responsible, and they stick to the schedules. They like to prepare and plan ahead.

INFJs Traits

- They are real visionaries who often try to make sense of life.

- They trust their gut instincts

- INFJs can understand and read other people easily

- They are cautious, courteous, helpful and sensitive

- Approachable, warm and caring

- They like creating and organizing systems

- INFJs are always passionate about dreams and ideas.

Creative and artistic, INFJs live in a world that has hidden possibilities and meanings. While INFJs place great value on order, they also are spontaneous; this is because INFJs intuitively understand things even without them being able to pinpoint why. It is because of this reason that INFJs are less orderly and systematic compared to the other judging personality type.

Intuition is one of the strongest values of the INFJs.

INFJs are very sensitive towards others feelings. They carefully do not hurt others through their actions and words. INFJs always lend a hand to others who need their assistance because they are empathizing and compassionate. They are good at sensing other's emotions and also good at analyzing people.

At the workplace, INFJs are very creative that makes them stand out from the crowd. They are strategists and planners who have respect for deadlines and rules.

ENFJ Personality–The Giver

These are focused on people. ENFJs are charismatic, outspoken, idealistic, extroverted, ethical, and highly principled, and they understand how to connect and interact with other people no matter their personality or background. They really rely on their feelings and intuition; they live a life full of imagination rather than in the actual world. Instead of the ENFJs concentrating on living in the "now" and want is happening currently, they tend to focus on the abstract and what could happen in the future possibly.

E–Extrovert: These kinds of people like to be around people. They have high energy levels and are very active. ENFJs like to take up the initiative. They are enthusiastic and outgoing. They tend to talk more than listen.

N–Intuitive: Introspective, imaginative, and creative. They are perfect at analyzing complex topics. They mainly focus on the future rather than the present. They trust their gut instincts.

F–Feeling: ENFJs tend to make use of their subjective criteria, values, and feeling when they are making decisions. They are mostly ruled by their hearts and not the head. They are very tactful, empathetic, and diplomatic. ENFJs are mostly motivated by appreciation, and they prefer to avoid conflicts and arguments with others.

J–Judging: They are disciplined, organized, and strategic. ENFJs are very responsible, and they stick to the schedules. They like to prepare and plan ahead.

ENFJs Traits

- They are good communicators

- They are very organized and effective with challenges when it comes to dealing with uncertainties

- ENFJs are very open-minded and highly accepting of others

- They are firm and passionate when it comes to principles and ideals.

- Generous, warm, focused and caring

- Highly reflective and intuitive

- Genuinely kind, influential, reliable, and loyal.

ISTP Personality–The Craftsman

These are very mysterious people who are normally logical and quite rational, but they are also enthusiastic and spontaneous. ISTPs often have the capability of humorously insightful observations about the universe around them. ISTPs traits are less easy to recognize than other personality types, even for those who know the traits very well cannot often anticipate their reactions. People with ISTP personality type, deep down they are unpredictable, spontaneous, but they tend to hide the traits from the outside world, often more successfully.

I–Introvert: Self-sufficient, quiet, and reserved. Their energy is drained by them socializing. So they tend to be comfortable when they are alone. They process their thoughts internally. They need time to be alone to recharge.

S–Sensing: They are aware of, trust facts, details, specifics, present realities, and past experiences. ISTPs are often pragmatic, observant, and realistic. They live in the now-and-here.

T–Thinking: ISTPs make decisions mainly based on logic rather than their emotions. They are ruled by their head and not by their heart. They are very concerned with truths facts rather than protecting other people's emotions.

P–Perceiving: Keeping options open, preferring spontaneity, and flexibility. ISTPs are very adaptive, and they go with the flow. They are playful and are less aware of the time. They prefer to begin a project, and they question the need for many rules.

ISTP Traits

- They are determined and independent

- ISTPs are more focused on living in the present rather than in the future

- They are normally laid back and are easygoing with most people

- ISTP is a risk taker who likes new and variety of experiences

- They are better troubleshooters who are easily able to get solutions to practical issues.

- ISTPs are result-oriented, highly practical and realistic

- They often put together facts about the environment and store them away for later use.

ISTPs are generous and optimistic; they believe that equality and fairness are vital. ISTPs have a strong drive to know well the way things work. They are perfect in logic analysis, are action-oriented, and they enjoy the practical application. ISTPs are adaptable, and they normally have good technical skills. They have a very compelling drive to understand the way things work.

ISTPs are usually easygoing with others and confident in their capabilities. Many people will describe ISTPs as friendly but quite calm, private but suddenly spontaneous, and very curious but not able to stay focused on formal studies.

Their decisions mainly stem from a sense of practical realism and a do unto others attitude. Equality and fairness are very vital to ISTPs. ISTPs are very loyal to their friends, but they may require a lot of time alone for them to recharge.

ISTP personality types are likely to be good at regulating the energy levels and saving the energy for things that they consider vital. This is particularly noticeable in events where ISTPs get an opportunity to work something they like, like a hobby project. The amount of energy and effort ISTPs they can expend in this kind of situations is very impressive.

CHAPTER 14:

Analyzing People Through Body Language

Body Language Clues: The Basics

When you try to know more about your goal and how they view the world, body language is going to be so crucial. Too many times we get caught in the words that someone else tells us and we won't concentrate on the other indications they also give us. There is so much that can be disclosed by these body language clues, and it makes a large difference in how effective you are in understanding and working with your goals.

Body language will refer to some of the nonverbal signals we use to interact with others. These nonverbal signals will take up much of the interaction we communicate every day. From the movement of our body to our facial expressions and everything in between, things we don't say can still share a ton of information during the process. Indeed, 60 to 65% of our interaction could be accounted for by body language and other nonverbal communications. So how do we learn to read this language to our own advantage? Let's begin by learning more about the various indications of body language, and how we can read this for our benefit. First off we have the facial expressions.

Think of a time, by the expression on your face, about how much data someone can convey. A smile is a nice way to show happiness or consent. A frown can imply the other way around. In some instances, facial expressions can show our real emotions about a scenario. While an individual may say he's okay, he looks like he's talking when he says this might talk otherwise. There are many feelings on our facial expressions, including:

1. Contempt
2. Desire

3. Excitement
4. Confusion
5. Fear

The expression that appears on the person's face helps us to determine if we trust and think anything the person says. In reality, one research discovered that the most credible of all facial expressions will be a small eyebrow raise and a slight smile. This is an expression that in many instances shows us to trust and friendliness.

The other type of body language cue will have to be the mouth. Mouth expressions and motions can be another vital component of body language reading. For instance, if you notice someone else chewing on his bottom lip, it may show that there are feelings of insecurity, fear, and worry. The individual can cover his mouth to be polite when he coughs, but sometimes the other person's disapproval. And smiling will be one of the best signals of corporeal language, but the smile and what it says about a person can be evaluated differently. Some of the stuff you can care about when reading someone else's mouth movements include;

- Pursed lips: If you see your goal tightened up, it's a sign of distrust, disagreement, and disgust.

- Lip biting: This is when you bite your lower lip, usually when you are stressed, anxious, or distressed.

- Mouth cover: Any moment someone wishes to conceal one of their emotional responses, they can cover their mouths in order to assist.

- Turned up or down: Even a slight shift in your mouth can be a subtle indication of how you feel right now. When your mouth turns up, it's a sign that you are hopeful or glad. It could be a grimace, disagreement, and even sorrow when the mouth turns down.

Another area to observe as body language cue is gestures. Gestures can be a very evident, direct sign of body language to be careful about. Waiving, pointing and fingering can be common and easy to understand gestures. Some may even be cultural. Some of the most popular gestures and the significances that come with them include:

- A clung fist: In most cases, this will show anger, but sometimes it can also imply solidarity.

- Up or down thumbs: This is used as a sign of approval and disapproval.

- The "all correct" gesture: This one will assist others to say you're fine in the United States. But it is seen in some other cultures as a vulgar gesture.

The next thing we have to do is look at the arms and legs of the individual you talk to. These can be useful if a lot of information is to be transmitted nonverbally. Crossing the weapons will often be a defensive maneuver. Crossing the legs away from another individual will also show a person's discomfort or a dislike.

Other subtle signals, including the large expansion of the arm, can sometimes help us to seem bigger and more comfortable while maintaining the arms close to the body. When you try to measure your body language a little, be careful about some of the following signals that your legs and arms will transmit to you from the target:

- Crossed arms: This will give you a signal that you're closed, safe and defensive. As a manipulator, you need to uncross the arms of the goal to make you feel comfortable.

- Standing on hips with your hands: This can be a good sign that the person is ready and controlled. This will sometimes be a sign of aggression.

- Clamp the hands so that they're behind the back: This will be a sign that your goal is angry, anxious or boring. You have to look at some of the other signals that come first.

- Tap fingers or fidgeting quickly: The other person is frustrated, impatient and even bored.

- Crossed legs: This is a good indication that someone feels closed or needs some privacy.

Posture is another thing you should look at. The way we hold our bodies will also be a significant component of body language. Posture refers to the way we hold our bodies and to a person's general physical shape. Posture can give a wealth of data on how someone feels and also suggests that a person's features are submissive, open or confident. For instance, if you sit directly, it can show that an individual is concentrated and is attempting to look after what is going on. Sitting down with the body, on the other side, will show that someone is most of the time indifferent or bored. Looking at your goal will assist you to understand whether you are interested in what you do or say, or if you need to move on to find a different destination.

Whenever you attempt to read some of the languages of your body, attempt and find out some signals that your goal's position is attempting to tell you. Some of them are:

- Open posture: This includes keeping the body's trunk exposed and open.

- Closed position: this one will require hiding the body's trunk and hitting the legs and arms. This posture will be more indicative of anxiety, discomfort, and depression in the objective.

CHAPTER 15:

Understanding the Self–What Does My Behavior Display?

In order to properly analyze others, it is important to seek understanding with your own body movements. In social settings, the way we position our body can be the difference between making friends and repelling them. Since we cannot see our body movements as well as others, it's important to become in tune with your feelings and perception. Many times, we may not even realize the silent signals we are giving off. Sure, we have the ability to speak our emotions, but we all know that the truth is seldom spoken.

Science has proven that we emit energy that can be detected, and is even contagious. When your inner energy is feeling tired or bored, your outward appearance will give evidence of that energy despite how "excited" you say you are. Technology has given us the grand opportunity to display rejection with the simple glance down at the phone. For example, when a friend is telling you a story that you are 100 percent not interested in, likely you will reach for your phone and begin scrolling. Your words are saying, "Uh-huh," occasionally, but your demeanor speaks volumes. You may believe you are listening when really you are showing outward disdain for your friend. This sign is often taken as disrespect and could create distance in the friendship.

Another common sign is the crossing of the arms. In social occasions, this can be translated as, "I don't want to be here." When in reality, you could simply be cold. Since this is what you are exhibiting, others are naturally going to view you as unapproachable. Do you find yourself doing this quite often? Crossing of the arms is another form of protection. It is almost likened to a comfort mechanism that we do when in an uncomfortable situation.

This can be attributed to a form of social anxiety and inner insecurity. Sure, you may be the most inviting person in the room, but you are not aware of that yet. Your inner, primal voice is activating your fight-or-flight response. You may be subconsciously uncomfortable with your outfit, afraid of others' opinions, or even fearful of talking to people. The importance of becoming aware of your deeper desires will work wonders towards your body language.

Another instance occurs during one-on-one communication. Do you notice your eyes drifting during a conversation? Or even your hand being placed on your face while someone is talking? This signals disinterest and could be extremely disrespectful to the person talking. In turn, your friend could become upset with you without you even realizing it.

Flirtation can be a fine and tricky art because many of the signals of genuine interest and attraction are often intertwined. For example, a young man was engaging in a conversation with a married woman at a public event. She was talking to him about a job opportunity she had available in her department. Being recently laid off from his job, naturally, the man was excited! He began to shift his body towards her as he leaned his head in. His eyes never left hers, and he had a slight smile on his face. Upon noticing, the woman's husband grew increasingly alert to their conversation. From the outside, all he saw was this young man, leaning in towards his wife with a smile. Unbeknownst to him, the situation was far from flirtatious.

This is a clear indicator of how our body language deeply affects the way people view us. When engaging in that conversation, the young man was extremely interested in the possible job opportunity, not the married woman. However, his body language signaled attraction. The importance of being aware of how your body is positioned when speaking to others is a subliminal sign of respect. One fantastic way to become aware of your body motions is to remember the three W's: who, what, and where. Let's consider them one at a time.

Who

When speaking with another person, it's key to remember who you are engaging with. Is it a close friend of the opposite sex? Is it your manager or maybe even an older person? In all of these instances, the way you position your body means everything. Take, for example, speaking with your manager. Do you find yourself naturally crossing your arms when he or she approaches you? This could be your way of protecting yourself against their authority, or you may actually dislike your manager. However, you want to keep your job and even appear interested in what he or she has to say. This instance is when acting and awareness play a major role.

When you see your manager coming, the butterflies may ensue. You may even become a bit clammy in the hands. Instead of allowing that feeling to overpower you, simply acknowledge it, and let it be. Don't try to manipulate the feeling as that causes further anxiety. Rather, acknowledge it, and place your hands by your side with open palms. Try your best to breathe and remain comfortable. Position your back upright with your shoulders aligned. Create an opening demeanor that opens the door for conversation.

What

When engaging in a conversation, try to feel what your body is doing. Are your hands clenched in a fist? Do you feel your face tightening as if you're displeased? When you become aware of what your body does when engaging in a conversation, you will be able to control those muscles. One vital question you can ask yourself is, "What is my body telling others right now?" By doing so, you can immediately change the way others perceive you.

Where

It's especially important to be cognizant of where you are when speaking to others. Oftentimes, certain atmospheres may warrant specific behavior. For example, during a blind date, it would be quite rude to scrunch your forehead and brows in disgust at your date's appearance. Sure, they may not be what you expected, but you never want to display your inner emotions. In addition, you wouldn't walk into a funeral with a big smile and open arms. Even if you barely knew the deceased, that demeanor may appear heartless to the grieving family. Making the connection between what your body is doing and remembering where you are is imperative for your reputation.

Body awareness is key to navigating your world. It is defined as "the sense that we have of our own bodies." It is an understanding of the parts that make up one's body, where they are located, how they feel, and even what they can do. Certain activities such as yoga and Pilates assist with connecting the bridge between the body and mind. When engaging in these exercises, you are mentally aware of the positioning of your body. You have full control over your balance which strengthens your mental and physical muscles. Engaging in these activities on a regular basis can assist with understanding your body movements. This will come in handy when evaluating what your body is doing in social settings.

To practice your own proprioception exercise at home, begin by balancing on one foot. What are your arms doing? Your fingers? Do you feel a tingle in your opposing leg? Become engrossed in how your body is working together to keep you balanced. By repeating this simple exercise daily, you'll begin to notice the movements of even the smallest parts of your body.

In order to fully understand the body language of others, you have to become connected with your personal movements. Body language is more than just reading movements. It's attributing a deeper meaning towards body posture that can speak volumes into a person's

CHAPTER 16:

Mirroring

One of the critical roles of mirroring the body language of the target person is that it alerts them that you are taking a deliberate interest in the person and want to strike a rapport with the person. Mirroring helps create a connection between the participating parties in a conversation. Akin to any other aspect of communication, one needs to learn the right way of mirroring body language to realize the maximum benefits of the concept.

First, start by building your connection through fronting. In fronting, you want to lend the other person, complete attention. Go ahead and square your body so that you are directly facing the target person and try to make them the focus of your universe. Then establish eye contact, which may first appear invasive. Eye contact is critical in communicating your level of interest in the target person by communicating that you are giving undivided attention. Eye contact is also thought to elicit warm feelings that enhance a close connection. You should go ahead and initiate the triple nod, which does two functions. When one does the triple nod, then the target person is likely to speak three or four times longer, making them feel that they are being listened, or that what they are communicating is important. Additionally, if one nods, then it communicates that you are in tandem with what the person is saying, and this creates a receptive environment for sustained communication. One should elicit questions that will invite nodding. For instance, start by asking if the weather is warm. Then, pretend, followed by not pretending. In this instance, you are fronting the target person and initiating the right eye contact and applying the triple nod will help strike a rhythm with the individual. In this instance, you are likely feeling a strong connection, but to realize its full benefit try using the power of imagination by pretending the target person is the most interesting individual you have ever met. Try to imagine it and act accordingly followed by ceasing the pretense. In all this, significant levels of mirroring are likely to happen naturally on its account, but the following techniques can help enhance the mirroring of body language to attain intended goals.

Relatedly, exploit the pace and volume as many times people think of mirroring body language as mimicking the physical actions. However, mirroring body language includes all aspects of nonverbal communication, such as pace and volume. For instance, mirroring the pace and volume of the target person's speech will help initiate a connection and rhythm between the two. If the target person is, a fast talker and loud then enhance your volume and animation and if they are soft and slow, then relax and match them at their level instead. Compared to physical actions mimicry, pace and volume matching are easier. Recall how you felt when one of your friends adjusted their pace and volume of speaking to match yours; at those instances you probably felt that they want to hold a conversation with you.

Additionally, identify the target person punctuator. Assuming that you have been carefully paying attention to the target person, you are mirroring all this time; then you will notice their favorite punctuator that he or she uses to emphasize a point. For instance, it could be an eyebrow flash such as quickly raising the eyebrows. The punctuator could also be a form of hand gesture, such as the one certain politicians use. For instance, it could be that each time the target person insists on an issue, he or she makes a certain finger gesture, then you can encourage the individual by nodding when he or she makes the particular sign. After his or her submission, you should mimic that gesture to suggest that you align with the submitted views. In all these interactions, you will not utter a single word but are connecting and communicating with the target person.

Equally important, you should test the connection with the target person in several ways. For instance, make an overt unrelated action to the conversation and observe if it is reflected. An example is where you are giving a keynote speech, and a member of the audience comes up to you, and you discuss the similarities that he and you had with your fathers that had both participated in World

War II. At that instance, while talking, you get an irritating itch on your nose that you quickly scratch but then you realize that he reached up and scratched up his nose all the while continuing with his story. Even though it seemed out of place, you go ahead to evaluate if the test was a fluke and a moment later, you scratch your head, and suddenly the target person does the exact thing. It appears odd, and you almost laughed aloud. It is important to avoid repeated testing as it will break the connection and make the entire exercise appear like a prank against the best of your intention. It is also necessary to only mirror positive body language and avoid mirroring negative nonverbal communication such as turning away, closing your eyes, locking with your arms folded, or looking away. Akin to any other aspect of communication, comprehensive practice is important for one to attain efficacy levels.

As indicated, mirroring helps create a rhythm with the target individual. The main intention of mirroring the nonverbal communication of the target person is to make them notice you and fall to your pace of communication—nonverbal communication. Recall your school days when in a sporting activity or a hall with a visiting school. One of the ways that you initiated a conversation was by looking directly at the eyes of the other student that you did not know, and he or she responded. You then slowed your breathing and blinking of eyes to mimic the target student until you felt as if you are talking to each other using words. All these actions constitute mirroring to create a pattern of communication nonverbally with the target person.

For instance, if you smile at a child, it is likely to smile back at you. A common example of mirroring is when you look at your baby or any baby directly in the eyes or smile at them. In most cases, the babies will replicate the same action that you posed at them. For instance, if you clap your hands, they will also clap their hands at you. Though for the case of babies, they may lack the conscious level to perceive what they are doing, it represents the efficiency of mirroring body language. Babies with difficulties reflecting your actions can suggest that something is amiss, enabling you to investigate their welfare deeper.

Compared to men, women are more likely to mirror each other with ease. It emerges that women are likely to mirror the actions of another woman enabling two strangers, women, to connect instantly. If you are a woman or have female friends, then you must have noticed that women appear to easily connect, and it is largely due to mirroring the body language of each other. For instance, if one of the women adjusts her hair, then the other is also likely to do the same and all these increase the likelihood of striking a rapport and creating a rhythm.

It is important to take into consideration your relationship with the target person when mirroring. When mirroring the target person's actions remember that the power relationship between the two of you. For instance, mirroring your supervisor may not be a good idea. At the same time, mirroring a colleague of the opposite sex may be misinterpreted to mean that you are attempting to flirt with them even if they are responding to the mimicry. Similarly, mirroring in some contexts may appear unprofessionally and a violation of work ethics. For instance, a teacher mirroring a student or a doctor mirroring a patient may appear as a mockery even if that is not the intention. Overall, the power relationship with the target person should mediate and moderate the level of body language mirroring.

As such, mirroring body language is an efficient way of building trust and understanding fast. From all these what we learn is that mirroring body language helps initiate trust between two people, especially where the two have a passive history of interaction. As indicated earlier on, you might use mirroring body language during a random interaction such as a sporting event, a party, and any social function where you want to initiate communication and rhythm of communication to build a long-term relationship. In a way, mirroring body language acts as a technique of testing waters before one can verbalize their intentions. Chances are that if the mirroring of body language backfires then the person is likely to the walkway and make the target individual understand it was just a prank or casual moment, but if mirroring body language elicits positive responses then the two individuals are likely to go ahead and connect.

Lastly, like any other form of communication, the feelings of the target person should be taken into consideration. Even though mirroring of body language is a nonverbal and mostly passive form of nonverbal communication, a human being is an emotional creature, and it is necessary to listen and respond to the feelings of each other. For instance, if the body language of the target person indicates anger, then you should cease or adjust your actions to show consideration and care for the affected person. If the target person that you are mirroring body language is happy, then you should also exhibit positive emotions to increase the shared ground spectrum and encourage the person to exude emotions that are more positive.

CHAPTER 17:

How to Read People's Body Language

B ody language is a universal language, while inevitably there are some regional nuances, for the most part, you'll be able to appraise a person and read into their thoughts solely from the displays of their body. We're going to break down some of the common, more applicable aspects of reading body language so that you're not bogged down with excessive, possibly useless information.

Context is key. A person will react to numerous stimuli in their vicinity. You have to be aware of the changes in the environment or just the status of the environment to know if your subject is reacting to you or an increased room temperature. As the detector, you have to keep track of the changes in the environment. You need to know if a light is flickering, it will be a distraction. You have to notice if the air has kicked in and it's getting colder in the room. Are there annoying sounds? Displeasing aesthetics? Anything and everything are important.

Importance of the Environment

So, the very first exercise in learning body language is to notice the things going on around you. Start up a conversation with a person you intent on observing and make sure you notice without missing parts of the conversation what is going on. Take a mental note if something changes so you can monitor the new baseline of behavior. If for instance, the air conditioner does kick on in the middle of your conversation with someone, take note of when it turns off again. Wait a few moments for things to baseline again, and then bring up the pervious parts of the conversation the person reacted to. If they rubbed their arms while they spoke, they may have been cold, but if they do it again and the temperature has started to warm up, it could be a sign of unease.

Learning a Baseline

Any successful interrogator knows to establish a baseline with their suspect before they move towards taboo subjects that may cause discomfort. Once a baseline is established all future gesticulations and motions can be compared to a truthful, foundational display.

You may not fully be aware of the baseline behavior of even people that are close to you. So, take some time to start conversations with individuals and establish their personality and baseline. Take the conversation to multiple topics. Start with very neutral subjects, move to more passion invoking ones and happier ones back to neutral.

Once you've spent some time getting accustomed to changes in the environment and establishing a baseline, you're ready to start learning what the gestures you've been noticing mean.

Primitive Movements

There are different kinds of body language. Most actions are conscious, meaning they can be faked or omitted at will. True liars versed in the ways of deceit know this and use this to their advantage. Everyday citizens who may only lie on occasion to save face, may not be as well versed. That is where our advantage lies. We want to be able to distinguish our usually loving co-worker's sudden interest in our project as a power play. Thankfully though, there are primitive reactions that happen subconsciously and are far more reliable some of the gesticulations that can be faked. For the sake of diversity, we'll cover both.

Freeze, flight-or-fight? More often than not, a person will freeze to evaluate whether or not fight-or-flight is the appropriate reaction to their situation. It could be a split-second freeze that happens just long enough for the perpetrator to send a signal to their brain to unfreeze. Look for the freeze.

Have you ever caught a child sneaking into the proverbial, metaphorical cookie jar? If they even start to hear someone's footsteps they may freeze before they react in any other way. If you've caught them and you speak to announce your presence, they are sure to pause and they'll probably even turn around slowly to discover your presence.

Just as a child will pause when caught, a manipulator will pause. An average person lying may not think anything of their sudden freezing movement, but a full-fledged manipulator may only let the freeze last a split-second, may play the freeze off as a different reaction, or even try to convince you there was a freeze at all.

People don't just freeze for a physical threat; they freeze at thoughts. Have you ever paused suddenly in the middle of an action because you remembered something? The same will happen to a manipulator if they think they've been caught or if they think they are in danger of being discovered.

A form of flight. Often times, when people are feeling threatened in some way, they will find ways to put distance between them and the negative stimuli or they will find a barrier. Distance can be achieved by simply taking a step back, leaning back or completely existing the room/situation. If while standing, you notice a person leaning back away from you, they may be starting to feel threatened.

Continuing with the child metaphor, have you ever watched a child try to hide or sneak? What do they do? They either cover their eyes, thinking that if they can't see you, you can't see them, or they try to make themselves smaller. If they hunch over and walk past you, suddenly they are camouflaged and you can't see them–or so they hope. You can watch a child who has done something wrong try to exit the room hunched over. The same is true for adults who are trying to get away with lying, however, with time to grow up, adults tend to change how they hunch over.

While, an adult in trouble is just as likely to try to become a turtle: pull their shoulders up and forward and tuck their head down as the try to gaze towards the floor, there are also other displays of trying to hide.

Barriers. Other times, simple barriers will do. Have you ever noticed someone put their ankle on their knee, forming a table on their lap? The shin facing outward is a barrier. It's a form of keeping threats at bay. So, if you're having a sitting conversation with someone and you notice they start to lean back in their chair and prop their leg up to form a barrier between you and them, you may want to take note of the topic. While this may be a sign they just don't agree with your view, it could also be worth exploring the topic a little more, especially if you've already got the sense that something is off.

Some people may pick up objects to act as a barrier between you and them instead of changing their body position. The same way children have security blankets or stuffed animal they can press against their chest, lying adults may also want a security blanket of sorts. Pillows on couches are often grabbed, if there are no items, the arms could be placed across the chest.

Check the Feet. Just as looking at the bottom of someone's feet will tell you where they've been, looking at the direction of the feet will tell you where they are going. While this phrase may seem obvious, looking at the direction someone's feet is pointing will tell you where they *want* to be. If a person is sitting on a couch, but have moved their feet to face the door, they may be ready to leave. This becomes especially true if they've moved their stance to prepare for standing up, like scooting towards the edge of the cushion and leaning forward, ready to shift their weight to their legs.

People can point their feet in the direction they want to go if they are uncomfortable and they want to leave the current situation faster. Just like leaving the scene of a crime before the law enforcement shows up. While not everyone is going to want to flee the conversation because you've brought up something they may be lying about, some will especially if they can use leaving as an excuse to not have to talk about it. Leaving gives them more time to think of what to say, how to say it and how to come off as truthful or convince you it was all a misunderstanding.

Locking. Women are more prone to locking their legs or ankles because they've been taught to sit this way, especially when wearing a skirt. However, if a man interlocks his ankles while sitting he is displaying a high level of stress and it should raise a red flag. For either gender, sudden locking of the ankles is a sign that something may be off. Prolonged ankle locking is a way of restricting movement.

Just as the freeze instinct suggestions, people tend to cease their movements when they are lying. If someone has been using gestures frequently and suddenly ceases, this may be an indication that they have started lying. If someone's feet have been moving regularly during a conversation, especially while sitting and they suddenly cease, take note.

Evolving

Joe Navarro an FBI agent trained in interrogation states that after every primitive response, there will be a pacifying behavior. These behaviors are mechanisms to calm anxiety or fear. They are big discomfort flags.

Going for the Neck. The neck is the most prominent pacifying area. Men like to rub their necks, touch their collars or pull on their ties, women will play with necklaces, or touch around their collar bone and center of the neck.

Sometimes, when a woman puts her arms across her chest, she is actually cupping her right elbow with her left hand. When she does this, she is putting a barrier between her and the person she is talking to. If things get really uncomfortable, she will move her right hand to her neck. She may play with a necklace or touch her fingers to her neck to display her discomfort.

The Cleanser. The cleanser is a well-known sign of discomfort or stress. Have you ever noticed someone rubbing their hands, or more accurately, their palms down their thighs? This action can be done once or repetitiously depending on why the reaction is occurring.

The cleanser could be used for two reasons, the person has started to sweat (possibly from anxiety), or because the person is using it to pacify. With either reasoning the cleanser is a behavior to notice. The subject may be more prone to use it if they think a table is blocking the view of their thighs and palms. An easy way to still notice the cleanser is to watch the elbows/arms and shoulders if their hands have disappeared under the table, you will still see a forward and backwards motion in these regions.

CHAPTER 18:

Basic Techniques to
Easily Improve Your Body Language

There's no specific definitive advice on how one must actually use body language because interpretation depends on the setting, situation, & cultural context. The way you use body language when talking to your own mother compared to when you talk to your boss, or a person you're intensely attracted to all differ from each other. There're simple ways that can help you communicate effectively with your body.

1. Be aware of your own body. Simply observe yourself—the way you sit, stand, & walk, how you use your arms, legs, & hands, & what your body does while talking to someone you know, for example. You may already be aware of some of your mannerisms & particular bodily quirks, like biting your nails when you're nervous, or pinching your nose when you're upset, or just twirling your hair when you're with someone you like, but you may be surprised to discover new ones. A lot of these quirks, mannerisms, & knee jerk reactions we cannot control, but when we're aware of them, we understand why we do them.

2. Maintain steady eye contact, but don't stare for too long. Eye contact is like a requirement when talking to someone, but the intensity & frequency of eye contact also depends heavily on your own relationship with the person you're talking, the setting or context, & the nature of your conversation.

    For some people, prolonged eye contact & being stared at makes them so uncomfortable or even creeps them out. On the flip side, if you don't maintain eye contact, you'll also more likely come across as insecure, timid, hiding something, or even lying.

What's the best thing to do then? If you're talking to several people, give some time to make eye contact with all of them to establish connections & gauge whether they're really listening to you & are interested. If talking with one person, find that balance between maintaining eye contact at the most crucial points of the conversation, & looking away every once in a while. That way, the other person will also know that you're still interested in the conversation & won't feel offended by your gaze.

3. Sit & stand up straighter. How many times have we been told to sit or stand up straight & not slouch? More often than not, a slouched posture is immediately associated with a lack of confidence. You wouldn't want to just give away that kind of impression especially during a job interview or a first date. Whatever situation you find yourself in, it's always better to be aware of your stance & your posture & fix it when you find yourself slouching. Keep your back & head straight, your spine aligned, & your shoulders level.

4. Keep your head up. Like a slouched posture, just keeping your eyes down on the ground is also associated with insecurity & lack of confidence. Keep your chin up, with your head straight & your eyes looking straight in front of you.

5. Don't be afraid to take up some space. Simply taking up a bit of space by sitting or standing with your legs apart is a sign of having self-confidence & being comfortable in your skin. Please don't worry about offending other people's sense of personal space, though. It's all still within the acceptable bounds of personal space as long as you just don't bump or graze into someone in the process.

6. Relax your shoulders. When you're tense, it's also most obvious in the way your shoulders hunch up or down. Try to relax & lose a bit of the tension by pulling your shoulders back & shaking them slightly. Also, leaning back slightly makes you look confident & at ease.

7. Avoid crossing your arms & legs. That's if you don't want to be perceived as defensive, guarded, or insecure in business & social gatherings or situations.

8. Give indications of interest in conversations. Nod, smile, laugh, lean your own head to the side, & react at

appropriate times during conversations. Insert sounds that indicate interest or agreement like "uh-huh," "yeah," or "ok." Also showing positive signals encourage people to listen & pay attention to you. Otherwise, the other person will unequivocally come to the conclusion that you aren't interested at all. Please be careful, not to overdo it though so as not to seem overeager or needy for approval.

9. Slow down your movements. This's helpful especially when you're feeling nervous, uncomfortable, or shy. Deliberately slowing your movements like just walking slowly, can make you look more at ease with yourself, calm, & confident.

10. Eliminate or even minimize distracting movements. As much as possible, try to be conscious of & avoid distracting mannerisms like fidgeting in your seat when you're nervous, drumming your fingers on a surface when impatient, touching your face when you're flustered, or even shaking your legs back & forth. Body movements such as these're not only distracting to others, but clearly indicate your level of discomfort.

11. Be aware of others' personal space. As a general rule, don't stand too close when talking to someone you aren't close with on a personal level. Especially at work & other professional settings, boundaries are always expected to be given respect & consideration.

12. Please always maintain a positive attitude. No matter what kind of situation you find yourself in, try to always keep your cool & a positive attitude. Strive to be relaxed & open. How you're feeling inside will also always find its way in your body language if not in the words you speak.

13. Learn to manage stress. Stress somehow messes up your physical, emotional, & mental well-being. It even compromises your ability to communicate well. The more you're stressed out, the more likely you're to misread people & send confusing, mismatched signals. If you're feeling overwhelmed by stress, just take a moment to calm down before joining the conversation again. Now once you feel more at ease, you can better deal with the situation or conversation you're involved in.

CHAPTER 19:

Body Language Applications

B ody language and self-esteem go hand in hand. This allows for a wonderful mechanism to observe and monitor how people behave and feel. Awareness of our body language is essential for becoming effective and persuasive communicators. Hence, there are several applications for using, reading, and changing body language.

Therapeutic Applications

Body language plays a major role in counseling, NLP, and hypnotherapy. For psychologists, body language not only allows them a way to read their clients' emotional state, but also gives them a way to build rapport. Observing the client's body language can help the psychologist to read how the client responds to a certain discussion or line of questioning.

Body language speaks when we can't. Health care professionals have known this for some time. A great many studies have been conducted in it, and psychology academic studies for professionals including modalities on body language.

Common issues which can be examined and treated through the use of body language include:

Bi polarity

Individuals with this condition suffer a chemical imbalance that leads to severe depression and the inability to make decisions. They often have a low self-esteem that accompanies this disorder, and it is incredibly difficult to understand effectively or treat correctly. Using body language, the person with bipolarity can be taught to manage their daily situations, and considering the link between body language and emotion, they can also enjoy relief by being trained to use positive body language. This is a way for them to use their own body language to persuade their emotions to stabilize and improve. For their families, body language reading is also an effective way to monitor their loved one's state and intervene before incidents happen. Depression can often go unnoticed and people will rarely speak out about it. They are not likely to say: "I'm feeling depressed."

Low self-esteem

Many of us have suffered the devastating effects of low self-esteem in one way or another. The first victim is our ability to progress in life. A positive belief in yourself is needed if you are to convince the rest of the world to believe in you. People can be trained in positive body language such as the open position, making eye contact, lifting the head. It's a case of faking it until you feel it. With enough repetitive use of persuasive body language, you can even convince yourself that you are stronger than you believe.

Trauma

Survivors of trauma suffer from a loss of power, feelings of inadequacy, and loss of confidence. They also have the burden of guilt where they hold themselves responsible for what happened to them. Whether the trauma is due to a violent act such as an assault or rape, a natural disaster or loss in their family, the emotional state of these individuals is reflected in their body language or the change thereof. Where body language may have been positive and inviting before the incident, the person may now display negative body language, such as crossed arms, slumping, excessive facial touching, and nervous ticks such as repetitive movement. With effective counseling, their progress to recovery can be tracked through counseling and monitoring their body language.

Abuse

Abuse can be physical, emotional, and sexual in nature, but whichever of these it is, there is bound to be an overwhelming sense of a loss of power. The victim may need to be convinced that they can regain their power and that it is okay to trust people. Body language is extremely efficient in this regard. Helping these survivors of abuse establish strong body language will increase their sense of their own strength. Suffering abuse at the hands of another human being is also linked to a loss of trust in people and the world around them. By helping the abuse victim to understand the body language of others, they can be aided in evaluating the world and those around them in terms of what they see, not what they fear. This is in itself already great empowerment to the abuse victim, as they can become a participant in life again, and feel like they have the power to make informed decisions.

Self-development

Being an effective communicator is one of life's greatest skills that will open doors and lead to the emboldening of the self. Self-development programs often include modalities on body language where the participants are trained in the uses of positive body language and assertiveness.

Group dynamics

People can be classed as two groups: introverts and extroverts. Introverts, as we know, are those people who tend to thrive in one-on-one communications and prefer to spend more time alone; while extroverts are the life of the party and go through life with a the-more-the-merrier attitude. Introverts often suffer a form of depression based on social settings. They do not do well in groups. As a result, their communication within a group dynamic tends to fizzle. Yet, communication is a learned skill. Like we learn the words, sentence structures, and grammar of a new language, we can also learn the way in which body language works.

Depression

People suffering from depression tend to convince themselves that they are not worthy, that they are to blame for some usually imaginary flaw, and that they are being judged by everyone around them. In the worst cases, this can lead to extreme paranoia.

People with depression sometimes think that everyone else has it good, while they alone are suffering. In creating awareness of body language, they can begin to see the world in a more realistic sense and realize that people everywhere go through trying times and that they are not alone.

By learning to focus on using positive body language they can also begin to manage their condition, as this will encourage feelings of well-being.

OCD

This condition is known for the repetitive behavior that someone engages in to make themselves feel in control of their lives. At the root of this tragic condition lies the fear of a loss of power and a profound distrust in themselves and in others. In extreme cases, this can even extend to excessive washing of hands to remove imaginary germs and then avoiding people because people have germs.

People with OCD tend to have a very negative view of the world, and their only safety comes from their repetitive behaviors. Using body language, they can be trained to notice positive feelings in others and to begin incorporating that into themselves. As they learn to project a positive self-image, they will feel their stress levels diminish, which will lead to a reduction of their anxiety-driven obsessions. When they feel more balanced, they will begin to develop trust in themselves and those around them.

Destructive body imagery (bulimia and obesity)

Poor body image is a tragic and very destructive condition to suffer from. It goes with low self-esteem, lack of trust, feelings of abandonment, and severe depression. Bulimia leads the sufferer to obsessively lose weight, while obesity is a condition where the sufferer wants to fill themselves due to their own emotional disabilities.

Both these conditions are associated with a loss of reality. These people begin to see the world not as it is, but as they believe it to be, and their world view is almost always negative. They eat, or refuse to eat, to hide from the world and themselves.

Body language is a way to find a connection back to the real world. In reading the body language being projected by those around us, we can begin to see that there are loads of people who are just like us. We are not alone. Using positive body language is one of the therapeutic ways to recover a sense of self that is realistic and beneficial.

The biological feedback mechanism of body language

Due to our loss of trust in other humans, we often turn to animals for comfort and assurance. We read into what people do, what they say, how they say it, and how they react to us. A salesman will do this on a second-by-second basis where they monitor the body language of the client and adjust their body language to match. Techniques such as mirroring, open position, advancing or retreating, and touching can be used to have an effect on the other person, and monitor how persuasive we are being on them. If they have begun to trust us enough, they will begin to do something we want; in which case, we will trust them since they've done something for us. This endless, nonverbal loop is known as a biological feedback mechanism.

Training and exercises

There are numerous academies and colleges that strive to train people in body language detection and application. They mention facts and case-studies, what to do and what not to do; however, not many of them detail exactly how to improve your body language in a step-by-step way. When considering the activities and desired results, we suggest the following steps be followed:

Observe

Look at the world around you. Notice the people in it and how they interact with each other. Identify people in similar situations to those that challenge you. This could be someone applying for a promotion at work, asking a girl on a date, and even haggling for a discount. Each situation will use the same skills but in different ways. It all boils down to body language. Take notes if you like, or snapshot the interactions to review later. This may seem like stalking behavior to some, but it is called vicarious learning in psychological circles. You learn from the behavior, whether successful or not, of others.

Practice

This will require some bravery, which is perhaps why people do crazy things in foreign lands where no one knows them. Find some friends, or set up a hidden camera if you have to, or go to obedience training with your dog. The goal is to place yourself in a situation where you can practice some of the skills and how they can be used. If you feel overwhelmed, you can practice at home with a mirror. You might even find some online help with an online counselor who can perhaps observe you over Skype.

Evaluate

Look at the recording you made of yourself, or talk to friends who are helping you. Don't look at your awkwardness; rather, focus on each body language technique, how you applied it, and what the response to it was.

You may even give yourself a score or write down what you need to focus on. Remember to celebrate the successes, no matter how small. Then it's time to repeat step two, practice.

It may seem like an incredibly arduous task to learn body language, but it certainly is worth it. These skills of using space, posture, facial expressions, eye contact, gesture, and touch are vital to leading a fulfilling life that has less conflict and misunderstanding in it

CHAPTER 20:

How to Control Your Body Language

Body language can enhance your communication skills in a great way. You can have effective communication skills, only if you can control your body language. Before, we look at the most used body language for manipulation. It is important to know how to take charge of your own body. Can we base these with the quote that, 'Charity begins at home?' Yeah, you cannot have an interest in understanding how to manipulate other people positively, yet you do not know how to take control of yourself. Let us kick off with understanding and having control of our body language.

How to Take Control and Manipulate Your Body Language

Research has shown that, when you are aware of the happenings of your own body, you can manipulate it by training yourself to have control, and even mold it to have effective communication. Further research recommends that you take some breathing exercises before going into a meeting or presentation. It will help you calm as well as have the ability to take note of your posture and gestures while on presentation. As you have noted by now, mirroring is a good technique. Always try to be keen on what the next person is doing non-verbally and copy that. It will help you become more effective in your communication with them. They will understand you better because this tunes your mind to the ability to communicate more truthfully at a place of relaxation.

However, you should be careful while shaping your body language. This is to ensure that the body language that you portray matches with what you are trying to present. A mismatch may bring confusion and may not be relevant at the moment. The person you are in conversation with may mistake you for meaning something else contrary to what you intended. The secret to having control of your body language is to take your time to learn it, to be aware of your non-verbal cues, as you apply what you learn.

The Body Language That Will Help You Take Charge of Your Space

Effective management involves individuals being able to encourage and have a positive influence. In planning for an important appointment maybe with your employees, management team, or partners, you are focusing on what to say, memorizing critical points, and rehearsing your presentation to make you feel believable and persuasive. This is something you should be aware of, of course.

Here is what you should know if you want to take control of your position, at work, at a presentation or as a leader.

Seven Seconds is What You Have to Make an Impression

First impressions are essential in market relationships. When somebody psychologically marks you as, trustworthy, or skeptical, strong, or submissive, you will be seen through such a filter in any other dealings that you do or say. Your partners will look for the finest in you if they like you. They will suspect all of your deeds if they distrust you. While you can't stop people from having quick decisions, as a defense mechanism, the human mind is programmed in this way, you can learn how to make these choices effective for you. In much less than seven seconds, the initial perceptions are developed and strongly influenced by body language. Studies have found that nonverbal signals have more than four times the effect on the first impression you create than you speak. This is what you should know regarding making positive and lasting first impressions. Bear in mind several suggestions here:

- Start by changing your attitude. People immediately pick up your mood. Have you noticed that you immediately get turned off after you find a customer service representative who has a negative attitude? You feel like leaving or request to be served by a different person. That is what will happen to you too if you have a bad attitude, which is highly noticeable. Think of the situation and make a deliberate decision about the mindset you want to represent before you meet a client, or join the meeting room for a company meeting, or step on the scene to make an analysis.

- Smile. Smiling is a good sign that leaders are under using. A smile is a message, a gesture of recognition and acceptance. "I'm friendly and accessible," it says. Having a smile on your face will change the mood of your audience. If they had another perception of you, a smile can change that and make them relax.

- Make contact with your eyes. Looking at somebody's eyes conveys vitality and expresses interest and transparency. A nice way to help you make eye contact is to practice observing the eye color of everybody you encounter to enhance your eye contact. Overcome being shy and practice this great body language.

- Lean in gently. The body language that has you leaning forward, often expresses that you are actively participating and you are interested in the discussion. But be careful about the space of the other individual. This means staying about two ft away in most professional situations.

- Shaking hands. This will be the best way to develop a relationship It's the most successful as well. Research indicates that maintaining the very same degree of partnership you can get with a simple handshake takes a minimum of three hours of intense communication. You should ensure that you have palm-to-palm touch and also that your hold is firm but not bone-crushing.

- Look at your position. Studies have found that uniqueness of posture, presenting yourself in a way that exposes your openness and takes up space, generates a sense of control that creates changes in behavior in a subject independent of its specific rank or function in an organization. In fact, in three studies, it was repeatedly found that body position was more important than the hierarchical structure in making a person think, act, and be viewed more strongly.

- Building your credibility is dependent on how you align your non-verbal communication   By the use of an electroencephalograph (EEG) device to calculate "event-related potentials"–brain waves that shape peaks and valleys to examine gesture effects proofs that one of these valleys happens when movements that dispute what is spoken are shown to subjects. This is the same dip in the brainwave that occurs when people listen to the language that does not make sense. And, in a rather reasonable way, they simply do not make sense if leaders say one thing and their behaviors point to something else. Each time your facial expressions do not suit your words e.g., losing eye contact or looking all over the room when trying to express candor, swaying back on the heels while thinking about the bright future of the company, or locking arms around the chest when announcing transparency. All this causes the verbal message to disappear.

What your hands mean when you use them

Have you at any point seen that when individuals are energetic about what they're stating, their signals naturally turned out to be increasingly energized? Their hands and arms constantly move, accentuating focus and passing on eagerness.

You might not have known about this association previously, however you intuitively felt it. Research shows that an audience will in general view individuals who utilize a more prominent assortment of hand motions in a progressively ideal light. Studies likewise find that individuals who convey through dynamic motioning will, in general, be assessed as warm, pleasant, and vivacious, while the individuals who stay still or whose motions appear to be mechanical or "wooden" are viewed as legitimate, cold, and systematic.

That is one motivation behind why signals are so basic to a pioneer's viability and why getting them directly in an introduction associates so effectively with a group of people. You may have seen senior administrators commit little avoidable errors. At the point when pioneers don't utilize motions accurately on the off chance that they let their hands hang flaccidly to the side or fasten their hands before their bodies in the exemplary "fig leaf" position, it recommends they have no passionate interest in the issues or are not persuaded about the fact of the matter they're attempting to make.

To utilize signals adequately, pioneers should know about how those developments will in all probability be seen. Here are four basic hand motions and the messages behind them:

- Concealed hands–Shrouded hands to make you look less reliable. This is one of the nonverbal signs that is profoundly imbued in our subliminal. Our precursors settled on endurance choices dependent on bits of visual data they grabbed from each other. In our ancient times, when somebody drew nearer with hands out of view, it was a sign of potential peril. Albeit today the risk of shrouded hands is more representative than genuine, our instilled mental inconvenience remains.
  Blame game I've frequently observed officials utilize this signal in gatherings, arrangements, or meetings for accentuation or to show strength. The issue is that forceful blame dispensing can recommend that the pioneer is losing control of the circumstance and the signal bears a resemblance to parental reprimanding or play area harassing.
- Eager gestures–There is an intriguing condition of the hand and arm development with vitality. If you need to extend more excitement and drive, you can do as such by expanded motioning. Then again, over-motioning (particularly when hands are raised over the shoulders) can cause you to seem whimsical, less trustworthy, and less incredible.
- Laidback gestures–Arms held at midsection tallness, and motions inside that level plane, help you–and the group of spectators–feel focused and formed. Arms at the midsection and bowed to a 45-degree point (joined by a position about shoulder-width wide) will likewise assist you with keeping grounded, empowered, and centered.

In this quick-paced, techno-charged time of email, writings, video chats, and video visits, one generally accepted fact remain: Face-to-confront is the most liked, gainful, and amazing correspondence medium. The more business pioneers convey electronically, all the more squeezing turns into the requirement for individual communication.

Here's the reason:

In face to face gatherings, our brain processes the nonstop course of nonverbal signs that we use as the reason for building trust and expert closeness. Eye to eye collaboration is data-rich. We translate what individuals state to us just halfway from the words they use. We get a large portion of the message (and the majority of the passionate subtlety behind the words) from vocal tone, pacing, outward appearances, and other nonverbal signs. What's more, we depend on prompt input on the quick reactions of others to assist us with checking how well our thoughts are being acknowledged.

So strong is the nonverbal connection between people that, when we are in certified affinity with somebody, we subliminally coordinate our body positions, developments, and even our breathing rhythms with theirs. Most intriguing, in up close and personal experiences the mind's "reflect neurons" impersonate practices, yet sensations and sentiments too. At the point when we are denied these relational prompts and are compelled to depend on the printed or verbally expressed word alone, the cerebrum battles and genuine correspondence endures.

CHAPTER 21:

Interpretation of Some of the Most Common Gesture When Greeting With Hands

Handshake With Both Hands

This type of greeting consists in giving one hand and also, to cover almost completely the other person's hand with your other. This gesture comes from comfort and certainty. This kind of handshake means the person wants to calm the other. You are transmitting you are very intuitive, that you are worry about how the others are really feeling. As a result, people see you as someone who is opening to them and they tend to trust you and to feel safe in your presence. You just know how to be around the other, how to help, but without your own limits and borders.

Push and Attraction

"Push and Attraction" is, basically, energy and enthusiasm. Rather than just moving hands up and down, many people like to make their hands run in horizontal. With this movement someone could indicate that is excited about seeing the other person. You, are honest and friendly, so, you want to share your positive energy with the other person through your greeting.

However, be careful you don't pull too much. Not everyone could share the same enthusiasm.

The Finger-Crushing Handshake

We believe there isn't even need to describe in much detail what the Finger-Crushing means. We are sure that at some moment you have found someone who did it with you. The Finger-Crushing is beyond a "firm" handshake. Sometimes your fingers even can end numbed. If, on the contrary, you are the one doing such atrocity with other people's hands, it means you have a lot of self-esteem and confidence. You mean business and want the other person to know that you want everything done and prepared. Squeezing the other person's hand is your way to say the rest of the world that come over, get into your ship or get out of the way.

The Happy Passive

This kind of handshake consists in submission. You barely take the other person's hand and let the strength conquer you. This kind of greeting says about you, you are an unconcerned one, that you tend to go along with whatever comes to your life, that you prefer being a passenger, rather than taking responsibility and control. You like to just go with it and don't worry about anything other people can think about you. Your lightly passive attitude can provoke jealousy from your stressed and filled with anxiety friends.

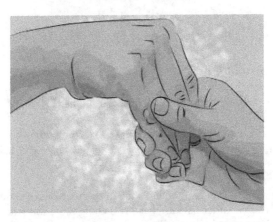

The Fast Handshake

The fast Handshake as its name says, is all about being in a hurry. You take the other person's hand and shake it quickly and almost furiously up and down to let it go very fast.

That kind of handshake means you are very busy and don't have time to chat or wasting time in banalities.

Actually, you never lose time, always want to get to the point during a conversation, either an informal chat or a professional meeting. You are not high about the clouds. You like to talk about specific topics and make them real as soon as possible.

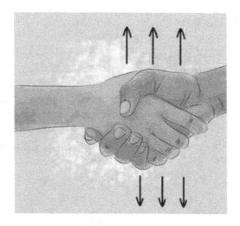

The Persistent One

The persistent one is just, the lack of social abilities.

One of the persons keeps the handshake for a long time and make it awkward for the other person, who try to let go. This handshake says you don't believe in social rules.

You just want to live the moment. And at this particular moment you want to take the other person's hand for a long time, and you are just doing it. You are a free soul, filled with warm and love.

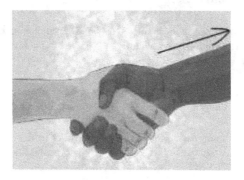

The Winner

This handshake is a teaching about people and hierarchy. The person in command takes control and demonstrates it putting the hand over the other person's. The weaker person (socially) ends with the hand beneath. This kind of handshake is a very subtle sign that you are in control of things without being too aggressive or violent. You are a person with a plan. You know best things in life come to those who know to be patient and work hard.

Fist Bump

Fist Bump is an informal handshake, common among close friends. Instead of doing a classical handshake, the two persons just bump their fists lightly. This greeting is how you express you are comfortable with the other person in an informal way. It indicates you are a good friend, since this class of interaction would not be made with a stranger. If you are a person who goes doing the Fist Bump to anybody, be prepare to receive strange looks.

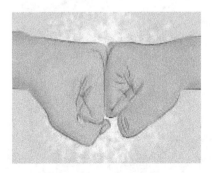

The Perfect Handshake

Even when we all know there is no perfect person, there are some who believe a perfect handshake exists. Here they are, the features of a perfect handshake, although you can take it lightly:

Keep a good posture, keep visual contact, keep your hand at reasonable distance, shake the other person's hand firmly, follow the two seconds rule, smile, say hello to the other person and repeat his or her name. However, although you know how to make "the perfect handshake", it doesn't mean you must resign to your own personal handshake.

CHAPTER 22:

Lie Detection and Deception

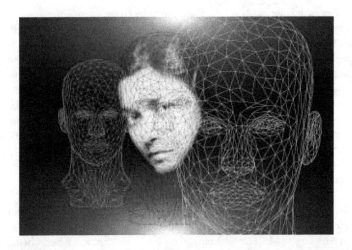

Notably, each one of us would like to easily determine deception at any level such as personal, social, and organizational levels but it is not that easy. Some professions that rely wholly on determining the truth in personal and social contexts such as law agencies, health agencies, and media agencies invest heavily in determining the truth value of their productions, but they fairly fail despite having immense resources.

There is only one reliable way to determine lying and deception, and that is establishing a baseline for the target individual and comparing against this baseline as well as doing the adequate prior investigation before confronting the person. Unfortunately, creating a baseline for each and conducting relevant background study is not always assured due to the time factor and resource constraints and this implies that a speedy analysis of body language and verbal communication can help determine a likelihood of a truth or a lie.

Verbal Hints of a Liar

Liars Tend to Respond to Questions That Were Not Asked

If a person is lying, then he or she wants to cover as much ground as possible, and this includes answering questions that were not posed. By answering questions that were not asked, the individual is prompting the speaker to a particular direction and does not want to be caught off guard. Answering questions that are not asked may also give the individual lying an opportunity to deny the speaker adequate time to analyze the answers given by continuously bombarding the interrogator with new information and ideas. Lastly, answering questions that were not asked also helps the layperson to appear well prepared and knowledgeable in what is being asked.

Liars Tend to Answer a Question with a Question

Expectedly, most liars will respond to a question with another question to shift the burden of thinking and responding to the interrogator. Most politicians employ this tactic when being interviewed, and it is meant to buy them enough time to recall information to the main question. For most liars, not responding is akin to affirming that they lack memory of what is being asked or what happened. The other purpose of responding to a question with another question is to irritate the interrogator and derail his or her composure. Responding to a question with a question is a defensive tactic indicating attempts to hide something.

Most Liars Tend to Make Self-corrections to Avoid Sounding Uncertain

As indicated, most liars want to ensure that each area is covered to eliminate any doubts because allowing room for doubt may expose them. For this reason, most liars tend to self-correct to ensure the information given is irrefutable. In most cases, liars will repeat the correction to ensure that the interrogator and the audience also capture the self-correction. As expected, the liar will blame the need to self-correct on a slip of the tongue or the fast nature of the interview. Another reason for self-correction by a liar is that the individual has a premeditated script and outcome and keeps forcing everything to align with the premeditated picture.

Liars Tend to Feign Memory Loss

As expected, most liars need a safe escape button when cornered and feigning memory loss is a favorite excuse for most liars. When a liar is cornered, then he or she will cite memory loss and later institute self-correction to attain the preformed script. Try watching interviews with politicians to appreciate how they feign memory loss to escape explaining something and pretend to have recalled the information when there is an opportunity to sound believable.

Most Liars Tend to Report What They Did Not Do as Opposed to What They Did

People that lie will give an account of what they did not do to avoid being held accountable. If a liar dwelled on what he or she did, then the individual can be held accountable, and this is not something that a liar wants. However, if a liar dwells on what they should have done, he or she has a large degree of freedom to give any answer and avoid scrutiny. Again, try watching a recorded or filed interview with any politician to appreciate how this technique is employed.

Liars Tend to Justify Their Actions Even When Not Necessary

Expectedly, most liars are insecure and are uncertain that they sound convincing. For this reason, they over-justify everything because they feel that no one believes them even when people have fallen for the lies. When examining a potential liar, look for signs of unnecessary justification, and again, politicians will provide a good case study of over-justification.

Most Liars Avoid Mentioning Emotional Feelings in Their Version of Events

Since a liar is faking everything, he or she will avoid mentioning feelings that were associated with what is being reported. Mentioning emotions may force one to show them. For instance, if you were talking about an exciting event that you witnessed, then your facial expressions and voice should manifest positive emotions, and this is not something a liar wants because he or she is not assured of the consistency of verbal communication and body language.

Most Liars Are Careful, and Will Insist on a Question to Be Repeated

Finally, liars focus more on what is being asked because they only want to accept a question that they are certain of responding to. Liars dwell more on what the question is and what the interrogator wants to help them generate convincing information. The other role of wanting questions repeated is to help the liar elicit a response by making up one because there is none.

Nonverbal Hints of a Liar

Liars Randomly Throw Gestures

The hand gestures are among the best indicator of positive and negative emotions and are difficult to fake in a consistent manner. If one is angry but is pretending to be calm, he or she will throw gestures randomly. Most liars get irritated when taken to the task of what they just said and are likely to throw random gestures in the air even as they try to sound calm.

Against the Norm, Liars Speak Faster than Usual

People that normally do not speak fast will suddenly speak fast when they are lying. Speaking fast helps, the person denies the audience adequate time to listen and analyze the information. Speaking fast also allows the liar to exhaust all of the rehearsed information, as any interjection will throw the liar off balance. Speaking fast also indicates that the person is uncomfortable with the audience or the message and wants to finish fast and end the experience.

Liars Sweat More Than Usual

People sweat, and it is normal. However, more than normal levels of sweating even when the weather is fine may indicate that one is panicking and feeling cornered. All these may indicate a sign of a liar.

Liars Avoid Eye Contact

Most liars shun eye contact or give a sustained stare to intimidate the target person. Shunning eye contact indicates that the person feels awkward or embarrassed about what he or she is presenting to the audience.

Pacing Up and Down

If one paces up and down more than necessary, then the individual is likely lying. All these indicate feeling uncomfortable with the message and the audience.

CHAPTER 23:

How to Spot the Liars

The reasons why people lie are intriguing and incredibly important. Lying is a hard part of human behavior to understand, and it helps to know why people do it and how often it generally happens. And not only why people lie in general, but more importantly, why are people lying specifically to you?

Often when people choose to lie, it has more to do with themselves. Yet, in other circumstances, there is something about you that prompts that person to lie to you. This is not always a bad thing though! When another chooses to lie to you it is in reflection of the best qualities you possess. And these qualities are things you do not and probably should not change. Your best qualities are things you should be proud of and share openly, regardless of the effects it has on others, particularly in terms of lying. However, this information is valuable in recognizing how your premier qualities and strengths can attract lying and liars. In addition, you might possess other qualities, which are not very positive that increase the likelihood that people will lie to you. These more negative qualities might be something you want to develop. Below are a few of the key facts regarding how you may encourage others to lie to you.

The Positive Qualities that Encourage Others to Lie to You

You have high regard as well as high expectations for the important people around you and with whom you interact.

You probably have people in your life who are important to you. Sometimes these are the people you the best of. You are "in their corner," or "have their back." Those people feel wonderful when they know how much you value them. They are aware of how much you care about their presence and that you want the best for them. They also know that you want the best from them as well.

Your standards are moral and "high."

Do you consider yourself to have "high" and moral standards for yourself and others? Even in difficult situations, do you try to do the "right" thing?

This is a great thing to have and to do! Your actions often express your integrity. Even the way you talk can alert others about your high standards, making them clear to other people about them. Sometimes you might do this when you say things similar to, "I do not lie to my family" or when you share your dislike of other people's "bad" behavior.

Your attractive qualities, beyond just physical attraction

Every person has qualities that attract other people to him or her. Some of these attractive qualities might include generosity, kindness, empathy, wisdom, wit, or quirks, including attractive physical traits. If you can think of anything that people have commented that they like about you, that is an example of an attractive trait you possess.

Your power or status

Do you hold a position of high status or power? Perhaps you are a boss or leader in your life. Or perhaps you have the power to sway the decision whether another person gets a pay raise or a promotion or something else desirable. Teachers decide students' grades. Bosses decide promotions and raises. Even writing letters of recommendation for someone can be seen as a position of influence or status.

The Negative Qualities that Encourage Others to Lie to You

Sometimes the qualities that encourage others to lie to you are not so good or can be called "negative." These are the qualities people often try to work on, even when some qualities are not something you chose or can do anything substantial about. For example, if you are going through a hard time, or if you people misinterpret your personal style, it may result in you becoming attractive to others lies.

You are a frightening person

Some people come across as frightening to other people. Are people often demonstrating fear when they are around you? Sometimes people can be frightening in negative ways, and they choose to do this purpose. For example, bullies. But sometimes others have a certain manner or demeanor that can appear scary. These people are not intentionally looking to appear mean or "off-putting," but it is the way they appear. It is possible you might come across like that. If you do, that can tempt people to lie to you if they think you might not respond well to the truth.

You are in an emotionally "bad" space

Do you consider yourself to be vulnerable? Do you easily get your feelings hurt? Are you sad and upset often? Perhaps you are not typically vulnerable, however, at this moment you are experiencing a challenging time.

If this describes you to some extent, and others recognize this is happening, they may be hesitant to share something with you that they think you will not want to know. If the other person thinks you cannot process honesty because you are too vulnerable, or it would hurt your mental health, they will be more likely to lie to you.

You do not want to hear the truth, and others can sense that

When you are vulnerable, you may not want to know the truth, but there are others who do not want to know the truth as well. Occasionally successful and confident people do not desire to hear the truth either. Powerful company owners or executives, for instance, may exhibit behavior that makes it obvious that they do not want to know about bad news regarding their organization. But when there are problems, those that could give that leader a warning are not motivated to do so. Instead, these people hold back important details, or they simply lie.

You present a message that there is some truth that is not meant to be shared out loud

Your behavior sends the message to others if you do or do not want to hear the truth. You may not realize your behavior is giving off the impression you do not want to know the truth, but it can be. In addition, if you struggle with telling the truth about certain subjects, others not only realize the lie but that those topics are ok to lie about to you.

Parents choose to do this to their children, particularly if something horrible is occurring. For instance, if a close friend or loved one is critically ill, or the family animal companion is dying, a parent does not want to share this with their kids. Trying to protect someone from discomfort or pain, particularly a person you love or someone who is vulnerable, like a child, is understandable. However, you must recognize how this instinct, no matter how good in intention, can end up making you that recipient of lying.

The Body Language of a Liar

Detecting a liar typically means people are focusing on the message body language shares, or the small behavioral and physical indicators that expose deceit. A few of the common ideas include the eyes shifting around, fidgeting constantly, and lack of eye contact. It was believed that these were fool-proof indicators that the person communicating is lying. Yes, the cues shared through body language can identify deceptions; some research indicates that several of the highly anticipated expressions are not closely tied to lying. Psychologist Howard Ehrlichman, a researcher dedicated to eye movements since the 1970s, revealed that the movement of the eye does not indicate lying at all. Actually, Ehrlichman hypothesizes that eyes shifting around reveal that a person is intently thinking, or more accurately, that the person is tapping into how or her long-term memory. A few of the most reliable cues for lying that people can observe include:

1. Vague behavior and communication. When someone is speaking and appears to leave out vital information intentionally, it is possible it is because they are deceitful.
2. Uncertainty in their voice. When someone appears uncertain or uncomfortable with what they are saying, they are often perceived as deception.
3. Appears to be indifferent. Posture that makes the other person appear to be bored, without expression, or is shrugging their shoulders can create the perception that the person is avoiding emotional displays and potential "tells."
4. Thinking extensively on a topic. When someone appears to be overthinking in an effort to add more detail to the story, it can be because the person is lying to you.

The take-away from this information is that even though body language can help, it is also vital to observe the "right" cues.

Researchers recommend not to rely heavily on these cues because they might limit your ability to determine deception.

How to Spot Lying

Request They Share Their Tale in Reverse

Detecting a lie is usually considered as a "passive" approach. Many take it for granted that he or she can watch the body language and facial expressions of a person they suspect to be lying, and they will see clear "tells." However, much research has shown that this is an ineffective method for detecting deceit. Instead, a more "active" process to discover lying can offer better outcomes.

It is More Difficult to Lie with an Increased Mental Load

Some research hypothesizes that when you ask potential liars to recall their tales in reverse order instead of chronological order it can improve your ability to detect lies. The studies predict that the nonverbal and verbal expressions that allow you to tell the difference between the truth and lying become more obvious as the mental load of the potential liar increases. The truth takes a lot less mental load than lying does. When you add more complex cognitive function, the expressions in the body and face become more enhanced.

Listen to Your "Gut"

Based on the published content of a study conducted in 2014, your instant "gut" responses could be more reliable than any acutely aware lie detection you may try. Within the study, those conducting the research required the 72 subjects to view recordings of interviews with pretend suspects of a crime. A number of these "suspects" had taken a $100 note that was sitting on a shelf whereas some of the "suspects" had not taken the money, nevertheless everyone one of the pretend suspects were instructed to inform the officer interviewing them that they were innocent and did not take the money from the shelf.

CHAPTER 24:

How Brainwashing Works

This phase is most likely to concentrate on the procedure of indoctrination as well as all the elements that feature it. With the media and also the flicks that are seen, many individuals see persuading as a wicked method that is done by those that are attempting to corrupt, impact, as well as to get power. Some that actually rely on the power of indoctrination think that individuals around them are attempting to regulate their minds as well as their habits. Generally, the procedure of indoctrination takes place in a far more refined method as well as does not include the threatening methods that most individuals connect with it. This phase will certainly enter into a whole lot even more information concerning what indoctrination is and also just how it can affect the topic's mindset.

What is Indoctrination?

Persuading in this manual will certainly be gone over in regards to its usage in psychology. In this relationship, indoctrination is described as a technique of idea reform with social impact. This sort of social impact is taking place all throughout the day to everyone, no matter whether they recognize it or otherwise. Social impact is the collection of techniques that are made use of in order to alter other individuals' habits, ideas, and also mindsets. As an example, conformity techniques that are utilized in the work environment can practically be thought about a kind of indoctrination since they need you to act and also assume a certain method when you get on the work. Persuading can come to be even more of a social concern in its most serious kind due to the fact that these methods operate at altering the method somebody assumes without the subject granting it.

For persuading to function properly, the topic is most likely to require to undergo a total seclusion and also dependence because of its intrusive impact on the topic. This is just one of the factors that a lot of the indoctrination situations that are understood about happen in totalistic cults or jail camps. The brainwasher, or the representative, should have the ability to acquire full control over their topic. This implies that they need to regulate the consuming practices, resting patterns, and also meeting the various other human requirements of the subject as well as none of these activities can happen without the will of the representative. Throughout this procedure, the representative will certainly function to methodically damage down the topic's entire identification to essentially make it not function right any longer. When the identification is damaged, the representative will certainly function to change it with the preferred ideas, perspectives, as well as actions.

The procedure of indoctrination is still up for dispute whether it will certainly function. Many psychotherapists hold the idea that it is feasible to persuade a subject as long as the best problems exist. Also, after that, the entire procedure is not as serious as it exists in the media. There are likewise various meanings of indoctrination that make it harder to establish the results of persuading on the topic. A few of these meanings call for that there has to be some type of hazard to the physique of the topic in order to be taken into consideration indoctrination. If you follow this interpretation, after that also the methods done by several extremist cults would certainly not be taken into consideration real indoctrination as no physical misuse takes place.

Various other meanings of indoctrination will rely upon control as well as threat without physical pressure in order to obtain the adjustment in the ideas of the topics. In either case, specialists think that the result of indoctrination, also under the optimal problems, is just a short-term incident. They think that the old identification of the topic is not totally gotten rid of with the technique; instead, it is taken into hiding and also will certainly return as soon as the brand-new identification is not enhanced any longer.

Robert Jay Lifton generated some fascinating ideas on indoctrination in the 1950s after he examined detainees of the Chinese as well as Oriental Battle camps. Throughout his monitoring, he figured out that these detainees went through a multistep procedure to indoctrination. This procedure started with assaults on the feeling of self with the detainee and afterwards finished with an expected modification in ideas of the topic. There are 10 actions that Lifton specified for the indoctrination procedure in the topics that he examined.

These consisted of:

1. An attack on the identification of the topic
2. Requiring regret on the topic
3. Compelling the topic right into self-betrayal
4. Getting to a snapping point
5. Providing the subject kindness if they alter
6. Obsession to admit
7. Funneling the shame in the desired instructions
8. Launching the topic of intended sense of guilt
9. Proceeding to consistency
10. The last admission prior to a renewal

Every one of these phases should happen in a location that remains in full seclusion. This indicates that every one of the regular social referrals that the topic is made use of to find touching are not available. Furthermore, mind clouding methods will certainly be used in order to speed up the procedure such as lack of nutrition as well as rest starvation. While this may not true of all persuading situations, typically there is a visibility of some kind of physical injury, which adds to the target having trouble in assuming individually as well as seriously like they generally would.

Actions Utilized

While Lifton divided the actions of the indoctrination procedure right into 10 actions, contemporary psychotherapists arrange it right into 3 phases in order to much better comprehend what takes place for the topic throughout this procedure. These 3 phases consist of the damaging down of the self, presenting the concept of redemption to the topic, as well as the restoring of the self of the topic. Comprehending each of these phases and also the procedure that occurs with each of them can assist you to recognize what is taking place to the identification of the subject with this procedure.

Damaging Down of Self

The initial stage of the indoctrination procedure is the damaging down of the self. Throughout this procedure, the representative wishes to separate the old identification of the topic in order to make them really feel much more susceptible as well as open up to the preferred brand-new identification. This action is needed in order to advance the procedure. The representative is not likely to be really effective with their ventures if the topic is still strongly embedded in their willpower as well as their old identification. Separating this identification as well as making the individual concern the important things around them can make it much easier to transform the identification in the later actions. This is done via numerous actions consisting of attack on the identification of the topic, brining on sense of guilt, self-betrayal, and after that getting to the snapping point.

Sense of guilt

When the topic has actually undergone the attack on their identification, they will certainly get in the phase of sense of guilt. The topic will certainly be continuously informed that they misbehave while experiencing this brand-new id that has actually been induced. This is carried out in order to bring a big feeling of sense of guilt on the topic. The topic will certainly be frequently under fire for any one of the important things that they have actually done, no matter just how huge or little the acts might be. The variety of the assaults can differ too; the topic can be slammed for their idea systems to the manner in which they clothe and also since they consume also gradually. Gradually, the topic is most likely to begin to really feel embarrassment around them every one of the moments as well as they will certainly really feel that all things, they are doing are incorrect. This can assist to make them really feel much more prone as well as most likely to support the brand-new identification the representative wishes to generate.

Self-betrayal

Since the topic has actually been converted that they misbehave which every one of their activities are unwanted, the representative is most likely to function to require the based on confess that they misbehave. Now, the topic is sinking in their very own shame and also sensation really dizzy. With the continuation of the psychological assaults, the hazard of some terrific physical damage, or a mix of both, the representative will certainly have the ability to compel the based on knock his old identification. This can consist of a wide array of points such as obtaining the based on knock their very own peers, close friends, and also household that share the exact same idea system as them. While this procedure might take a while to happen, once it does, the topic will certainly seem like he betrayed those that he really feels dedicated to. This will certainly additionally raise the pity along with the loss of identification that the target is currently really feeling, better damaging down the identification of the topic.

CHAPTER 25:

Body Posture

Body Alignment

The way your body align while speaking words, is a powerful tool. Unconsciously it will be sending out nonverbal messages. It can show you if feel relaxed, tense, aggressive or disinterested.

Open

A confident person with a friendly outlook will not show signs of tense body language. Their posture should be open and relaxed with the feet apart and head held high as they look forward. They're not afraid to face the person standing before them. If seated then they are likely to have their palms open and lean forward as they speak to others. Or may sit in an open and relaxed manner, such as for a man he might open his legs whilst keeping his arms relaxed at the sides.

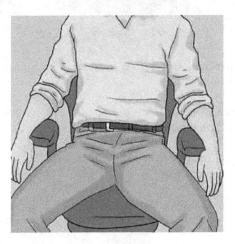

Closed

As you would guess, this posture is exactly the opposite. Vulnerable parts of the body will be covered in some way. Perhaps arms crossed over the chest. If their arms do hang loose, they will likely cover the groin area.

When seated they may cross their legs or arms. The head may lean downwards with eyes looking at the floor.

If standing they may position themselves side-on when speaking with someone else.

Other signs could be clenched hands, hands covering parts of the face, feet tucked in if seated.

A closed posture will not invite friendliness but rather show disinterest or even hostility.

How the body comes together as a whole, including the head, arms, and legs, will give away those all those revealing nonverbal signals.

Head

The position of a person's head's an important clue as you also attempt to read their facial features.

Are they looking at the floor? They could be shy or not want to appear confrontational. Or, are they showing signals of boredom from their conversation with you?

The higher a person raises their chin, as they speak, the more confidence they have in themselves. They're not afraid to lift their head up high and make themselves look tall.

A tilt of the head when speaking to someone can reveal all. It could indicate that they find the other person interesting, or at the very least that they are paying attention. People who are not interested in each other will look away quite a lot, as their mind wanders. They may even turn their heads away physically, so their face is not pointed in the other's direction.

Neck

Even the neck will reveal a secret or two as this is where our vulnerable throat lays. When someone fiddles with their own neck it shows they're a little unsure of themselves, so they're loitering near their vulnerable throat. If they're covering the throat then they may be feeling a little exposed. They want to protect themselves from whatever's going on around them. A man may fiddle with his tie, or stroke his chin. A woman might fidget with a necklace, or the neckline of the top they're wearing. All are indicators that they feel uneasy.

The throat itself can give obvious nonverbal signals by how much a person swallow. When anxious, people tend to swallow more than usual. Unless we cover up our throat area, other people can read this signal because they can see us gulping.

Trunk

The trunk of the body is much like the pointing feet. If you're comfortable with someone you're more likely to lean towards them, and vice versa. Leaning towards a person is a sign that you are engaging with them. It's a good indicator that you're listening because you're interested in what they have to say.

How your clothing hangs on your body can also be an indicator of your demeanor. If your shirt is open casually at the top, then you're probably feeling relaxed. Whereas buttoned right up to the top can only mean, "Keep out," or "Don't come near me." Much the same as a man's tie, if it's loose then he's relaxing, but he wouldn't wear it like that in the middle of a business meeting.

The trunk of the human body is where the most important vital organs are encased. It's understandable that we're wary of allowing another person close to them. We may keep a distance from someone we don't particularly care for, or know. Only those we trust and love can stand close to those vulnerable organs, such as our heart and lungs.

How we hold our body when we embrace someone can reveal this message better. The closer we allow another person to get to our own body, the more relaxed we are about them. Other silent indicators will be the arms as well. There's the hug that only involves a little pat on the shoulders. At the same time, the bottom halves of the two people will have a distance between them. It usually indicates the two people don't know each other that well. They're hugging as a social nicety.

Then there's the hug of a person you are familiar with, such as a loved one or a long-time friend. In that instance, we tend to wrap our arms tight around the other person's back. The top half of each person's body will touch. We know this person can be trusted so we allow them close without even thinking.

The hips will play a major part in that hug. That's because your genital area is reserved for intimacy. You might allow your spouse or partner's hips to touch your own, but it's unlikely you will allow anyone else in such close proximity, even your offspring.

Consider the complete opposite of a hug. This would involve turning your back on someone. Is it a coincidence that if we turn our back on someone who we're annoyed with? In a sense, we are protecting our vital organs at the front, and showing them our spine. This body posture is known as ventral denial.

In Eastern cultures, people are more likely to bow the torso to a stranger, than to hug one. Bowing is considered a sign of respect. Yet in Western cultures bowing is only for meeting royalty.

As with the facial expressions, the use of hands, fingers, head, neck, legs, and the sway of the body are all complex. There are so many combinations of movements that it could take a lifetime to learn them all. Given that, it shows it's not simply the pose, but the tone of the pose. For instance, if someone is crossing their arms, what does their face say about their mood. Poses show emotions and they speak loudly about our nonverbal language.

CHAPTER 26:

Interpret Body Language and Decipher Different Gestures

E ven when not a word comes from your lips, your body speaks. And when it is spoken, you always speak two different languages—once the words are spoken and meanwhile the body is talking. Body language can be a vicious betrayer if what you think and feel is not put into words. Your body brings out your real emotions and thoughts in posture, facial expressions and gestures.

You curl your lips, raise an eyebrow, inflate the nostrils or wrinkle your nose, and the person opposite you knows your true thoughts and emotions. A harmonious overall picture is only created if the body language matches the words spoken. Authenticity and credibility are the results. In communication, body language is of great importance, whether in conversations with colleagues, at job interviews, in negotiations or contact with customers. Even in small talk, attention is paid not only to the words said but also to the language of the body.

To detect manipulation, it is important that you correctly interpret and decipher facial expressions and gestures. This will help you to quickly recognize what the person you are talking to wants to achieve with their words.

Body language is seen as a success factor since gestures have indescribable power. However, when it comes to body language, the spirits are divided into two camps. One camp believes that the hype about facial expressions and gestures is greatly exaggerated and the effect is often overestimated. Voices from the other camp, on the other hand, think that body language is an important factor for effect and individuality. They practice and train hard because in their opinion, their success is closely linked to convincing body language. Somewhere in between lies the truth about body language. In the same way, the statement "You cannot "not" communicate" by Paul Watzlawick is correct. Because gestures and posture speak for themselves, even when no words are spoken. There are so-called high-status gestures, which are also called power poses.

Not only do they have a great effect on other people, but they can also increase your self-esteem. The following gestures express a very high status and especially a lot of power:

- An upright and still head position

- A powerful voice

- Elegant and slow movements

- Open, uninhibited smile

- Smooth movements

Various gestures are used in the game of recognition and status. If these are used in a controlled manner, it is much easier to win over other people for yourself. However, body language has two very different sides. One side is even very dangerous. The hidden signals that are sent out with posture, facial expressions, arms and hands are aimed at manipulating you and winning you over for your cause. People who can manipulate correctly do not need words to make you feel bad and to influence your thoughts. Be aware that body language is manipulative. In this way you will encounter obvious signals, but also those that are much more subtle.

They have a hidden influence on your thoughts and perception. You have no control over this influence. Always remember that you are influenced by everything you perceive. Because the brain not only records the words you say but also the gestures and facial expressions. If a stimulus is strong enough to upset the balance of ions in the cell membranes, a very special reaction occurs. This refers to the biochemical process that processes sensory impressions. As soon as a reaction is triggered in a cell by a stimulus, a hidden influence is established. If the stimulus did not exist, there would be no manipulation.

Not only are you being manipulated by body language, but you are also manipulating yourself. For example, other people can read the current mood from your posture. The signals that you send out trigger stimuli in other people. You, for example, use these stimuli to get the most out of them. Body language can therefore manipulate. However, it cannot be used to elicit a particular reaction that does not correspond to your interests, values or innermost desires.

That is why manipulation through body language alone is not so effective because inner values have greater power.

Manipulation through body language only works if there is already an inner inclination in this direction.

This is especially true for advertising. For example, you can watch an advertisement for beer for hours without immediately feeling the desire for a beer. But if you watch an advertisement from Zalando or About You, there is no stopping you.

Always remember that body language is largely unconscious. Or have you ever thought about your posture, the movements of your hands and arms, or your current facial expression?

This gives other people a deep insight and allows them to read your thoughts and emotions unfiltered. If you want to prevent another person from manipulating you, you should learn to become aware of body language and use it in a way that you can benefit from it.

This makes it difficult for a manipulator to force you into the role of a victim. By now you have learned so much about how to protect yourself from manipulation by saying things.

Now it's just a matter of using body language correctly. The following tips will help you do this:

1. Get to the same level as your opposite. This is meant literally. This is meant because it enables you to compensate for differences in height and ensures that what is said is perceived correctly and is no longer twisted. As soon as you are at eye level with the other person, the threatening, superior effect disappears. If someone tries to manipulate you, starts rumors about you and you want to confront this person, you should not look up or down. Because you will weaken your position.
2. A true multi-talent of body language is the smile. And the best thing about it: you can use it consciously and purposefully. This way you radiate self-confidence, inner strength and self-assurance.
3. Just like facial expressions, gestures and other aspects, body language also requires a certain distance, which should be respected. In plain language this means: Do not let anyone get too close to you and keep the distance to the other person.
4. Are you aware of your body language? To use body language perfectly, you need to understand its effect on others. That is why you should find out what signals are sent through your body language. Those who feel small and have little self-confidence express this through body language. Manipulators who are looking for a new victim will find you immediately.

The Interpretation of Body Language

There are quite a few people who have a perfect command of power poses and gestures of power.

Politicians, superiors, company bosses and all those who want to convince other people of something.

Often these people owe their popularity and the position they hold to this ability.

Nevertheless, body language cannot always be deciphered clearly and correctly. Sometimes it is a premonition or a strange feeling in the pit of the stomach that leads to the assumption that something is wrong.

It is noticeable that the words said to express something quite different from body language.

Harmony is missing. Even the smallest nuances are registered by the subconscious.

Never look at body language separately, without the words that have been said.

This will tear facial expressions and gestures out of context. But by training your sensors and expanding your mental radar, you can localize negative and positive signals. With the acquired knowledge you will be able to react appropriately.

The following nonverbal messages should be remembered. You are guaranteed to notice them in many people who have a perfect command of body language:

Positive	Negative
The person stands or sits with you and physically moves to your level.	When you sit, the person stops to demonstrate hierarchy and power.
Eye contact is maintained and thus interest is symbolized.	There is hardly any eye contact, there is blinking and the lips are formed into a narrow line.
Instead of stopping in front of the room, you enter it without hesitation. A symbol of trust.	During the conversation the arms are crossed or the hands are supported on the hips. A sign of skepticism.

Quiet, non-extending movements. The hands are open and possibly the palms of the hands are visible. This shows confidence.	Hands are hidden under the table or in the trouser pocket, fingers are crossed or hands are clenched into fists. The gestures show nervousness and are asymmetrical. This is an expression of mistrust.
Rubbing hands means satisfaction.	Impatience and annoyance are expressed when fingers are damaged by objects.
Oblique head posture in conversation testifies to satisfaction	Scratching your head or nose is a sign of doubt
Adaptation of body language and gestures equals sympathy	Spreading out documents means demarcation
Loose stand and lean over symbolizes familiarity	Looks over your shoulder, turn away and achieves a distance
The person stays close to you and thus symbolizes affection.	It is not introduced and hardly spoken; this is a sign of dislike

CHAPTER 27:

Body Language Codes

The Secret Question Code

How will you know what others are thinking about, how will you know what they are trying to find, and what will offer you a clear picture of the roadway, which you will follow in the persuasion procedure?

There is an answer to each question, and this rule is a principle; you call it (A response for each issue). Regrettably, some salesmen are characterized by exceptional sales ability to speak, and you find them throughout meetings, talking, and talking without stopping, presenting more and more details. Sometimes they succeed and very frequently, they stop working. Yes, everybody thinks that the sales guy has to speak without disturbance, but this is entirely incorrect. You talk, and the client listens, you come out from the conference without the smallest idea in your mind of what the customer wanted.

Technique #1 (The Question)

This Strategy supplies extensive research on the depth of the mind of the other party for a clear photo of the way of approaching to persuade this person. How do you get this picture? Yes, it holds, through a question. For that reason, it is merely asking the question as many as you can. Here is how to implement this method. From now on, you will begin any discussion with anyone else with questions. Do not talk about yourself; simply start by asking questions consistently. We will discuss what you will be asking about. Let us assume you want to persuade someone of your product, and you just have 10 minutes. If you are a normal male, you will start immediately to discuss your product, and you will duplicate a lot of times about how much fantastic and efficient is this product is, and so on. The possibility that the customer will purchase this item has to do with 50%.

If you are an expert in the science of persuasion, as you will become later, you will spend the first 6 minutes listening to your customer after each concern you asked. Then you will discuss your product based on his responses for 2 minutes. You will sign the contract and take the cash and provide him with the item in the last two minutes. The success rate is 90%.

In any discussion from now on, we will divide time into areas: 60% of the time will be committed to get to understand much better the other party through using several strategies, including concerns. We will find out in particular when, where to enter, how to end, and from where to come out. We will draw a map of the other individual, to collect information about him/her, and to understand how to operate? 30% of the time will be for persuasion, and the last 10% will be to close the discussion. Let us know more about this technique: Questions used by the persuasion expert include:

1. Determine the worth and primary requirements
2. Determine the direction of the conversation
3. Understanding the internal system for decision-making
4. Knowing rejection elements and clarification.

"People do not understand what they think in and do not know why they believe this!"

Therefore, we use concerns to clarify the values, beliefs, and views to comprehend the other party and manage the discussion better. Did you understand that it is impossible to ask a concern without getting an answer to it? Even if the other individual does not talk, he will answer it with his mind and his body language. Now I'll leave you with this discussion that occurred to me in among the conferences. Think deeply, and diligently with creativity, and I desire you to concentrate on the way the questions and how I could handle to talk and look for the golden piece of information, the secret to encouraging this customer to buy my item:

Client: Let me think about it!

I: Of course, you need to think of the subject; however, what avoids you from making a choice now, is it the power of the business that I represent?

Client: No, of course, I am confident that your company is one of the most influential businesses in this location; however, I require some time to believe!

I: So, it is our service that you do not like?

Client: Of course I like it, this is an excellent service, and we need it, I told you I require a long time to think about all the possibilities

(Notice here how I make the client reveal that he desires the service, and it is a fantastic Adherence to the concept Law)

I: Are we talking here about the regular monthly payments and costs?

Client: Yes, in reality, I think I need to consider how I can manage these payments

I: How much precisely do you anticipate that you will be able to pay in one month?

Client: I believe we will have the ability to provide over $ 800 a month

I: Gorgeous, however, you require this service, and as I stated, you need it now, (he did not say that–inject the memory with false information)

Client: Yes, we require it, but the payments.

I: So, we are discussing $ 860 a month. Do you think that your requirement for this service will make you save $ 30 a day to get this service?

Client: Haha, I do not believe that this is hard for sure!

I: What do you think about signing the order now, so I can schedule the service for you today when I return to the workplace so you can be able to get it tomorrow!

Have you seen what happened? If I were not a specialist of persuasion or having the wisdom to understand questions, and how to use them I'd wouldn't have changed the course of any discussion; I will not have the ability to change the customer's decision from allowing me to think of it (and 80% this means that he will not purchase) to (I do not believe that this is undoubtedly challenging). I asked about the reason for the rejection and a question after another until I got the result where I can resolve it and succeed in signing a contract.

Therefore, the questions manage the conversation and lead to the manner you have to take. However, there are some cases whereby impractical question get you to the outcome when the other party is connected emotionally to his opinion.

For example, you talk to a lady in one of the cafés and to convince her that you are a nice person. She has to drink a cup of coffee with you. Rationally, she is convinced but declines your request because she is emotionally connected with somebody else. You talk with somebody to sell your luxurious and stunning car, and he refuses to purchase it because this person wishes to have Porsche and absolutely nothing else. Logically, you will get him to the point that your car is the best option for him, but he is associated emotionally with something else. Sometimes you can change the point of view of someone; however, for the most part, you will not have the ability to reach a satisfying result for both parties. Therefore, you need to ask and then ask over again until you are familiar with the other party very well; to know how he believes, behaves and responds, what he desires, and what he cherished. Throughout the following codes, we will give many examples consisting of drawing the road map to the other party through questions; however, I choose to mention them promptly.

Communication Styles Code

How do other people talk? What does it mean? How do they speak, or how do they behave? This does not matter to others, but, as a professional in persuasion. You have to know who the other person is.

As you know, it is much easier to put people in appropriate boxes, groups. In truth, it is difficult because everyone is different from each other in personalities and communication designs. But we share some of the qualities that, as a specialist in persuasion, I can figure out the portion of which 70% of who the other person is, sometimes it can reach up to 100%, and possibly down to 1% at different times.

But what concerns me is that I won't know who is sitting before me in a meeting or a service lunch. It may take years to develop a connection and relationship. I will only need essential headings to know which group that person is, so I can determine the proper interaction design to get approval. Of course, as I stated, it is difficult to give a test of character for each person you want to know how to talk to. However, we'll know a little; the essentials which will enable us to develop our discussion techniques to match others.

According to Psychology Experts, Human beings' characters are divided into four primary types:

- Leader
- Analytical
- Friendly

Everyone falls in one of these groups. Many have a leadership personality. Others are friends, and many may have a bit of this and that. However, no one is beyond these groups. Before you learn more about the qualities of each of these four groups, we need to understand that there is nobody who is a leader, or only an expert, preferably one may have a mix of all attributes in various degrees and percentages. All we need to do is to have a short conversation with this person before we start speaking about what we wish to do to encourage him/her. We have to know which of these groups has a higher percentage forming his/her character; this code is intriguing! Because you'll see yourself first, where you are, who you are, you will discover your friends, your employer at work, you will see where your husband is, and after that, we will learn how to convince everybody about these groups.

The Leader

The main qualities of this person are:

- Does not lose time
- Desires the results at any expense
- Constantly in charge
- When he/she is accountable for the work, it encouraged that the work ends with positive and satisfying results
- Always positive of himself/herself
- Independent in his/her way of thinking
- Likes obstacles
- Decides quickly and right away
- Anticipates everyone to deal with all his or her capabilities
- They are considered to be in one of the most antagonist group compared to the rest groups
- Develops his/her world around him/her and takes pleasure in being in control
- Desire everyone to know his/her achievements
- Thinks quickly
- Makes the decision based on the information available to him/her now
- Is successful in any job as long as he/she is in charge
- Expects everyone to be on time and pay attention to those who do not
- You will find him/her in a position like Chairman of the Board of Directors, a supervisor of the company, or a group supervisor.

CHAPTER 28:

Facial Expressions

Take into account your looks on the outside. Think about how much a person can pass on with just an external appearance. A smile may reflect happiness or approval. A fake smile can flag unhappiness or hopelessness. Our physical appearance can now and again show our specific feelings about a particular situation. While you're pretending, you're feeling fine the whole phrase could tell people something else. Some examples of emotions that can be conveyed through physical actions include:

- Joy

- Gloomy

- Getting angry

- Shocked

- Disgusting feeling

- Anxiety

- Feeling confused

- Happiness

- Aspiration

- Contempt

A Scientist went on and found help for the completeness of a number of outward appearances linked to individual emotions, including euphoria, anger, fear, pain, and sadness. A study even suggests that we use their appearances and articulations to make decisions regarding the current knowledge of individuals. One study found that people with smaller faces and increasingly visible noses were expected to be deemed astute. Individuals with smiling, serene resonance were also selected to be more positive than those with articulations of frustration. Physical attributes do the share of a lion's responsibility in transmitting data to the next man. A regular person will not be able to explore the legs or arms' non-verbal communication. However, almost everyone can see the sign shown on an individual's heart. It is therefore of great importance that we maintain a reasonable and sufficient outward presentation in the event that we are abhorred by everyone because we are not receptive. The key articulation that everyone in a person is looking for is the smile. A smile can recover, but it can be difficult at the same time. A lady with a stiff-lipped smile that does not show any teeth is emblematic of her lack of enthusiasm for the debate, although it may seem to a normal individual that she is charmed by the continuous conversation.

Real and Fake Smile

There are numerous attributes of a unique grin. At whatever point individual grins normally, with no deliberate power, wrinkles are made around the eyes. This is because in a unique and real smile, the corners of the lip are pulled up and the muscles around the eyes are contracted. In a phony grin, just lip developments occur. Individuals giving phony grins grin just through their mouth and not eyes. Imagine a scenario where the individual who you are conversing with attempts to deliver a phony grin by wrinkling their eyes willfully. There is a stunt to distinguish this too. At the point when a grin is veritable, the plump piece of the eye between the eyebrow and the eyelid moves descending and the parts of the bargains additionally plunge to a slight degree. Research has demonstrated that the more individual grins, the more positive response he/she gets from the others. There is one all the more method to identify false grins. At the point when an individual attempt to counterfeit a grin, the right side of the hemisphere of the cerebrum–the one work in outward appearances sends flag just to one side of the body. Henceforth, a phony grin will consistently be more grounded on one side and more fragile on the opposite side. Be that as it may, in a certified grin, the two pieces of the cerebrum send signals and thus, the grin is similarly solid on both sides. If by any chance individual's eyes are turning away from you, at that point you should understand that the individual is exhausted from you and it is smarter to either change the subject of dialog or leave. Be that as it may, if the lips are marginally squeezed, the eyebrows are raised and there is a watchful eye of eyes at you alongside the head erect or somewhat pushed forward, at that point this suggests enthusiasm of the individual in you.

Eyes

Eyes have such an enormous significance in any discussion or association that if the language of the eyes turns out badly, the whole discussion and the notoriety of the individual turns out badly. Eyes communicate in a language that is inevitable from others' eyes. Eye to eye connection manages discussion and clues about accommodation and strength also. What individuals see about another when they meet just because are the eyes. Also, subsequently, both the gatherings included make speedy decisions about one another dependent on the eyes. Eyes are thus, the vehicle of passing on data about other individuals' frames of mind and contemplations. Give us a chance to take a gander at a portion of the messages passed on by the eyes.

The Dilating and Contracting of Pupils

At the point when somebody gets energized, the pupils get expanded and can widen up to multiple times the first size. On the other hand, when an individual is furious or in some other negative state of mind, the pupils contract. Thus, if you find that the other individual's pupils have enlarged, it implies the individual is keen on you or in your discussion. In any case, if the pupils have contracted, at that point, it is smarter to comprehend that the individual isn't intrigued.

The Flash of the Eyebrow

In pretty much every culture, a long separation "hi" is passed on by the brisk ascent and fall of the eyebrow. This is called as the eyebrow streak or flash. The brief instant development of the eyebrow is a method to welcome one another. In any case, in Japan, it has a contrary undertone and thus, must not be utilized with individuals from Japan.

The Eyebrows Game

The rise of your eyebrows during discussion suggests accommodation. Then again, the bringing down of eyebrows connotes predominance. Those individuals who deliberately cause a rise in their eyebrows are found to seem compliant and the individuals who lower their eyebrows are commonly viewed as forceful.

There is one trick here. At the point when women bring down their eyelids and cause a rise in their eyebrows simultaneously, it passes on sexual accommodation. This articulation must, henceforth, be kept away from informal and professional workplaces.

It is constantly prescribed that an individual must keep in touch with the other individual to show a degree of intrigue and expectation. Be that as it may, if you continue taking a gander at the other individual for quite a while, it might put the other individual at some inconvenience. The other individual might be threatened by your look. In many societies, it has been discovered that to construct a decent affinity with the other individual, your look must meet the other individual's look for about 60% to 70% of the time. If you continue looking at them with intrigue, different individuals will feel that you like them and subsequently, they will respond with their look also. In any case, if you find that the other individual isn't taking a look at you for a specific timeframe and is somewhat turning away from you constantly, at that point the discussion needs to end or the subject of the discussion needs to change. If you are uncertain of to what extent you should take a glance at the other individual, the most secure wager is to take a look at the other individual for the time the person is taking a look at you. Turning away during a cross-examination likewise gives away the signal that the individual is lying.

The Sideways Glance

The sideways look can be seen as a declaration of intrigue or even threatening vibe. At the point when a sideways look is joined with a grin or somewhat caused a commotion, it can convey intrigue and is additionally an acclaimed romance sign. Notwithstanding, if the sideways look is joined with a grimace, downturned eyebrows, and downturned lips, it can pass on doubt, analysis, or even antagonistic vibe.

The Blinking Magic

The rate at which your eyes squint is additionally a transport of important data. If you are keen on somebody or somebody's discussion, you won't flutter your eyelid as frequently. Be that as it may, on the off chance that you are not inspired by somebody, your pace of squinting the eyes will increment drastically. Increment in the squinting pace of the eyes passes on a lack of engagement or fatigue.

The Dart

If the eyes of the other individual start to shoot from one side to the next, it suggests that the individual has lost enthusiasm for you and is searching for break courses to be away from you. This uncovers the other individual's instability.

The Authority Gaze

One approach to radiate authority is to bring down your eyebrows, slender the eyelids and spotlight intently on the other individual. This gives an impression of what predators do right before assaulting their prey. The flickering rate needs to diminish and there must be a consistent spotlight on the other individual's eyes.

Eye to eye connection and eye developments are a significant piece of our relational abilities and furthermore, our non-verbal communication. Thus, it is of most extreme significance to keep in touch with the other individual, without threatening that person. Eye to eye connection assumes a critical job in deals interviews, prospective employee meetings, and easygoing discussions too.

Fingers

Regardless of whether the eyes, arms, and legs are at a legitimate spot, the fingers can in any case play as a spoiler. The hands and the fingers together give away a great deal of data about us and different individuals too. Besides, when we talk with our hand signals and finger developments, it is simpler for the other individual to hold what we have spoken about. Thus, hand developments help in the maintenance of messages as well. Give us a chance to investigate the distinctive hand motions that are regularly seen in the world over.

Scouring of Palms

The scouring of palms against one another is seen to be an indication of hope. Scouring of palms together is representative of having the desire for positive results. This articulation is very regular in deals pitch also. The business groups of numerous associations advise about an idea to other individuals utilizing collapsed hands and palms scouring against one another.

Scouring the palms at a quicker rate shows that the individual is thinking about the advantages for the other and is an amicable individual. On the other hand, a moderate rub of hands with a grin passes on that the aims are insidious and the individual is narrow-minded.

Thumb and Finger Rub

The scouring of fingers and the thumb against one another shows that the individual has a hope of getting cash. This is one motivation behind why this signal must be utilized with an alert before individuals

CHAPTER 29:

Microexpression

Microexpressions are a special category of facial expressions, which have been the subject of considerable and specific scientific research during the past fifty years. We define microexpressions as subtle muscular movements in the face with a duration of half a second or less. Microexpressions often occur unconsciously and reflect emotions that we are feeling at that particular moment. If you compare the face to a screen, the brain is the projector of our emotions, which cause our facial muscles to contract for just a brief instant.

There are seven basic emotions that are shown in the same way in the face in all cultures. Research conducted among blind people has proven that microexpressions are not culturally learned, but are a biological phenomenon which each of us is equipped with from birth. They are the physical reaction to the way our brain translates emotional impulses. What's more, most people are unable to control these unconscious contractions of the muscles, because they are directly generated by the emotions.

Microexpressions display most of the basic emotions. Robert Plutchik was the first to develop the theory of eight basic emotions: sorrow, dislike, anger, fear, anticipation, pleasure, acceptance, and surprise. He even developed a specific graphic in color for each emotion to reflect the fact that they could be combined to create new emotions; for example, fear + surprise = alarm or pleasure + fear = guilt. Since it was not possible to observe anticipation and acceptance as a universal code visible in the face, the only positive emotion that remained in Plutchik's theory was a pleasure, later more commonly referred to as happiness. This term covers a whole family of positive emotions, including acceptance, anticipation, approval, pleasure, and joy.

Today, microexpressions are grouped into seven basic and universal emotions: anger, dislike, fear, surprise, happiness, sadness, and contempt.

What we now refer to as microexpressions were first identified in the nineteenth century by Duchenne de Boulogne, a famous French neurologist. He combined his huge knowledge of facial anatomy with his passion for photography and his expertise in the use of electricity to stimulate individual muscles in the face. He recorded his conclusion in his book *The Mechanism of Human Facial Expression*, published in 1862.

The second person to write about microexpressions was Charles Darwin in *The Expression of the Emotions in Man and Animals*, published in 1872. Darwin noted the universal nature of facial expressions and listed the muscles that were used to generate them. In the findings of their 1966 study, Haggard and Isaacs reported how they had been able to observe "micro-moment facial expressions" when examining films of psychotherapy sessions, initially searching for signals of nonverbal communication between therapists and their patients. Ekman and Friesen conducted numerous investigations into facial expressions and were eventually able to confirm that seven basic emotions are displayed facially in the same manner in twenty-one different cultures.

In 1960, William S. Condon conducted pioneering research into interactions that last for fractions of a second. He reduced his groundbreaking conclusions to a film fragment lasting just four and a half seconds. Each of the constituent images he had analyzed and recorded lasted for just 1/25 of a second. After having examined this film fragment minutely for eighteen months, he reported on what he called "interactional micro-movements"; for example, how a woman raised her shoulder at almost exactly the same moment as a man raised his hand. According to Condon, this interplay of micro-movements in combination with each other made possible a series of micro-rhythms.

Paul Ekman's later research into emotions and their relationship to facial expressions took Darwin's work to a higher level and proved beyond question that certain emotion-related facial expressions are not culturally determined, but are biological in origin. These expressions are universal and transcend cultures. On the basis of his work, in 1976 Ekman developed his Facial Action Coding System (FACS) with Wallace V. Freisen. FACS is a system for classifying human facial expressions and is still used today by psychologists, researchers, and animators.

We look at the most common variations of three of the seven basic emotions, which can occur regularly in day-to-day conversation. If you have already had microexpression training, you will notice that our approach to identifying and interpreting short muscular movements in the face is designed to make things as simple as possible. This is because we refer to all facial expressions of half a second or less by the generic term microexpressions, even though from a purely scientific perspective some of them can better be described as partial expressions, subtle expressions, or masked expressions. While there are slight differences between the different types of partial, subtle, and masked expressions.

Neutral Face

The Neutral Face Is Your Basis for Comparison

It is important to be able to identify when someone is wearing a neutral face because this gives you a basis for comparing or noticing the difference when the facial microexpressions activated by emotions kick in. Sometimes, wearing a neutral face may express the fact that the person is experiencing no emotions at that particular moment or has no opinion about what she is hearing. In such situations, it can be useful to check if she is really paying attention to what you are saying. It is always possible that she is simply not listening to you or has not properly heard what you said.

You have probably experienced when someone deliberately puts on a poker face. Most of us are capable of producing our own variant of this, when necessary. For this reason, it is important to be able to make a distinction between a neutral face and a poker face. A neutral face will appear more relaxed and more spontaneous than a poker face. With a poker face, you often get the impression that the person concerned is wearing a mask. The muscles in the face are more tensed and you can notice that the person is deliberately trying to suppress reactions to what is happening around him. He will not answer questions spontaneously, but will first take time to think about how he wants to respond, while at the same time attempting not to react with his face.

This is also the reason why people with something to hide often wear dark sunglasses so that people cannot see part of their faces and, in particular, their eyes.

Happiness: Corners of the Mouth Turned Up

You can read happiness in someone's face when both corners of their mouth are turned up symmetrically to the same level. If you can recognize it, this microexpression is extremely useful in everyday life. For example, if I ask my partner what she wants to do tonight, "Shall we meet up with friends, stay at home, or go to the movies?" and if I see both corners of her mouth turn up when I mention *friends*, then I know that she has already made her nonverbal choice.

Both Corners of The Mouth Turned Up Indicate Happiness.

Compare This with a Real, Wholehearted Smile of Joy

This is not a microexpression, but we show it as an example, so that you can see the difference between a microexpression that lasts for half a second or less and a microexpression that lasts for significantly longer. The photo is also useful to see the difference between a real and a false smile.

When you see the orbicularis oculi (the muscle around the eye) contract, you know that you are looking at a real smile, a so-called Duchenne smile. The contraction of the orbicularis oculi muscles makes the areas of skin between the eyes and the outer edge of the eyebrows stretch and lower slightly, often accompanied by the slight lowering of the eyebrows as well. These two movements are a reliable indicator that someone is experiencing pleasure in the left prefrontal cortex of their brain, so that the happiness they are expressing is genuine.

This Is Not a Microexpression.

How Good Are People at Recognizing Microexpressions?

The average score when people first do a microexpression test is just 24.09 percent (based on 2,664 unique test results worldwide in 2012).

Fewer than 12 percent achieve a score of more than 50 percent. This leads to the conclusion that in their daily conversations most people pay little attention to microexpressions, or else they are not aware of the significance of these small muscular contractions, which are nevertheless the most reliable indicators of the way people are feeling.

CHAPTER 30:

Micro-Expressions and
Body Language Signs

Micro expressions are tiny little features within our face that give us a better indication of what somebody else might be thinking or wanting to do. Whether it's a small wrinkle in their forehead or the way that they move their mouth, we can start to pick up on these tiny micro expressions to better understand what somebody is really thinking inside their head.

There are seven different emotions that we can pick up through micro expressions. These include anger, fear, disgust, sadness, content, happiness, and surprise. These micro expressions will show people in different ways. However, there are specific indications that we can use, which will help us better understand what somebody might be feeling.

Let's first discuss anger. Anger is something that we can pick up on by the way that a person uses their eyebrows and their mouth.

If eyebrows are pointed down and inwards towards the nose, then this is a sign of anger. The lower lid might also become raised up and closing over their eyes, in a way that makes their eyes look a little bit more squinted. They'll often keep their lips sucked in and tight around their mouths. They might have a frown in the way that their cheeks are tense and their mouths are pointing downwards. Let's move on then to discuss something that we do when something might smell bad, or if we simply don't like the information that somebody is telling us.

We can show disgust in the same kind of way that we do anger in terms of eyebrow usage. Disgust will often leave the person with their mouth hanging open a little bit more. They'll have tense cheeks and a wrinkled nose. Their face is basically recoiling away from the disgusting thing that they're hearing.

Fear is going to have similar eyebrow movements as well. However, they'll be raised extremely high and flat.

If somebody's forehead is wrinkled, and their mouth is slightly open, then this can also tell us that they are feeling fear. Look at the rest of their body to indicate if it's fear, or if it's just surprise. Surprise looks a lot like fear but a little bit more positively. When somebody is surprised, they'll have curved eyebrows versus flat eyebrows as when they're fearful. They'll have their mouth open, but they might have the corners of their mouth turned up a little bit as well. Even when we receive bad news, we can still sometimes have a smile. The smile might manifest simply because we're trying to work through that emotion in our brain. Sadness is like anger turned downwards. You'll have those arched eyebrows; except they'll be hanging a little bit looser and closer to your eyes. A more relaxed cheek is seen in sadness, but the corners of their mouth will also be turned down. Content is sort of like complacency. You're satisfied with the moment, but you're not necessarily happy. You feel comfortable, and you're not really angry or anything like that. Content is when we keep our mouths flat. You might have one side or the other raised. Not in a smile just sort of half expression.

This is because we don't have that much emotion at the moment, but we're trying to show the other person what that emotion might be in our face. And finally, let's discuss happiness. This is undoubtedly one of the easiest micro expressions we can pick up on. Somebody who's smiling is going to be a happy person. The bigger the smile, the easier it is to understand how they might be feeling. Let's take a more in-depth look into what smiling can tell us about another person.

Fundamentals of Body Language

Body language is a main form of communication and you can get so much more from paying attention to body language than you can with any other form of communication. A person's body doesn't lie. If they are perturbed, their body will show it. If they're angry, the body will show it. The body will show what a person does and doesn't want to do, if they are tired, interested, bored, etc.

Body language is part of our everyday transactions and interactions. You probably already observe and analyze so much more body language than you think. If you are walking and you see a certain swing in the hips in another person, this can be enough to give you a whole idea about what that person wants. A small change in eye direction can be a huge mark of body language. These are very subtle movements that result in the transmission of ideas and attitudes.

If you have any experience with acting, you know that how a person leads with their body can tell you about their personality. If a person "leads" with one part of their body, you might notice it in how they walk; one person might lead with their head, and you will notice that will be the most prominent part of the body as they transport themselves. Another person might lead with the hips. People tend to accentuate one part of their body when walking, and this can tell you a little something about their personality. For example, if a person is leading with their hips, you might find that they are a particularly sexual person and that sexual and sensual drives are how they make their way in the world and how they use their bodies and minds in space. If a person leads with their head, you might find that they are more cerebral and like to use their cognitive skills to attack a problem. If a person leads with their feet, they might be telling you that they are a little cautious and aren't going to jump into anything quickly, not exposing themselves until they find that the coast is clear.

These are all examples of the ways that body language can be analyzed. Remember, body language is an art. In purveying it and reading it, you must remember to use artfulness and artful considerations when encountering this. There are no formulas, there is only intuition. You must develop the side of you that can intuitively read people and trust that part of you through the process. There are some archetypes that you can look for in deciphering body language. These are archetypes that people play into in their personalities. Sometimes, they are accurate, while sometimes, there is more to the story.

Conclusion

This guide should open your mind to a daily process that we all take for granted. Our nonverbal communications. When you find out how much information you are signaling, without even realizing it, you will see how important it is to disguise those clues. Most especially if you desire to be successful in your life.

Interpreting someone else's complex body language is not easy. You will need to identify some of the small, almost invisible, movements we have written about. Then, you must try and fit them according to the situation you are in.

Whether at a business meeting or a romantic liaison, you can learn to read between the lines of what people are saying. It takes a good deal of practice to make sure you don't misinterpret what you're observing. So, don't think you can learn this skill overnight.

Once you feel confident that you're reading the right messages, you can then begin controlling your own nonverbal signals. Make sure you always come across as confident and clear, by knowing what to give away and what not to make so obvious.

If you're intrigued by the mysteries of body language, then you're not alone. It's only one small part of the intricacies of communication between people. Our ability to feel so many emotions is what makes humans such a convoluted species. This is a small part of understanding what we're all about. If you can master the secrets of nonverbal communications, you will get to know other people better than they know themselves.

As you become more aware of the people around you, business associates or your social circle, you will be better able to help them. That's because you can read when they have conflicting emotions. If you've read this book through, and taken in the advice and techniques we have shown you, then you'll know to do.

Whilst we think our verbal words instruct others on what we wish to communicate, they only cover a small part of our message. Emotions are not conveyed in a verbal language unless we chose to do so. Yet, in nonverbal communications, we give our emotions away without knowing it. Once you can comprehend that, then, and only then, will you get the full picture of what people are expressing. They do this every day, so you have a lot to learn and understand.

Use this guide to improve your own communication skills. Better understand what others communicate with their movements, that they're not saying with their words. You might find one or two surprises within these pages. Use them as a guide to make you a better person for this new skill. We all have room for improvement, so long as we never stop learning.

PERSUASION

TECHNIQUES

Nlp For Beginners. Control People's Minds And
Influence Them Through Dark Psychology,
Emotional Manipulation, And Persuasion With A
Focus On Hypnotherapy And Mind Games

STEVE BROOKS

Introduction

Persuasion can be found in everyday life, and it's a beneficial force as well as a significant impact on the subject and community. Advertising, mass media, legal decisions, and politics will be affected by how persuasion works, and in turn, it will work on encouraging the subject.

As can be seen, there are some crucial differences between persuasion and the other types of mind control.

Brainwashing and hypnosis will need the based on be in isolation to change their minds and identity. Control will also work on just one individual to get to the final goal. While persuasion can be done on one subject to change their mind, it is also possible to use persuasion on a bigger scale to persuade an entire group or even society to change what they believe. This can make it a lot more effective, and perhaps unsafe because it can change the minds of lots of people at one time rather than the intention of just a single subject.

Many people fall under the fallacy that they are unsusceptible to the effects of persuasion. They think that they would have the ability to see any sales pitch that is thrown their way, whether the representative is giving an item or some originality, after which they can comprehend the circumstance that is going on and discover the conclusion through their reasoning.

In some situations, this is going to be real; no one succumbs to everything they hear, they use logic, specifically if it goes totally against their beliefs, no matter how intense the argument might be. Also, the majority of subjects will be able to avoid the messages about purchasing televisions and expensive automobiles or the most recent item on the market. Most times, the act of persuasion is going to be far more subtle, and it can be more challenging for the subject to form their viewpoints on what they are heard.

They will think of a conman or a salesman who is trying to convince them to change all their beliefs and who is going to push and bother them till the change takes place. While this is one way to think of persuasion, this procedure can often be used in a positive way rather than in a harmful way.

Public service campaigns can prompt people to stop cigarette smoking or recycle can be forms of persuasion that can improve the lives of the subject. It is all in how the procedure of persuasion is used.

Aspects of Persuasion

Like other forms of mind control, some aspects to be looked out for when it concerns persuasion.

One of the essential things that make persuasion different from the other forms of mind control; the subject is typically enabled to make their own free choices in the matter even if the strategies of persuasion are going to work to shift the subject's mind in specific instructions.

The subject can choose which way they wish to think, if they want to buy an item or not, or if they feel the evidence behind the persuasion is strong enough to change their minds.

CHAPTER 1:

What is Dark Psychology?

P sychology underpins everything in our lives, from advertising to finance, crime to religion, and even from hate to love. Someone who can understand these psychological principles is someone who holds onto the key to human influence.

Learning all of the different principles of psychology is not necessary. Start with the lessons in these pages, and you'll have a solid foundation. You have to be able to read people, understand what makes them tick, and understand why they may react in ways that may not be normally expected. And even then, you may need to spend time taking classes and reading through countless books to gain a complete understanding.

So, if only a few people understand psychology and how the human mind works, why is it so important to know what this is? It is because those who do know what it is and how to use it can choose to use that power and that knowledge against you.

While some people are going to use these dark psychology tactics to harm their victim, there are times when you may use these tactics without the intent of negatively manipulating another person. Some of these tactics were intentionally or not added to different variety of means that could include:

Using the tactics may have been unintentional in the beginning, but when you found that it worked to get you what you wanted, you would start to use those tactics intentionally.

Some people, such as a politician, a public speaker, or a salesperson, would be trained to handle these types of tactics to get what they want.

Dark Psychology Tactics That Are Used Regularly

Love flooding: this would include any buttering up, praising, or complimenting people to get them to comply with the request that you want. If you want someone to help you move some items into your home, you may use love flooding to make them feel good, which could make it more likely that they will help you. A dark manipulator could also make the other person feel attached to them and then get them to do things that they may not normally do.

Lying: this would include telling the victim an untrue version of the situation. It can also add a partial truth or exaggeration to get what you wanted.

Love denial: this one can be hard on the victim because it can make them feel lost and abandoned by the manipulator. This one includes withholding affection and love until you can get what you want out of the victim.

Withdrawal: this would be when the victim is given the silent treatment or is avoided until they meet the other person's needs.

Restricting choices: the manipulator may give their victims access to some options, but they do this to distract them from the options they don't want the victim to make.

Semantic manipulation: is a technique where the manipulator is going to use some commonly known words that have accepted meanings by both parties in a conversation. But then they will tell the victim, later on, that they had meant something completely different when they used it.

Reverse psychology: is when you tell someone to do something in one manner, knowing that they will do the opposite. But the opposite action is what the manipulator wanted to happen in the first place.

Who Will Deliberately Use Dark Tactics?

Many different people may choose to use these dark tactics against you. They can be found in many various aspects of your life, which is why it is so important to learn how to stay away from them. Some of the people who can use some of these dark psychology tactics deliberately include:

Narcissists: these individuals are going to have a bloated sense of their self-worth, and they will need to make others believe that they are superior. To meet their desires of being worshipped and adored by everyone they meet, they will use persuasion and dark psychology.

Sociopaths: those who are sociopaths are charming, intelligent, and persuasive. But they only act this way to get what they want. They lack any emotions, and they are not able to feel any remorse. This means that they have no issue with using the tactics of dark psychology to get what they want, including taking it as far as creating superficial relationships.

Politicians: with the help of dark psychology, a politician could convince someone to cast votes for them merely by convincing these people that their point of view is the right one.

Salespeople: not all salespeople are going to use shady tactics against you. But it is possible that some, especially those who are getting their sales numbers and being the best, will not think twice about using dark persuasion to manipulate people.

Leaders: throughout history, there have been plenty of leaders who will use dark psychology to get their team members, subordinates, and citizens to do what they want.

Selfish people: This could be any person that you come across who will make sure that their own needs are put before anyone else's. They aren't concerned about others, and they will let others forego their benefits so that they can benefit. If the situation helps them, it is okay if it helps someone else. But if someone is going to be the loser, it will be the other person and not them.

How Is Dark Psychology Used Today?

When you were a child, you would see how adults, especially those close to you, behaved.

When you were a teenager, the mind and your ability to understand the behaviors around you were expanded indeed.

You were able to watch others use the tactics and then succeed.

Using the tactics may have been unintentional in the beginning, but when you found that it worked to get you what you wanted, you would start to use those tactics intentionally.

Some people, such as a politician, a public speaker, or a salesperson, would be trained to use these types of tactics to get what they want.

Practical and Theoretical Overview

Murder, rape, incest, abuse are all words that can send chills up your spine. As a culture, we have saturated ourselves with contrary ideals for entertainment purposes. We sit and watch horror movies, crime shows, and reality shows diving into the deviant's minds. The darkness within these becomes an obsession for some, and though they don't reenact or find the actions preferable, there is a connection that few want to recognize outwardly. While the majority of human beings have a buffer in their mind, knowing fact from fiction and right from wrong, some lack it.

Imagination is one thing. Combining the worst fears of people to find what scenario can be the scariest and most grabbing is something fiction writers and creators do. Often, though, when watching these dark psyches at work on the screen in front of you, the human mind finds a specific recognition of why the predator or villain did what they did. Some movies and books even prey on the idea of the worst human condition. Depraved and distraught, the father who witnessed his family's murders climbs out of his ominous depression to wreak havoc on those that committed the acts to begin with. There is a satisfaction for people in the revenge of heinous acts.

But then, doesn't that apply the same dark psyche to the perpetrator, regardless of the reasoning behind it?

Dark Psychology has no pointed targets and cares little for the reasoning behind the actions. It is the actual act of manipulation, deceit, and harm that carries the weight within the dark psyche. The idea of revenge has been around a very long time. Some significant points in history are considered a requirement of honor if the wrong was done to you. Prominent examples of the "eye for an eye" concept is still in existence today. The death penalty is one example, though its root is broad and doesn't currently encourage the private actions of one person to another. The federal organization as a whole is in charge of carrying out the punishment. But long before that, laws were erected in civilizations that based themselves on the idea of revenge.

Psychological Definition

The human condition is studied continuously, broken down, dissected, and used in the psychological community. Dark Psychology subscribes to this as well. However, in the studies of dark psychology, its focus relates to the nature of the predator vs. prey relationship of the human condition. Psychologists with a focus on the dark psyche move their research toward people that perpetrate crimes or abnormal activity with little or no instinct or care of the social norms. Most people have that buffer protecting others from these ideals, while the perpetrators lack this ability to keep control of their most basic sexual instincts.

You may be thinking that basic instincts do not include the often-heinous acts performed by someone with a dark psyche. And while you are correct, there is a significant difference with the .01% of criminal acts performed by dark minds of particular interest, and if you think about the most primal human from millions of years ago, they lacked one major player that we all deem reasonable. The very early primitive human beings did not have a societal construct that had been bored into them from birth, augmented with religious ideals, and regulated by high functioning governments. Their most primal instinct was survival.

In a world fraught with danger, both natural and nurturing, the human mind protected the body at all costs. There were most likely times that an act of manipulation and deceit are worse committed in an uncalled for the situation. However, our brains are wired to perceive danger and either act on that or flee. Survival back then had more to do with the ability to fight off animals and find food, water, and shelter. There were no other societal norms.

Since our brains are the same brains that were also inside the Neanderthal man, our perception of danger is the only thing that has changed. In a world where almost everyone has food, water, and shelter at their disposal, the fight for those types of situations is lower. In today's society, we see the instinct of survival manipulated into a course where we fight for more, better, and more. Frequently the crimes committed outside of the realm of revenge or the .01 percent are based solely on those theories.

CHAPTER 2:

Dark Traits Psychology

For a long time, psychologists have referred to the dark human traits as "the dark triad," which consists of three negative personality traits; narcissism, Machiavellianism, and psychopathy. However, in recent years, many experts in the field have been insisting that garden-variety sadism should also be added to the list of major dark psychological traits. As a result, we are now moving away from the dark triad and toward the "4 dark psychology traits."

Narcissism

Narcissism is the dark trait that is displayed by individuals who are narcissists. Narcissists display high levels of grandiosity, superiority, dominance, and entitlement. Narcissists tend to be charming people who have a positive outlook, which is why they are good at fooling other people. According to psychologists, narcissists are usually on the lookout for people to feed into their "narcissistic supply" because they want to use those people to build their egos. They also lack empathy for others.

One main characteristic that you see in narcissists is that they are quite good at building and cultivating relationships, and they can initially blind people to the fact that they are acting out of self-interest. We all tend to have narcissistic traits to varying extents, but there are few among us who have Narcissistic Personality Disorder.

The terms Narcissist and Narcissism come from Narcissus, a character in Greek mythology. Narcissus was a hunter and a very attractive young man. He was so attractive that everyone seemed to fall in love with him. However, he only treated people with contempt and disdain, and he never returned the love that others showed him.

Because of this, he was cursed by Nemesis (the goddess of revenge) to fall in love with his reflection in a pool of water.

Just like Narcissus, modern-day narcissists are in love with themselves. However, psychologists have come to discover that narcissists don't love the real versions of themselves; they are in love with perfect versions of themselves, which only exist in their imaginations. It's easy to assume that narcissists have high self-esteem, but that is not the case; they have a perverse kind of self-esteem that is not predicated on accepting or loving who they are but loving a fictitious grandiose version of themselves. When a narcissist acts out of self-interest to someone's detriment, it's usually in pursuit of that grand vision of himself, even though he knows for a fact that it's not real.

Narcissists have an exaggerated sense of self-importance. They think they deserve to be treated better than everyone else around them. They have an exaggerated sense of entitlement, and they truly believe that when they receive favorable treatment in certain situations, it is for the common good. A narcissist thinks that when he is taking advantage of you, he is actually doing you a favor. This way, he can rationalize a lot of selfish and evil acts. In a relationship, a narcissist will think of himself as more important and more deserving than the other person. In the workplace, a narcissist will think that he has more natural talent than his colleagues, and he, therefore, deserves to be put in charge of projects or to be promoted ahead of everyone else.

The interesting thing about narcissism is that in some cases, it can make someone successful. Narcissism can be a self-fulfilling prophesy. When a narcissistic person believes that he is smarter than everyone else, he may work hard to prove it, and in the end, he may be more accomplished in his career. When a narcissist believes that he should be in a leadership position, he may exude confidence and acquire leadership traits, and the people around him will become truly convinced that he deserves to be their leader.

Because of this fact, some have argued that narcissism could be a positive trait in an ethical person. The problem, however, is that most narcissists seem to believe that their needs come before everyone else's, so sooner or later, they are likely to do something unethical, and to betray the trust of those who hold them in high esteem. Narcissists who seem confident at the beginning will often turn out to be arrogant. A narcissist who seems ethical at the beginning will throw ethics out of the window as soon as he feels that his dominance is being threatened.

Narcissists believe that they are special, and to reinforce this belief, they surround themselves with people who tend to be agreeable. They want to be around people who will validate their inflated sense of self-worth. Now, even the most agreeable people have the ability to spot flaws in others, and after spending some time with narcissists, they will stop affirming the negative actions of the narcissist. To prevent this, narcissists try to control the thoughts and actions of the people around them.

Machiavellianism

Machiavellianism is a dark trait that involves deceitfulness and manipulation. Machiavellians tend to be very cynical people (not that they are skeptical or they have doubtful curiosity; they just don't care for the moral restrictions that the rest of society adheres to). They tend to be amoral and self-interested. They don't have a sense of right and wrong; they'll take any course of action, as long as it serves their interests.

Machiavellians are cold, unprincipled, and they are naturally adept at interpersonal manipulation. They believe that life is a zero-sum game and that the key to success is manipulating others. They approach all kinds of relationships with a cold, calculating attitude, and to them, when they desire a certain outcome in a given situation, the end invariably justifies the means. Machiavellianism is named after Niccolò Machiavelli, the Italian political philosopher who is best known for writing The Prince. The book offers advice on how one can control the masses and manipulate people to gain power over them. The book teaches people to be cunning, manipulative, and deceitful, as long as they get what they want. It argues that in pursuit of one's interests, it's morally justifiable to harm others. In this sense,

Machiavellianism is similar to narcissism because, in both traits, there is an underlying belief that one's interests serve the common good, even if people are hurt in the process.

People with these traits are likely to cheat, lie, and harm others to achieve their goals. They are emotionally detached from the people around them, so if you are in a relationship with them, you may notice that all your experiences are shallow. They won't hesitate to harm others if it's expedient for them. Where narcissist, sadists, and psychopaths may harm others for their enjoyment, because they lack empathy, or to fulfill certain emotional needs, Machiavellians will do it for a rational and arguably pragmatic purpose. They have little consideration for the emotional collateral damage that they leave behind; in fact, they only care about others' emotions if they know it will come back to haunt them.

Machiavellians seem to have "cold empathy" as opposed to "hot empathy." Cold empathy is an understanding of how people may think or act in certain situations, or how certain events may unfold. On the other hand, hot empathy refers to be being aware of and caring about people's emotions in a given situation. Normal people have hot empathy, which means that they understand how others feel, and they take care not to negatively impact the sensibilities of those around them. Machiavellians tend to understand the moves that others are likely to make in specific situations, but they don't resonate with other people's emotions. As a result, they tend to come across as unfriendly, emotionally distant, and harsh.

Psychopathy

Of all the dark traits, psychopathy is the most malevolent. Psychopaths have very low levels of empathy, so they don't care for others. On the other hand, they have extremely high levels of impulsiveness, and they are thrill-seeking individuals. They are very callous, very manipulative, and they have a heightened sense of grandiosity. They seek thrills without caring about the harm that they inflict on others in the process. Psychopaths are more difficult to spot than you might think. They tend to keep normal outward appearances; even though they lack empathy and a conscience, they learn to act normally by observing others' emotional reactions. They can even come across as charming when they are trying to manipulate you. They are volatile, and they have criminal tendencies, although this isn't always the case. There is a lot of interest and fascination with psychopaths, which is why you see so many depictions of them in pop culture. However, with fascination comes misconceptions. We tend to think of psychopaths as serial killers, bomber, super villains, certifiably insane people and the danger here is that we forget that most psychopaths are just normal (at least by all appearances), and they can harm us in other ways. People who like starting fights, who disregard your emotions and those who consistently lie to you may turn out to be psychopaths. Adult psychopathy cannot be treated. However, when psychopathic tendencies are observed in children and young people, they can be put through certain programs that teach them to be less callous and more considerate of others. A key thing you need to understand is the difference between a psychopath and a sociopath. In colloquial conversations, these two terms are often used interchangeably, but in psychology, they have different meanings. A sociopath is a person who has antisocial tendencies. Now, these antisocial tendencies are usually a result of social and environmental factors; for example, a person who has a bad childhood may turn out to be a sociopath because he doesn't trust society in general, or he has developed certain psychological issues as a result of the unfavorable upbringing. On the other hand, psychopathic traits are innate. People don't become psychopaths; they are born psychopaths. However, social and environmental factors may contribute to a person's particular brand of psychopathy. For example, people who are born with psychopathic traits and are brought up in an environment that is chaotic and violent, are more likely to have more pronounced manifestations of their psychopathy. Experts agree that three main factors contribute towards psychopathy; genetics, brain anatomy, and environmental factors.

CHAPTER 3:

How to Use Dark Psychology in Your Life

People around us may use dark psychology tactics every day to manipulate, influence, persuade and intimidate us to take advantage and get what they want. As you get to know that dark psychology includes the science and art of mind control and manipulation. Whereas psychology is different from dark psychology as it is the study of human behavior and our actions, interactions and thoughts are centered on them. Some people get confused and don't know the difference between psychology and dark psychology. However, if you want to manipulate others, you need to know how to use dark psychology.

Here are a different kind of people who know the tactics of manipulating others:

a) Manipulation is an art and you need to know the tactics to meet your needs first, even at someone else's expense. Though these kinds of people are known to be self-centered, and they are good when it comes to manipulating and intimidating others. These people are not bothered with the outcomes, but they have an agenda of self before others, no matter what.

b) People who are good public speakers use dark psychological and persuasion tactics to maximize the emotional state of the listeners, which leads to an increase in the sale of their product (whatever they were selling to the audience). These people also know the moment and time of taking advantage of the emotional turmoil of other people.

c) Some people meet clinical diagnosis, as they are true sociopaths. However, these people usually are intellectual, alluring but alongside they are impulsive. Just because these people do not have much ability to feel remorse and lack of emotionality, they build a superficial relationship and take advantage of innocent people by using dark tactics. They are not concerned about anyone's feelings and are least bothered with what others might do once the innocents know about their true face.

d) People in politics (usual politicians) use dark tactics to persuade people that they will do the needful and perform the activities in favor of the common people just to get a vote and to become the ruling party.

e) Some lawyers or attorneys focus solely on winning their case regardless of knowing the truth and even after knowing the truth, using dark manipulating tactics to get the outcome of what they want to win the case. They are not bothered about justice but are only concerned about their reputation and self-esteem.

f) People in corporate offices who are in a higher position and deployed as the companies' regional head use dark psychological tactics to get compliance, higher performance, or greater efforts from their subordinates. They are not cared about 'what their subordinates deserve' or 'is their salary justified as per the work they are performing within the organization.'

g) People who are involved in the sales department are usually well aware of many of these dark influencing tactics to persuade and convince other people to buy whatever they are selling. They could even disguise the customers, as they are only concerned with selling their product and earning a profit.

Now that you got to know about different types of people who may deceit you by using these dark tricks, here are the different dark psychological tactics to manipulate the people and make them do what you want them to do:

1. If you want to sell your product and wish to manipulate your customers to make them surely buy your product, you can use a decoy option. You can use it as the third option. For example, if you are facing a troublesome situation to sell the more expensive of two products, by adding the third option you can make the expensive product more captivating and appealing. You just need to make sure that the decoy option should be the same price for the more expensive option but assuring that it is less effective. It is a good strategy to increase the sale and enticing more customers towards your expensive product.

2. To win an argument, speak quickly so that the opponent has no other option left but to agree with you. If you speak faster, it will give the other person less time to process what you are saying and they will agree with you. While you should do the opposite in case when the other person agrees with you, speaking slowly is better as it will give them the time to evaluate and analyze what you are saying.

3. You can copy the body language of people whom you want to manipulate. Imitating their body actions shall impress them and will make you closer to them and they may start liking you. If you subtly imitate the way the other person is talking, sitting, and walking, they would probably not notice that you are copying them and it may get them to do as per your wants.

4. Scaring the other people to make them give you what you want and need is one of the dark psychological tactics to manipulate people. Anxious people often respond positively to requests afterward as they may be occupied thinking about the danger they are surrounded with. It would make them feel scared and would do as your saying. In addition, sometimes, even if you will not say anything, they will understand what you need and do what you would have spoken them to do for you.

5. To get people to behave ethically with you, you need to display an image of the eyes. It means you should create your image as a person who watches, notice and observe the other person by posting a picture of eyes nearby. The other people could never take you like a side option and will return all borrowed items on time.

6. Tweak such an environment for the people so that they would act less selfish. For example, if you were bargaining in a coffee shop, needless to say, you would be less aggressive as compared to what you would be in a conference room. Usually, people tend to act less selfish when neutral items surround them, whereas if work-related objects occupy them, they incline towards more aggression and selfishness.

7. Try to keep your point complicated and do not make it very easy for the people to understand in a first move. To comply with people with your request, confuse them. For example- instead of keeping a price tag of your product for 4 dollars, make it 400 pennies, so that people would first analyze how much dollars would 400 pennies make and if they bargain, they will do that in pennies rather than in dollars. Or they may just think that the price given is a deal to go for.

8. If you help someone to achieve their goals or sort their problems out, the other person tends to return your favor, as they would feel obliged by what you have done for them. This way when the time comes, you may manipulate the other person and is one of the tactics.

9. Try to ask a question or request a person at a time when they are mentally drained and exhausted. They would never question the request or the chances of denial for your request are very less.

10. Always make the other person focus on their gaining not losing. Moreover, declare the price of your product at last after telling all the features and benefits of your product. For instance, if you are selling your car in 1000 dollars, always let the other person know about its features, specifications, and benefits first. Then declare its price. The benefits will entice the customer towards the car, and then the price shall not be a constraint.

11. Do not use verbs; try to use more nouns to change the behavior of the other person towards you. If you use nouns, it will reinforce the identity of the person for whom you may be using it. It will also indicate a specific group, which shall be eloquent.

CHAPTER 4:

Differences Between Persuasion and Manipulation

The line between persuasion and manipulation is so thin that it often gets blurry. Distinguishing these two concepts can often be difficult, especially depending on the circumstances and your perspective as an individual. Persuasion and manipulation are alike in that in both cases, someone is trying to influence the decisions and behaviors of another. The key distinction between the two is that manipulation is seen to be highly driven by self-interest, where one party is willing to go through any length to benefit themselves, including putting others in harm's way. Persuasion, on the other is the nicer cousin of manipulation—there is a desire to influence self-interests, but there is often a line drawn to mark boundaries. Persuasion is the more ethical way to go about it, many will argue. When all's said and done, however, the two concepts seem to intertwine, especially depending on the techniques used to achieve either of them.

The ethics of manipulation and persuasion are a topic we have explored throughout these pages, but know that for our purposes, persuasion is changing someone's beliefs, while manipulation is changing someone's actions. This is easy to remember because NLP involves the neural pathways for both language (belief) and programming (action).

If you want your subject to change their behavior, you have to get them to change their thinking about their behavior. They are a thinking person just like you are, and while they have mental shortcuts that can get in the way (just like they can for you), your subject is entirely capable of talking through their judgment calls with you. In a conversation with you, they can come to re-evaluate their actions, and if you go through the conversation the right way, you will have the opportunity to convince them to change.

When it comes to manipulation, there is a slight difference from persuasion. The difference is that at some points, it is the right thing to ask them to change their behavior directly. Now, you don't want to pull this out as your first move. This is something you build up to after a long conversation—after you accomplish steps zero and one, just as you do for persuasion. But the big difference between changing someone's ideas and changing their behaviors is here in step two: more often than not, you should directly tell them what you think they should do differently.

When NLP newcomers learn this at first, they are taken aback. They think, how could I possibly be told to tell them directly to change their behavior? But if you think through it a little longer, it makes sense. What is the difference between belief and behavior? Persuasion changes belief by getting close to someone's mind and changing what is in there and manipulation is getting closer to their mind and changing what is in there, too.

But with manipulation, there is the added hurdle of getting them to follow up on the change in thought. While it is true that all of our behavior ultimately comes from our minds, our brains are still not simple masters of our actions. Rather, our actions are determined by multiple factors other than simply what our brain tells us to do. The reason you eventually have to ask your subject to change their actions directly is that for new behaviors, a change in thought is just not enough.

Social bonds are incredibly important to human beings. If you want to manipulate someone's behavior, unlike when you persuade them into having new thoughts, these thoughts alone are not enough. You telling them what to do is not enough, even once they have recognized you as like them. If you want to change their behavior, next, you have to change the social environment of the person with the undesired behavior.

This is not a catch-all for manipulation, because nothing is. After all, not in every situation will you be able to change the social environment of your subject. If they are not friends or family, but rather a co-worker, this could prove much more challenging. It is only fitting since manipulation is a more difficult and complicated task than persuasion.

All of this is to say that when you are not in control of a person's social environment, directly telling them what action they should take is a necessary and challenging part of the process. It is so challenging because there is no way around it, and it is also very easy to do the wrong way.

You have to work hard not to work too hard for them. If they can see how badly you want them to change their behavior, they will want to continue acting the way they do out of spite. Don't give them this opportunity.

Recall how with persuasion, we said never to address objections to your frame. In fact, if at all possible, you don't want to address the frame itself. That's because if you address the frame itself, you are acknowledging the fact that it is not the naturally-occurring reality that you want your subject to see it as. However, with manipulation, the situation is different than it is for persuasion.

With manipulation, you have to respond to objections directly, because you have to tug harder than you do with persuasion. You see, persuasion is a subtler, quieter art than manipulation. This is a direct way of saying that manipulation is loud and aggressive because it is not.

But you can't be quite as gentle with manipulation. You want them to change their habits to get your subject to understand the gravity of the situation enough to trigger the behavior change, you must be slightly pushier than you are with persuasion. Again: don't be pushy, but you can't be as subtle as you are with persuasion.

Even when you deal with their objections, you are better off preparing for them before they come up. When you are ready for any question or complaint your subject can haul at you, it is a signal to them that you are like them, you see things from their side, and perhaps, you know better. This is Step One yet again. If you demonstrate that you are like them and can reason things out better, they will listen. You are almost ready to get into the techniques of manipulation, but before then, you need to get into the personality of the NLP manipulator.

CHAPTER 5:

What Is the Persuasion

Persuasive speakers can help influence more than just one person at a time. Instead of sharing your positive ideas and helpful mindset to one person, if you are skilled at persuasion, you can influence groups of people at a time. The world needs positive influencers. We are desperate for role models, especially when you look at some of the most popular people in the world today.

If you have what it takes to be someone who can elicit positive change, you must know how to be persuasive and influential. You are already an inspiration, but now it is time to grow your sharing skills and sharpen your ability to spread new thoughts and ideas to other individuals.

Persuading groups of people to do things is more challenging, and not everyone is able to do it. Most of the time, the most influential people are that way on accident, whether they are doing well or spreading bad perspectives. When you really practice your persuasion skills and grow to become an admirable and influential person, you can have the ability to step in as the leader that many people need.

Since people learn in different ways, it is important to know how to be persuasive in a way that everyone understands. When complete understanding occurs, amazing things can happen. You may not think that it is possible, but if you continue to practice your influencing skills and grow your ability to persuade, you can become very powerful.

If you simply tell everyone what to do, they don't necessarily want to listen. Persuasion is on a personal level, with skilled tricks to get people to buy into who you are for them to be influenced by what you have to say.

Even when your persuasion fails, you have still offered information that may have caused people to think differently. Sometimes you won't be able to convince another person to change, and you won't have the ability to cause them to gain a new perspective. What you will have done, however, is caused them to think.

You forced them into a place where they had to confront their feelings and make judgments based on their beliefs. Even if you didn't convince them about what you had intended when you first started persuading them, you still got them thinking, and in the end, that can be the most influential factor of all. It is not always going to be what you wanted when you set out to influence, but it is still a positive result.

Help People

When you see someone, who might not have the courage to stand up for themselves, your persuasive tactics can come in handy. With these techniques, you can convince those who are taking advantage of a person or situation to stop. You can help encourage the victim to stand up for themselves by persuading them to speak their mind when they are feeling low.

When you have a positive influence on those who need it, you fulfill their lives while filling a part of yours as well. Some people are more susceptible to influence than others, so it is important that you step in as someone positive rather than wait around for easily influenced people to get taken advantage of by someone who might be a master manipulator.

When done right, persuasion and influence can be a form of problem-solving. If you have to confront a group of people that are set in their ways, it might be hard to tell them otherwise.

Instead of listening to what you have to say that might fix the problem, they will instead find ways to prove you wrong and discredit whatever it is you might be trying to convince them of doing. If you use a subtler method of persuasion and influential tactics to show why your way is better, it can help encourage them to make the decision themselves rather than latch onto the opposition with a more combative strategy.

Other people who see your positive influence can start to change their ways too. We think of babies as mimicking everything they see, but this mimicking can occur through adulthood. If you live a lifestyle in which you help people, others will start to follow along.

By persuading others to help, they will end up persuading more people to help too. Manipulation can easily spread from person to person as it is a learned trait and sometimes a survival tool. If you spin the situation positively and encourage people to do what is best for them, as well as for you, it will be much more powerful than it would have been if it led to abusive, manipulative behavior.

Some people are set in their ways, but being influential offers them a different perspective. Imagine a world where we didn't have positive influencers who were willing to change their thoughts. We would still live in a world where sexism, racism, and homophobia were all acceptable social acts.

Positive influencers encourage change, and without them, many people would still be set in their ways. When one person's mindset changes for the better, they have figured out a method of living that is more beneficial than how they were living before. They can then help others "see the light," or live a better life if they persuade them to start thinking the same way.

Ethical Foundation for Using Persuasion and Influence Strategies

Since persuasion and influence are powerful tools, you must be careful with how you use them. They are tools, just like any other item you would pick up to use for a task. A knife can be useful to cook and help prepare a delicious meal, but it can also be used to fatally stab someone.

When you aren't careful with who you are persuading or how you might be doing so, you can alter things for the worse. When persuasion turns negative, it can become manipulation, which can be damaging too many different people. Some individuals are more sensitive to influence than others, which may result in them getting taken advantage of by the manipulator.

If you are taking from someone else, then you have to question your ethics with your method of persuasion. People should think for themselves, but some people have moments where they aren't able to easily do so. Just because we might not have those same moments of weakness does not mean that we should be taking advantage of them.

Humans are entitled to free choice. When we take that freedom away from someone, are we really getting what we want? Are you fulfilled if you take something from another person?

When you manipulate and control someone too much, they start to lose their identity. They are no longer themselves and have become a version of you, scared to displease you or not live up to a certain standard. When this shift in identity happens, it can be hard to recover.

Not only is it a bad situation for the person who was manipulated, but the negative persuader has also become dependent on controlling the other person, leading to a toxic relationship. Influence should only be done when it is carried out in a positive, healthy way that mutually benefits both individuals.

When you are intentionally altering the way someone thinks, you have to be careful. All of our minds work very differently, so even though you might feel like a form of manipulation is harmless, it could be doing damage to the other person. For example, many people think that belittling someone is a way to get what they want from them.

Always consider the outcome. Make sure every time you influence someone that you question if you are doing the right thing. If you are going to be gaining all the benefits and the other person is going to end up suffering, have you done the right thing? You might have gotten exactly what you wanted, but did the other person?

Make sure that you have looked at all outcomes before you decide to try and persuade or influence. Make sure that you are compromising with yourself before embarking on a path of influence. Look at what they want and look at what you want and make sure to choose a path that is mutually satisfying so that no one ends up getting hurt.

We just have to make sure that we are not trying too hard to persuade ourselves that what we are doing is right. When you become a good influencer and are trained with different persuasion tactics, it becomes very simple to convince others what to do.

However, when we want to believe something, we can persuade that inner voice that questions our decisions to become silent. Sometimes persuaders become wrapped up in what they believe because they have tricked themselves into thinking something. Look at master manipulators like Charles Manson, for example.

Not only did he convince his followers that he should be idolized, but he manipulated himself into thinking so to the point that it wasn't wrong for him to persuade others to murder people. Be careful not to influence yourself too much, and try to remain as objective as possible.

Not Manipulation

Manipulation can be an abusive tactic that is not morally correct to use on other individuals. Some people are easy to manipulate, especially children, which is why most kids grow up having the same beliefs as their parents. At an early age and throughout their developmental years, they were taught a certain ideal.

Once an idea is put in their minds, it is harder to remove, and a little voice will always be in the back of their heads, reminding them of the manipulation. When you manipulate someone, child or adult, you are altering the way their brain thinks.

You can alter their chemistry, biology, and the overall function of the different parts of their brain through manipulation. You never want it to have negative results from which it is difficult to recover. Instead, you should be doing your best to try to persuade people to do well and think positively.

CHAPTER 6:

History of Persuasion

H istorically, persuasion is rooted in the ancient Greek's model of a prized politician and orator.

To make the list, a politician or orator needs to master the use of rhetoric and elocution in other to persuade the public. Rhetoric, according to Aristotle, is the "ability to make use of the available methods of persuasion" to win a court case or influence the public during important orations. On the other hand, elocution (a branch of rhetoric), is the art of speech delivery, which may include proper diction, proper gestures, stance and dress. Although Grecian politics and orations seem clearly to be the genesis of persuasion, its use in the rapidly developing world of the twenty-first century goes beyond politics, oration and other human endeavors.

Persuasion, in the business domain, refers to a corporate system of influence aimed at changing other people, groups, or organizations' attitudes, behavior or perception about an idea, object, goods, services or people. It often employs verbal communications (both written and spoken words), non-verbal communication (paralinguistic, chronemics, proxemics and so on), visual communication or multimodal communication to convey, change or reinforce a piece of existing information or reasoning peculiar to the audience. Persuasion in business can come in different forms depending on the need of the management. For instance, business enterprise sometimes uses persuasion in cases like; public relations, broadcast, media relations, speech writing, social media, customer-client relations, employee communication, brand management and so on.

Persuasion, in psychological parlance, refers to the use of an obtainable understanding of the social, behavioral, or cognitive principles in psychology to influence the attitude, cognition, behavior or belief system of a person, group or organization. It is also seen as a process by which the attitude and behavior of a person are influenced without any form of coercion but through the simple means of communication. For instance, when a child begs his mother for candy and the mother refuses but instead proffers a better food for the child to eat while also encouraging him that it will make him grow bigger.

In the world of politics and governing today, persuasion still retains its role as one of the important means of influencing the behavior, feelings and commitment of the populace through the power of mass media. For instance, politicians sometimes use social media, television, radio, newspaper, magazine to persuade the populace to sponsor their political campaigns. Persuasion in modern politics is also observed through the use of authority in such situations where opponents of one political party influence on cross carpet to the other party with different promises in the form of power and immunity. In addition, the court still entertains the use of persuasion during the prosecution or defense of an accused. Another way to see persuasion is through the intentional use of the means of communication as a tool of conviction to change attitudes regarding an issue by transferring messages in a free choice atmosphere. The verbal, non-verbal and visual forms of communication are manipulated just for the sole purpose of persuading an individual, group, or organization. Although communication is the most important and versatile form in which persuasion is manifested, it is worthy of note that not all forms of communication are intended to persuade. For instance, the celebration of a newly inaugurated president or governor circulated on the news cannot be classified as persuasion unless it is intended to impact something on the citizen of the country or react in certain ways.

We go further to look at other possible definition of persuasion in the circular world.

Persuasion is a concept of influence that attempts to change a person's attitudes, intentions, motivations, beliefs or behaviors. When a child begs his parent for candy and the parent says a big no to him, but the child insists on having candy even while knowing it might not be good for his health, persuasion is beginning to take place. Along the course of all of this, the parent will try to proffer a better food for the child to eat instead of the candy, the child gets excited and goes for the new alternative. In this way, the parent has won a banter of persuasion.

Persuasion, on its own is a branch of communication and also popular as a method of social control, so it is worthy of note that not all forms of communication intend to be persuasive. Persuasion is also a process by which the attitude and behaviors of a person are influenced without any harsh treatments by simple means of communication from other people. Other factors can also determine a person's change in behavior or attitude, for example, verbal threats, a person's current psychological state, physical coercion, etc.

Having to discuss the meanings of persuasion, it can be observed that persuasion extends beyond a specific field as there is an intermingling of ideas from different areas of study. However, communication and psychology seem clearly to be in use for persuasion to take place.

While communication provides the model as to how interlocutors in the art of persuasion get messages understood, psychology provides the model for the mental processes during the persuasion.

CHAPTER 7:

Principles of Persuasion

The psychology of persuasion is based on six principles, namely:

- Scarcity

- Reciprocity

- Sympathy and like-ability

- Authority

- Commitment and consistency

- Social proof

Reciprocity

We are compelled by social norms to react to favor and respond with another favor. We do that naturally so that we do not seem as being ungrateful. It is much easier to have someone do something for you after giving them a gift or doing something for them. This makes them feel obligated, and such a feeling of obligation inclines them to consent to your request.

Initiating a favor can result in so many reciprocations of the favor in the future. This principle is widely applied in sales and marketing, where free samples and giveaways are used to initiate transactions. When using the principle of reciprocity to influence others, it is good to be careful. First, you should have a clear understanding of your target audience, what they want, and why you want to influence them.

Consistency and Commitment

There is a tendency in every human being to want to appear consistent before others. There is an inherent need in us to be consistent with want we have bought, what we said and what we've done. We feel the pressure to act following our prior commitments when making new decisions. For example, you can keep old customers with ease that you can attract new ones.

Commitment is fueled by the desire to appear or look like someone consistent in behavior and attitudes over time. We are more likely to consistently go through a plan after we commit to it publicly. For example, let us say that you have five restaurants where you can call to order a meal. You call three of them to order supper, for three different types of food. By the time you pass by each restaurant to collect your foods, you find that only one restaurant has prepared the food well and it is ready, but for others, you will have to wait for thirty more minutes. The chances are high that next time when you need the same service, you will not call the two restaurants where you were delayed for thirty minutes. You will feel compelled to call the one that served you well because you think that they will be consistent in their commitment to serve you well.

Social Proof

When we are faced with uncertainty, and we really don't know which decision to make, we observe what others are doing for some social proof or evidence of whether something is good or not.

For example, let us say that you arrive in a new city unfamiliar to you. You go looking for a restaurant, and you come across two restaurants that look quite similar. One is empty, and the other one is almost full. Which one will you choose?

At that moment, you will rely on what others are doing to make your decision, and you will find yourself choosing the almost full restaurant. To be accepted by our society or social sub-groups, we tend to act in the same way as our community does, even if it is wrong. Also, if you know the truth, you may find yourself doing wrong with the masses, other than turning around and telling them the truth. We tend to follow trends, and marketers have mastered the art harnessing the power of social proof.

Sympathy/ Like-ability

The chances are high that we can get influenced by the people we like. If someone you love wants or asks you to do something, you are more likely to do it. Even something superficial as the physical appearance of someone can influence you to do something for them. When you like someone, you want to reflect on them. If the people you like are doing something, you also want to be part of doing it because you want to be associated with them. You will be influenced by the ease to support a cause that your family, colleague, and friends also support so that you can find safety in them by reflecting on what they are doing and doing it as well. Companies use this principle with great success when they send sale agents in their communities. It is more likely that people will buy from others who are like themselves, people they know and respect or friends. Sympathy is, therefore, key to influencing buyers. People will rarely buy something from someone they don't like.

When you reflect someone else's behavior, such as dressing in a way that aligns with their interests, speaking the same language, or copying their body language, they will like you and sympathize with you.

Authority

People tend to believe people with authority or someone they trust and respect. The ordinary individual will tend to accept what is being said by any individual showing authority without questioning it. A figure of authority can be a politician, a celebrity, or any other local hero, well known to the people. You can influence people in a great way by using a figure of authority to deliver your message, other than having to do it yourself.

In general, people tend to obey authority figures, regardless of whether those authority figures are questionable. It is human nature.

That is why companies use persons with the authority to advertise their goods. The opinion of such professionals and experts is critical and acts as a testimony to guide customers who are not sure about a purchase.

Scarcity

People want something more when they realize that their supply is inadequate. When there is a perception that something is limited, it is the nature of human beings to want it more. To buy something when it is the very last one, or in a situation where perception has been created that the special expires soon is a common human behavior. Businesses use such techniques to make huge sales within a short time. When customers or supporters get some wind that there is limited stock, tickets to an upcoming event are limited, or just a few volunteer positions remaining to be filled, they get a feeling that they might miss out and act quickly to secure their items or positions.

Elements of persuasion

The first element of this theme is that persuasion is often symbolic. What this means is that persuasion utilizes words, sound as well as images to get the message across to the specific victim. The logic behind this is quite simple really. For one individual to be able to persuade another into acting in a particular way, they will need to show them why they should act in a said way and not vice versa.

The second key is that persuasion will be used deliberately to affect how others act or think. This one is quite obvious; you don't use persuasion to get them to change if you don't deliberately try to affect others. In order to get the topic to believe the same way they do, the persuader will attempt distinct strategies. This could be as easy as having a discussion with them or presenting proof supporting their point of perspective. On the other hand, to change the mind of the subject, it could involve much more and include more deceptive forms.

The distinctive thing about persuasion is that it enables some type of free will for the topic. In this way, the topic is permitted to create its own decision. For the most part, they don't have to go for it, no matter how hard somebody tries to persuade them of something. The subject might hear about the best car to buy a thousand commercials, but if they don't like that brand or don't need a new vehicle at that time, they won't go out and buy it.

Examples of persuasion can be found everywhere, including when you talk to individuals you know, on the Internet, on radio and television. It is also feasible to deliver persuasive messages by nonverbal and verbal means; although when verbal methods are used, it is much more efficient

The ability to influence someone during a conversation and make a decision is necessary to become one of the most important people in the world today. This ability is useful in business negotiations, and in everyday life.

In general, the impact on people is not so obvious. The basic idea is that people's behavior is often guided by their subconscious simple desires. And to achieve your goals, you need to understand the simple desires of people, and then make your interlocutor passionately wish for something.

It should be noted that to influence people, you should NOT try to impose or force them to make a hasty decision. It may seem incredible, but the person that wants to reach mutually beneficial cooperation becomes a huge advantage compared to those that are trying to impose something on others. If you are willing to put yourself in the shoes of another person from whom you want to get something and understand his/her thoughts, then you do not have to worry about your relationship with the person.

The secret lies in the ability to help the self-affirmation of the interlocutor. It is necessary to make sure that your companion looks decent in his own eyes. First things first, six basic principles that will absolutely affect any of your interlocutors.

To achieve their goals, people often use the influence of psychology, which helps to manipulate a man. Even in ancient times, it can be seen that priests ruled the people, instilling in them that religion is harsh, and everyone will be punished if they cannot follow the established rules and practices. Psychological influence strongly acts on the subconscious, causing the victim to be influenced to be led by a skilled manipulator.

If you want to succeed and learn how to manage people, these words of the great American entrepreneur should be your credo. You will grow your personality only when you are in close cooperation with the community. From childhood, we develop the basic patterns of behavior and outlook, produced by the long historical, biological and mental development of humankind.

To have influence and control over another person, it is required that you know their personality and behavioral traits. Most importantly, learn how to use this knowledge to master the specific methods and techniques of influence and control the behavior of the other, based on his outlook, character, personality type and other important psychological features. If you want to learn how to manage people, secret techniques in this article will let you know not only the theoretical aspect of the question but also allow the use of this knowledge in real life.

To help people to look beyond the limits of consciousness, professionals use a variety of methods and techniques. One of the most effective of these is hypnosis. This method of direct influence on the psyche, whose essence consists of the introduction of human narrowed state of consciousness, makes it is easy to control someone else's suggestion and management.

Persuasion may involve the use of powerful symbolic words such as freedom, justice, and equality, nonverbal visual signs such as the holy cross, and the flag, and familiar images. Symbols are the tools of the persuader to drive the attitudes and mold opinions.

CHAPTER 8:

Subliminal Persuasion

Subliminal persuasion is a term that's mostly found in advertisement. It's often associated with the idea of tricking someone into picking up a message without their awareness. The persuasion is done on a level that those being persuaded can't initially, or easily, pick up on.

It is yet another manipulative tactic that many people use on those around them. Subliminal persuasion isn't as invasive or harmful as other forms of manipulation, but it can still be dangerous.

Of all the other forms of manipulation, this might be one of the hardest to detect as well.

The idea of subliminal persuasion is that its influences are below the detectable conscious human level.

Those who are being subliminally manipulated won't be able to realize what's going on until it's far too late. In some cases of manipulation, one can recognize while it's happening. For the most part, many people can go years before they realize that they were subliminally persuaded.

The Subconscious Mind

Our subconscious mind works so much harder than our conscious one. It pretty much never shuts off and is constantly making decisions for us before we even realize what's going on. Even while we rest our conscious mind, our subconscious one is putting on various movies for us in the form of dreams. The subconscious has so much information that it has to create these delusions, daydreams, and other forms of dissociation in a way to process all that it knows.

Our brain is pretty much limitless. There might be a number of how many things we can know, but we haven't found it quite yet. We've only made assumptions on how far we think our brain can go. Even though we can pack information into our brain all day, never feeling like we know too much, most of us will just use what we have already.

Our subconscious is powerful. It consumes about 95% of our brains, yet we don't have complete control over it. Our subconscious mind could be why we develop certain fears or might make up why we have certain addictions. For every time you felt as if you didn't know why you had a certain thought or emotion, there's a good chance your subconscious brain knew exactly why.

Your subconscious mind has been working this whole time you've been slacking off! Remember that one time you stayed up all night to get a test done? You might not have a specific recollection of that night, but your subconscious does. It's what's reminding you to get your work done on time so that you don't have to endure the pain you felt the day after pulling an all-nighter ever again.

The key to most of our conscious issues lies directly in our subconscious. Why might a person think dogs are so scary? They can usually look to their subconscious mind and realize that they internalized something dark in their past to make them fearful of dogs.

We'll never be fully aware of our subconscious or the way it works, but that doesn't mean we shouldn't try. The more we can understand about the inner-workings of our brains, the better we'll be at fixing it in the long run.

Subliminal Advertising

Subliminal advertising uses our subconscious against us. They sneak certain thoughts, feelings, and emotions into the things we consume to buy into their products more. Some countries have even banned subliminal advertising, knowing just how dangerous this manipulation tactic can be.

Advertisers know how to get into our heads, literally. They sometimes even pay people to watch their advertisements while their brain function is monitored. This is to get an idea of how our brains work while watching advertisements. They'll track eye movement to see what part of the commercial is being studied. All this information is then used against us to specifically sell something. Advertising has broken into our brains, understanding how to sell us something better than our understanding of capitalism, and what it means to be a consumer.

Think of a chocolate commercial as an example. The advertisement might be nothing more than a picture of a peanut butter cup. You see the logo for a moment, but nothing else that tells you to buy the treat. You still get the idea of the candy bar in your head, forcing you to end up buying one next time you're at the store.

While it is most easily recognizable in advertisement tactics, many people continue to use subliminal persuasion to get what they want.

Social Media

Social media has seemingly taken over the lives of many people. Not only do people create social media for themselves, but they make pages for their dogs as well! Social media isn't all bad, but it's agreeably inescapable.

The people that you follow on social media are likely using subliminal persuasion on you without you even realizing it. They can alter what the world sees of their life, using pictures, quotes, videos, and other small glimpses into their lives. We see more than we would see of their life in any other context, so we start to use this as our identifying factors for a specific person. Many people still keep in touch with those on social media that they haven't spoken to in a decade. Their in-person perception has faded and now all that exists is who they know them for as a social media personality.

Social media has allowed us to create new worlds. You get to pick and choose what other people see. You only post the good stuff if you want, or you can share the bad stuff too in an attempt to make yourself vulnerable and more relatable.

All many users see is a happy face of a baby, but they don't see that the same baby puked all over its mom and the new white rug once the camera turned off.

This manipulation makes many people feel less than themselves. They feel inadequate after comparing themselves to the people online that are living so happily. Many use this form of subliminal persuasion to make themselves feel better.

Altering Perspectives

This type of perspective-altering is seen in ways other than just social media. There are plenty of manipulators that only give others little bits of information, using a ton of energy to cover up some big secret that they don't want everyone else to know. Everyone deserves their privacy, and not all secrets are meant to be shared. Certain things can change a person's perspective, and it's not always fair to keep this from other people.

Friends and family might only tell you certain parts of their life that they want you to hear, not anything bad. Your sister might tell you on the phone that she's doing amazing when really, she and her husband have been sleeping in separate beds.

Celebrities are the biggest culprits of subliminal persuasion. They go as far as having teams of makeup artists, hairstylists, wig specialists, and wardrobe coordinators to create a seemingly "effortless" look.

How You're Being Subliminally Persuaded

Whether we're comfortable admitting it or not, most people are being subliminally persuaded in one way or another. Many forms of passive aggression can also be forms of subliminal persuasion. Maybe a person's mother comments how they saw someone at the store they hadn't in a while, commenting on their weight gain.

This could also be a subliminal message about how the mother feels about her daughter's weight. The subliminal persuasion, then, is that the daughter's perception is now altered. She might feel as though she does not meet her mother's standards of beauty and will alter her life as a result of this mild manipulation.

Those that are doing the subliminal persuasion are usually so lost in their delusions that they'll never recover. They won't be the first to admit that they might carry around some manipulation tactics.

Asking for More

One method that a subliminal persuader uses is to ask for more than they need. Perhaps someone needs $5,000, but they know that's a big amount to ask for. So, they'll end up asking for $12,000, knowing that's a massive amount of money for someone to borrow. The person they asked might feel bad that they need so much money and instead, offer half of $6,000 still wanting to help even though they can't give the full amount.

The person that gives in is then under the impression that they have to give at least something. They feel bad for not having enough to give for the original offer. The master manipulator knew all along that they only needed $5,000.

The person that was subliminally persuaded might end up feeling guilty because they couldn't give more. Even though that person already asked for something once, they can come back because the person that was manipulated still didn't feel like they had given enough.

Doing Favors

Someone that might subliminally persuade another person might first ask for a favor. In some manipulation cases, a person might blatantly tell another what to do, or at least manipulate them in an attempt to get what they want. A subliminal persuader might just ask for the favor, giving the illusion that they require some sort of help. The person being manipulated feels like they should help out, as they might have a need to care for others. They are also giving the illusion that they are worth doing the favor for.

Those that were subliminally persuaded then might feel as though they're special because they had the privilege of helping another person. They feel good about themselves, like they had value and were helpful to someone. The manipulator just used that need to care to their advantage, getting what they wanted from the person that was manipulated.

This method is seen most amongst bosses. They'll appoint a member of their team to a special position, making them feel like a superior employee. In reality, it was a task anyone could do, and the boss just didn't want to do it themselves.

If you think you might be being subliminally persuaded, it might be a good idea to ask if the person that asked for the favor can do it themselves.

Why might they be asking you? What personal gain do they have when you specifically do the task?

Being Flattered

Flattery is great, but many people use it as a manipulation tactic. They think if they can build someone up and make them feel good about themselves, then they'll be able to get anything they want out of them.

Children are great at flattery and learn at an early age how to trick people into doing what they want. They understand using charm can lead to happiness in other people, which will lead to them doing things for the manipulator. Most children become aware of this behavior, but many adults continue to practice this subliminal persuasion. A young woman might flatter an older man that isn't all that attractive, but maybe he has money.

CHAPTER 9:

Persuasion Techniques

Firstly, I think it's a good idea to state exactly what persuasion is. It's simply the process or action taken by a person or group of people when they cause something to change. This will be in relation to another human being and something that changes their inner mental systems (attitudes, values & beliefs) or their external behavior patterns (actions & habits). The act of persuasion may also create something new within the person or may just modify something that already exists in their mind.

In my experience both types of persuasion have its own set of problems and obstacles, getting somebody to do something completely new can be challenging as they have no prior reference point for it and will naturally be cautious or even dubious about trying it. Similarly getting a person to change or modify an existing thought pattern or behavior can be equally as tough as they are already set in their ways. Remember humans are pattern seekers by nature and are looking to connect the dots and find evidence to back up what they already believe as it's easier than re-thinking the whole thing. It's your job to go along with these patterns of thought when you can but disrupt, break up and redirect them when you cannot (pointers on this to come).

In terms of the process, persuasion is usually comprised of three parts:

1. The communicator or source of persuasion

2. The actual persuasive nature of the appeal

3. The target person/audience of the appeal

All three elements need to be taken into account before attempting any high-level persuasions. It's good practice to look around you in your daily life and watch out for when these subtle (and sometimes overt) persuasions are happening. It's good training for when you want to employ similar tactics yourself or just as important to make sure you are not at the end of something you do not want to be.

The 3 Aristotelian appeals

"Character may almost be called the most effective means of persuasion."

Aristotle

The ancient Greek philosopher Aristotle is perhaps the most famous arguer and persuader of all time. He believed that there were generally three ways a person could approach things when they indented to persuade and change the opinion of another person.

Ethos

The first of these appeals he described is Ethos, which focuses on attributes such as character, integrity and trust. It focuses on the reputation of a person, what they may have done in the past and what others speak about them today. Reputations can be a very important thing to protect, especially for politicians in high office or anybody in the public eye who wants to maintain any degree of influence over others. It's OK to show character, that you are a human being just like everybody else and even have some flaws. The trick is to ensure that they are small enough or irrelevant enough for the target audience not to care too much about, but large enough to show you as a person of good values and virtues.

Lastly, Aristotle explains how credibility can play a large factor in someone's persuasive power. Much like Cialdini's modern principle of social proof, people will more likely believe something that is coming from a perceived expert in that field. So make sure you cultivate this impression where you can through strong affirmative communication and gestures.

Pathos

Pathos is a quality that is more concerned with evoking the emotions of the listener, seeking in some way to excite them or arouse interest in what you are saying. This can most effectively be done through storytelling and referencing situations where injustices may have occurred or innocent people adversely affected. In turn, you may use Ethos to condemn such action and describe your high values and beliefs about the matter.

Linguistics also plays a big role when it comes to the Pathos appeal as language is such an effective tool for eliciting emotional responses. A good speaker and orator will always plan their words carefully by using hot and cold keywords to either amplify (intentional, anger, fire) or subdue a situation (careful, smooth, irrelevant). The next time you are watching a politician in a parliamentary debate or taking questions from the press, watch how they inflate or downplay whatever they are referring to depending on the spin they want to put on it. It was my job to coach this into certain foreign leaders who weren't quite ready for release yet.

Logos

The final approach is Logos, which is an appeal to logic, rational explanation and evidence towards the argument at hand. As well as being a philosopher, Aristotle was also a prominent scientist of his time and believed highly in the use of empirical evidence to prove a point. He tried to encourage this as much as possible within law-making and common discourse alike. The courts were especially interesting to him as all three appeals could come into play. Pathos being evoked when somebody is trying to put a positive or negative spin on a statement, Ethos to establish a witness's credibility and finally Logos to provide the evidence.

So, after reviewing some of the overarching persuasion principles, it's now time to delve into some of the specific strategies that you can apply in the everyday discourse, which also helped me carve out useful relationships in the field.

Persuasion is both an art and a science. It is a science because you must first learn the high-level skills and principles required to persuade someone effectively. It is an art to know exactly when to employ the strategies for the best results. In a day, most of us find ourselves in many types of persuasive scenarios. So, go over the following techniques and see how best you can apply them to your situation.

Start Small (Foot in the door)

The first principle is just like what it sounds, before asking anybody for any large favor or request, you initially ask for a smaller one first. By doing so, the person will develop a helpful mindset towards you. Once the small task is fulfilled, they will commit to fulfilling any larger task at some point in the future. It will also be easier for you to approach someone with a smaller task compared to asking for something bigger and more cumbersome, so that's where you should start.

Going about it systematically can help with getting the favor approved. This technique was tested out in 1966 when two Stanford professors divided 156 women into 4 groups. They asked the first 3 groups various simple questions about their kitchen. A week later, they asked the same women to catalog their kitchen products, no quick or easy task for these individuals. The first three groups showed a 52.8% success rate in cataloguing the products while the fourth group showed only a success rate of just 22.2%. This shows that asking for a smaller task before the bigger one can help increase the chances of getting it done.

This is the main premise of a confidence trick that con artists often employ. They will initially ask for a small amount of money, a hundred dollars or so to bet on a certain stock on your behalf due to some "insider" knowledge. They will obviously return a win for the mark often doubling or tripling the initial stakes. They will then go back to the mark some weeks later to ask them to invest a little more, this time a few hundred dollars and turn around a similar result. This will escalate until enough trust is built within the relationship when the con artist will now offer the mark the big prize, the real inside bet that will make them millions. So, the mark gladly hands over any winnings they've accumulated thus far and usually their entire savings to boot. However, unsurprisingly they never usually see the con artist or their money ever again…

Anchoring

I touched on this within "Negotiation; An-Ex SPY's Guide." Anchoring refers to a technique where a person uses a benchmark to influence another person. This technique is widely used in many circumstances as it can be very efficient in garnering a positive result. Say, for example, you are trying to sell a ballpoint pen that is priced at $10. The customer negotiates it to $8. The customer will walk away happy knowing that a product's price was reduced to suit his or her need, but in actuality, the price of the pen was increased just that morning from $6 to $10. So, in effect, you manage to make a profit on the product and satisfy the customer at the same time, all by initially anchoring the price at a higher point to begin with.

This theory was tested by a group of economists who offered students 3 annual subscription selections to pick from when signing up for a popular magazine. The first option was to choose a web-only version for just $59, the second was to choose the printed option for $125 and the third was to choose web and print for $125. 16 students ended up choosing the first option while 84 chose the third (nobody went for the second option). After a few days, the second option was eliminated. It was interesting to note that the vast majority of the students who choose the third option stuck with it as the second option was a mere decoy placed to enhance the value of the third option. It worked as an anchor for students to compare with the third option.

Reversal Tagging

Reversal tagging is a simple and subtle sentence phrasing trick that can be used to gain compliance or agreement from somebody in general. It is a method that uses two opposing structures to a sentence, the first component being an affirmative statement and second being a tag question. The premise here is to make the initial statement to open the line of questioning but add the tag question to give the person a binary choice when answering. That way, you can reframe whatever response they give to make it sound as if they are agreeing with you all along.

You might say to your spouse, "You like this house, don't you?" They might reply, "Yes, I like this place," to which you respond, "As I thought, you like this place." However, if you had gotten the opposite response i.e., "You like this house, don't you?" to which they replied, "No, I don't like this place" you simply say, "As I thought, you don't like this place."

Statements like this are designed to have a negative reversal element to them, such as "he did call you, didn't he?" If done correctly, the structure of the statement should hide the command in the form of a rhetorical question, by first telling the person what they should be thinking but inserting the question that offers a level of disagreement but also implying that this is not wanted (as it would be contradictory towards the already made assertion).

Reverse Psychology

This one should be familiar with just about everyone as it is a common psychological tactic used when trying to get another person to take an action.

CHAPTER 10:

Dark Persuasion and Personality

Trigger methods are often used by other names and are called forced strategies and stimulating tactics. There is only one way to convince someone to think or act in a particular way, which by persuasion. Persuasion can talk to the subject while providing evidence. To change the mind of the object, they can use some kind of force or pull on the object. And they can do some service for this problem or use different tactics. This segment details the different stimulation modes available for each method and their effectiveness.

Use of Violence

In some situations, persuaders may decide that it is better to use some form of violence to reflect on the problem. This can happen if the ideas don't fit properly, if regular conversations don't work, or if the agency is fit. Dissatisfaction or regret about the mode of conversation. Violence is often used as a kind of horror tactic because the topic has less time to think logically than during normal conversation. Coercion is often used when persuader has little success with other coercions. However, violence may be available. Otherwise, you can use violence when the agent feels out of control or when the agent provides contradictory evidence, and the agent is angry.

Responding violence with violence is often not the best idea

For the stimulation process, many subjects view the use of violence as a threat, after all, they have no choice but to require the use of violence. The attraction you want is to choose a path to the lesson, but as power is added to the mix, you lose the freedom to choose. Instead of feeling threatened. If the material is perceived as intimidating, the agent is less likely to hear or think about the agent. For these reasons, the use of violence in the area of coercion is generally not recommended and not avoided. Different from other mental controls.

Influence weapon

Another method that can be used to convince a subject to lean in a particular way is to use available impact weapons. Robert Chardini created these six influences in his influential book. Techniques of persuasion have six goals. Persuaders can accomplish these. The six weapons of influence are reciprocity, commitment and persistence, social evidence, empathy, empowerment, and lack. The agent must be part of these six influential weapons.

Mutually

The first weapon of influence is mutual politics. The principle is that when a persuader offers something to another person. If there is a value, the object tries to return the agent. This means that a persuader occasionally feels obliged to perform a similar service for the agent when a persuader provides a service in a matter. Although the two services are not the same, they are the same.

Everybody is equal

The tour ultimately creates a sense of duty for the subject and can be a powerful tool if persuader wants to use the trigger. Interactive rules are very useful as they help the agent get the subject in the right mood for coercion. Inject the sense of duty into this thing and drown it. In this case, a feeling of duty tends to make persuader believe that they will act or behave in a certain way.

Another advantage of persuader is the use of interactions

A moral position to impose obligations on objects; this is a position supported by social norms. Persuader does not have to worry about whether there is an appropriate code of ethics to return the favor. If the subject does not consider this necessary, persuader has various tools at its disposal to implement them. As a community, people hate people who don't pay back or pay for gifts and services. If persuader doesn't feel that classes are going to and from them, they can involve them in their social group. You can do this by telling other friends and colleagues how you like the topic. However, the material will not be returned if necessary. Persuader is now promoting socialization classes by turning to helpers, further increasing their chances of persuading them to do something.

In most cases, the lessons are readily returned to the agent

Without the need for external strength. If it is found, the agent looks for ways to repay the agent. The score becomes uniform and does not appear greedy or selfish. Persuaders can provide an easy solution to repay these debts. The lessons appreciate this simple solution, and persuader is more likely to do what they want.

Commitment and sustainability

Persuader must use both if they want to persuade someone to change. From their point of view. When things are smooth, they are easy to understand, and the lessons help them improve their results. It does not change the fact that persuaders always use it or change other information that requires material to process. Instead of helping. The process of persuasion, which maintains consistency, makes the agent look like a liar or an untrustworthy person, which leads to the failure of the induction process.

One of the most important aspects of the stimulus process is persistence.

Reason

Hard work is invaluable in society: in most cases, people want things to be a certain way.

There are many types of everyday life, but people believe that the whole thing is more consistent.

They can remember what happened, know what to expect, and be prepared for change. If there is no consistency available, it is very difficult to plan things,

It is always a confusing problem. If you want to believe in a topic, you need to make sure your facts are consistent and meaningful.

Stable

It benefits the everyday attitude of most people. Have you ever tried to plan a day when something unexpected happens? It makes things almost impossible and ends. Feel like a disaster. People love patience because they know what to expect and what to do.

They know when to eat when to work and when to do other things.

Stability provides an invaluable summary of the issues of modern existence. Life is enough without it

Then add those that aren't. If people can live a sustainable life, things will be much easier.

Sustainability is a great tool because it can make the right decisions and process information. If so, the agent wants to successfully persuade the topic. He needs to make sure the message is consistent. There is no room for false evidence to appear later and destroy the entire process. Keep the facts true and accurate and believe that the topic is very good.

Related to permanence is engagement. It takes some commitment to know that the title is concrete and worth the effort. Advertising means buying a product, and politics means voting for product-specific candidates. Commitment depends on the type of trust. Under the concept of sustainability, a person may value a commitment if involved in writing or verbally turned out to be more true written duties, titles can be very psychologically specific, and there is solid evidence that they have agreed to the promise. It makes every sense. Many people verbally promise, fix, or do something, but they don't. Of course, some people will do what they said.

You are more likely to make verbal promises than if you do not, but often it is difficult to achieve the desired result. Furthermore, there is no way to confirm this because there is only one verbal agreement, there is disagreement, and no one can win. On the other hand, if the agent can confirm in writing, they have enough evidence that the thing is over.

The persuader must agree to the obligation, as subjects are more likely to act in a manner that meets this obligation when a new approach is committed. Afterward, the important thing is that the topic continues, and you can convince yourself of this. You and others will provide a variety of reasons and reasons to support your involvement to avoid agent problems. If the agent can solve the problem in that location, there is little that the agent has to do.

Social evidence

Stimulation is a form of social interaction, so it must follow the social rules that occur. This thing is influenced by those around you. What they want others to do instead of doing it themselves. In classes are based on their beliefs and actions, what others around them do, how the same people behave, and how they feel. For example, if your subject grew up in a city, you behave more like the rest of the neighborhood. On the other hand, those who grew up in a very religious community

Time to pray, learn, and help others

With this belief, the term "power of the crowd" is very useful. Classes always want to know what others are doing around them. It is almost hysterical to do what others do in this country. How people differ and what they want to be as individuals must agree.

Examples of what people do are heard on the phone because other people are doing something. Host "Waiting for the operator; please call now." You can feel like an operator is sitting there doing nothing because nobody is calling. This makes it more difficult for them to make a call because they should not make a call when there is no one on the phone. The host changes only a few words, and instead: "If the operator is busy, call again." Very different results. Here the Chancellor assumes that the operator calls several clients. The system must, therefore, be appropriate and systematic. Subjects are more likely to make calls regardless of whether they pass or need to be suspended immediately.

Induction technology

The effects of social evidence can be very useful in situations where the object is uncertain, or there are many similarities to the situation. In ambiguous or uncertain situations with many choices or possibilities, the subjects often choose what others are doing. The decisions are very similar, so they all work, but assume that the decisions made by others are correct. Another way to use social evidence is with some similarities. For example, classes are about some people, and they are more likely to change. If someone resembles a responsible person, the person is more likely to listen to and follow them than the responsible person is very different. Persuaders can use social resource ideas to support the process of coercion. You are the first way to do this

CHAPTER 11:

What Is Manipulation?

A manipulation is a form of social influence that is designed to change either behaviors or perceptions of other people through methods that are, in some way, deceptive. Usually, the purpose is to allow the manipulator to get what he or she wants, even if it is at the expense of his or her target. Effectively, it is finding a way to coercively and secretly exploit someone else into doing what you want or need them to do. It can be valuable to understand the art of manipulation to understand how the mind works, or how manipulators will attack, but ultimately, the use of true manipulation is not recommended.

When you manipulate someone else, you have your own ulterior motive that you are pushing. You want to ensure that your desired result happens, regardless of whether it impacts you versus your child. Telling your child that he must tell the truth or you are going to die would be a form of emotional manipulation. You are putting excessive weight on the consequence that would never happen to coerce your child into telling you something. You may be trying to get him to tell the truth, but you are also doing so in a way that is emotionally harmful to the child.

Sometimes, manipulation is a bit more difficult to spot—it can be finding ways to use insecurities against the victim without them being spotted. No matter what, however, what holds is that manipulation is designed to override everyone's inherent right to free will. This is not something to be proud of or to accept—if you are on the receiving end of manipulation, you should be trying to protect that free will as much as you can. If you are the manipulator, you may need to reconsider your motives and tactics.

Keep in mind as you read through the rest of this that this does not condone the active and excessive use of manipulation. Controlling people is typically considered quite underhanded and cruel, and it should not be occurring on the regular, or at all if it can be avoided. It can be valuable to understand the art of manipulation to understand how the mind works, or how manipulators will attack, but ultimately, the use of true manipulation is not recommended.

How Manipulation Works

Several psychological theories explain how successful manipulation works. The first and perhaps the most universally accepted theory is one that was put forth by renowned psychologist and author, George Simon. He analyzed the concept of manipulation from the manipulator, and he can up with a pattern of behavior that sums up every manipulation scenario. According to Simon, three main things are involved in psychological manipulation.

First, the manipulator approaches the target by concealing his or her aggressive intentions. Here, the manipulator seeks to endear himself to his target without revealing the fact that his ultimate plan is to manipulate him or her. The manipulator accomplishes this by modifying his behavior and presenting himself as a good-natured and friendly individual, one who relates well with the target.

Secondly, the manipulator will take time to know the victim. The purpose of this is to get to understand the psychological vulnerabilities that the victim may have to figure out which manipulation tactic will be the most effective when he ultimately decides to deploy them.

Depending on the scenario, and the complexity of the manipulation technique, this stage may take anywhere between a few minutes to several years. For example, when a stranger target you, he may take only a couple of minutes to "size you up" but when your partner or colleague seeks to manipulate you, he or she may spend months or even years trying to understand how your mind works.

The success of this second step depends on how well the first step is executed. If the manipulator successfully hides his intentions from you, he is in a better position to learn your weaknesses because you will instill some level of trust in him, and he will use that trust to get you to let down your guard and to reveal your vulnerabilities to him. Thirdly, having collected enough information to act upon, the manipulator will deploy a manipulation technique of his choosing. For this to work, the manipulator needs to be able to marshal a sufficient level of ruthlessness; this means that the manipulation technique chosen will depend on what the manipulator can stomach. A manipulator with a conscience may try to use methods that are less harmful to manipulate you. One that completely lacks a conscious may use extreme methods to take advantage of you. Either way, manipulative people are willing to let harm befall their victims, and to them, the resultant outcome (which is usually in their favor) justifies the harm they cause.

Different Manipulative Personalities

Falling for a manipulative person can be very detrimental. It could mean that you lose out on a promotion, end up making a bad investment, and find out that your significant other is cheating, or you can be traumatized or physically hurt. When people hear about somebody conning others, they always ask, "How were they able to get away with it? Couldn't somebody stop them?" Yes, somebody could have, and the best way to do that is to stop the manipulation before it causes problems.

To use body language to figure out if a person is manipulative, there are three things you need to do: norm, observe cues, and spot verbal signals.

Norming

Everybody has a baseline on how they act. To norm a person, you have to figure out what their baseline is, or how they are likely to act when at ease. To be able to spot drastic changes in a person's actions that can warn us of manipulation, you must learn to listen to your gut instinct. When you norm somebody, scan across their body and look at:

Their Feet – Where are the feet angles? Do they have then crossed? How wide are they standing? Feet those are about 12 to 18 feet apart shows confidence.

Their Hands – Do they have the open or clenched? Are they carrying a weapon? Are they trying to cover a body part? Are they doing something to self-soothe like picking at their nails or ring?

Their Torso – Is it angled towards or away from me? The direction of their belly button is the best indicator of who has their attention.

Their Head – What type of expressions are they making? Do they have a narrow gaze? Are their lips pursed? Is their smile genuine or fake?

Their Tone – When they talk, is it normally high pitched? Are they trying to come off as confident? Do they sound agitated?

Their Verbal Cues – Why don't they want to give me a straight answer? What was the purpose of the things they said?

Start to get into the habit of watching how people act in a public place so that you can build your norming ability. Once you know a person's norm, you can easily spot sudden behavior changes.

Common Deception Cues

If you were to see a person exhibit these signals, it doesn't always mean that they are manipulative on purpose. However, it can show that they are uncomfortable, nervous, or trying to win somebody's approval. You have to be the one to decide how you want to use the information. The practiced manipulator will typically go against everything we have been taught. So how can we spot them? Look for people who seem too helpful or an uncomfortably friendly person.

Common cues include:

- Having a false smile. This means that the muscles around the eyes aren't contracted. When a person is truly smiling, the muscles around the eyes will contract and create smile lines.
- The constant mirroring of your body language.
- They keep a deep gaze or strong eye contact.
- They violate your space to try to make some false intimacy like leaning in too close, moving into your bubble even after you move back to reestablish it, and repeatedly touching your shoulder or arm to create rapport.

Chances are when you experience these types of people; there will be a voice inside of you, screaming, "This feels wrong!"

For a person who is unpracticed at manipulating, others may show signs of discomfort. This can include:

- They create some type of barrier using a cup, their arms, books, or any other object they can reach.
- They have unnatural, limited, or stiff body movements.
- They rub their nose.
- They take their fingers and hands up to their mouth to try to "block" their self from telling the truth.
- They avoid eye contact.
- They will self-soothe or self-touch.

If you start seeing these cues in clusters, then you should make sure you keep a watchful eye out on that person.

Verbal Signals

Now, we need to put everything together that we have learned about our manipulative person. Even the most skilled manipulators will leave us clues. If you are vigilant, you will be able to spot those verbal breadcrumbs that they leave behind.

Sociopathic Bragging: master manipulators, or sociopaths, take a lot of pride in all of their abilities, especially those to try and control you. If you listen closely, these people will share information that can save you a lot of misery. Things like "I always get what I want," "I can talk anybody into anything," or "I love controlling people," are all warning signs.

Discrepancy: the best way to spot manipulation is spotting when a person doesn't match their words and actions up. It is okay to forget different aspects of stories when something is retold, but obvious changes should be red flags that the story is made up of.

Offering unsolicited help for a price: have you ever had the misfortune of somebody offering you something for free, you accept it, but then they demand something in return? People who gain control over you will sometimes offer you some sort of assistance to build rapport and then try to exploit this by "connection" by preying a person's sense of reciprocity. If a person ever says, "Hey, I helped you. Let me in to get a drink," it is a red flag.

They mumble or change pitch: you know their norm, so intense emotions will change their pitch of voice. Manipulators understand that people with a deep voice are seen as trustworthy, so they may try to make their voice deeper to gain trust. A sharp increase in pitch or being monotone can signal that they are nervous.

A lot of details: too many descriptors to prove the truth of what they are saying are common for manipulators.

CHAPTER 12:

Manipulation Techniques

We all manipulate people and situations at various points of our lives, like telling a white lie to save your skin or using flattery to make someone like us. For some people, however, manipulation is a way of life and a weapon they use to overpower their victims. Sociopaths, psychopaths, narcissists, and other social predators are critical users of manipulation. While the predators may have a range of techniques with which to overpower their victims, they only target particular personalities. This is because they aim to manipulate quickly and easily, having established the specific vulnerabilities in a person that could render them ripe for manipulation. People with low self-esteem, naivety, low self-confidence, and people pleasers are quickly manipulated.

The Techniques

Here are several techniques the predators use to manipulate:

The Fear-Then-Relief Technique

The fear-then-relief technique is one of the oldest, most foul manipulative techniques. It preys on a person's emotions by the manipulator causing some high stress and anxiety on the subject then providing some temporary relief. Once the individual goes through these sudden mood shifts, he or she is disarmed and less likely to make rational or thoughtful decisions. The person will respond in the affirmative when requests are placed to him or her. Suppose you are walking along the corridors of your university and people start jumping from every corner around you, dancing and doing all kinds of stunts. At first, when they start dropping from all corners, you may be frightened, thinking that you have been caught up in a rowdy mob and that you stand to be harassed. On learning that they are singing and dancing to you, you will get some form of relief. If after this someone you have been dating comes up and presents a ring, you are likely to say 'yes' compared to if the person had asked you upfront in another setting when you would have given some thought before accepting the marriage proposal.

The fear-then-relief technique is the good cop/bad cop technique you see on TV all the time. The bad cop scares the hell out of the victim while the good cop tends to be helpful and considerate to the victim. With this mixture of emotions, the person becomes more cooperative and willing to talk. This is also the technique bosses use to get you to agree to their unfair demands. Your boss could let you know that your job is on the line, for example, then comment that you have been working very well, before asking you to work overtime. The Foot-In-The-Door Technique This is a manipulation technique where the person uses a small request to prime you before presenting the real request. It is a simple, subtle, but tricky technique. Cons use this technique when they ask you to purchase some lottery tickets that could get you to win some grand price. Once you have bought into the idea, you end up buying one ticket after the other without gaining any significant thing, in the hope of winning the grand prize. By the end of the exercise, you will have spent all your money buying a nonexistent award, and the manipulator will move on to the next victim and repeat the process.

Social Exchange

The social exchange technique is built on the premise of causing you to feel guilty. This technique is popularly used by unethical marketers and con artists in which the first person presents the second with a physical or psychological reward so that when the first person asks the second for a favor or request to comply, the second person will feel the pressure to give in. Doing favors and other good things for other people without expecting things in return is typical in human society, but crooked manipulative people can use these social cues as a means to get their way. For example, a bad friend could start informing people in a gathering about how helpful he was when he got you some bail money you needed to get out of jail after an arrest or a court ruling once you and those around you hear that, you will be too embarrassed not to give in to his requests when he immediately brings up his need for 500 dollars to get himself out of bad debt. You also see this trick in many movies when someone is forced to do things out of character to return a favor. A character could be forced to cover up murder as a favor to someone who helped them hide or falsify evidence in a case that would have sent the first person to jail. There are many other examples we could give.

Lowering or Utterly Destroying Your Self-Esteem

Lowering or destroying your self-esteem is a technique used to downplay you and everything you are about. The manipulator uses it by pointing out your defects instead of offering some positive criticism. For example, a manipulative parent could say that his 18-year-old son cannot drive by himself and will need supervision, not because the son needs it, but because the parent wants to accompany his son and monitor him wherever he goes, whatever he does. This is more like hovering than being a good parent.

Projection

Projection is a diversion tactic that the manipulators use to shift the shortcomings and deficiencies in their own lives to other people. Rather than take responsibility for the mistakes and the errors made he or she made, the manipulator prefers to plant the case on another person so that the manipulator can avoid taking the blame. Their failures and faults are often projected to other people. Projection is a psychologically abusive tactic that makes the manipulator look clean and innocent while making the victim look dirty, silly, and unfortunate. The manipulator is very quick to identify a person to be blamed. For example, a manipulative employee will lay blame on his supervisor when the section the employee works is underperforming. He will say that the supervisor is lazy and doesn't give them targets. He might also say that he works hard, but others around him are lazy; they leave him to do all the work. A projecting father might say that the reason his children are misbehaving and failing in school is that their mother does not parent them properly. This parent completely disregards his responsibility and role in raising the children and places all the blame on the mother. A projecting relationship partner, instead of admitting his or her need for intimacy in the relationship, will choose to make it appear like you are too touchy, clingy, or that the partner is only intimate with you as a favor. The idea here is to cause you to appear weak and vulnerable, but for the partner to appear strong and independent. However, the truth is that the manipulative one is the weaker one. The same is the case for people who are always finding fault and correcting others. They do it as a way to project the failures and negativity they see in themselves. For example, when a person is quick to note low self-esteem or pride in another person, it is because the person is proud or has low self-esteem, and is only looking for a victim who can bear the shame or the poor image that comes with that.

Intimidation

If a manipulator considers you a threat, intimidation is one trick he or she will use to silence you. One way to do this is to remain very close to you and to speak to you in a manner that is both aggressive and subtle. When you want to defend yourself, the person will look at you strangely, in a way meant to make you lose your train of thought or stop debating with them. This trick mainly works well with victims who are easily flattered or frightened. Once the manipulator has seen that you easily scare, threats and intimidation will follow. One way to avoid this is to overcome your fears and learn to stand amid intimidation. Avoid revealing your weaknesses and fears to someone you cannot trust because the person will look forward to using it against you in the future.

Intellectual Bullying

You may think that the person who often comes up with facts is so smart, but no, he is just a manipulator. Intellectual bullying is a common trick used to manipulate victims with intellectual facts that are not necessarily accurate. The person knows that you do not have any access or chance to access that information to verify the validity of his claims, and for this reason, they appear to you as having some authority of a kind. This kind of manipulation is often used at points of sales or in financial institutions. You could easily fall for the sweet talk and the facts laid on you. The only way to avoid intellectual bullying is to be informed. You do not have to know everything, but you should have an idea about everything. When you are informed, when a person comes to you with some alleged facts, you will know the validity of the information being given to you, and you can avoid being swept off your feet based on lies.

CHAPTER 13:

What Is Emotional Manipulation?

Telling signs that you are under the influence of an emotional manipulator:

- Killing with kindness

- Convenient neediness

- Projecting a calm, cool and collected composure

- Always "just joking"

- They play emotional blackmail – "I can do nothing without you," "I will kill myself if you leave me," "I will die without you," etc.

- Homing you (home-court advantage)

- Tugging on your heartstrings (it will be heartless of you to do this), "if you have a heart, please don't leave me alone," etc.

- Excessive compliments and flattery

- Excessive generosity

Types of Emotional Manipulation

Within these major categories of emotional manipulation techniques, psychologists have also identified a wide range of more subtle variations that we all likely encounter daily. These techniques include:

- **Lying:** dark Triad personalities, particularly psychopaths, are highly skilled at lying and cheating, so often we may not detect their intent until it is too late. Beware of those who have demonstrated a pattern of dishonesty.

- **Lying by omission:** lying by omission is a little more subtle. The predator may not say anything that is untrue but may withhold information that is necessary for an effort to cause you to fail.

- **Denial:** often the damage from emotional manipulation is inflicted after the fact. When you confront someone with evidence of their dishonesty and abuse, their refusal to admit wrongdoing can cause even greater psychological harm.

- **Rationalization:** the increase in popular news media has led to the growth of public relations and marketing firms who produce "spin" to deflect criticism in both political and corporate environments. A rationalization is a form of spin, in which a manipulator explains away their abuse.

- **Minimization:** like rationalization, minimization is a form of denial, which the predator understates the seriousness of their offense.

- **Selective attention and/or inattention:** manipulators will pick and choose, which parts of an argument or debate should be considered so that only their views are represented.

- **Diversion:** manipulators often resist giving straight answers to questions, particularly when they are confronted by their victims. Instead, they will divert the conversation to some other topic or change the subject altogether.

- **Evasion:** more serious than diversion, a manipulative person confronted with his or her guilt will often completely evade responsibility by using long rambling responses filled with so-called "weasel words," like "most people would say," "according to my sources," or other phrases that falsely legitimize their excuses.

- **Covert intimidation:** many manipulative people will make implied threats to discourage further inquiries or resolution.

- **Guilt-tripping:** a true form of emotional manipulation, a manipulator will exploit the integrity and conscientiousness of the victim by accusing them of being too selfish, too irresponsible, or not caring enough.

- **Shaming:** although shaming can be used to bring about social change when large corporations or governments advance abusive or discriminatory policies, manipulators may attempt to intimidate their victims by using sharp criticism, sarcastic comments, or insults to make them feel bad.

- **Blaming the victim:** this tactic has become increasingly common. When a victim accuses a predator of abuse, the predator will attempt to turn it around by creating a scenario in which the victim alone is responsible for the harm that came to him. The predator may also try to accuse the victim of being the aggressor by complaining about the violation.

- **Playing the victim:** using the opposite tactic of blaming the victim, the predator will lure a conscientious person into a trap by pretending to have been grievously wounded and cultivating feelings of sympathy. The real plan, however, is to take advantage of the caring nature of the conscientious person by toying with their emotions.

- **Playing the servant:** this tactic is common in environments marked by a strict, well-established chain of command, like the military. Predators become skilled at manipulating this system by creating a persona of suffering and nobility, in which their bad actions are justified as a duty, obedience, and honor.

- **Seduction:** this technique does not always have to involve sexual conquest or intimacy. Emotional predators may use flattery and charm to convince people to do their bidding, and they often look for people with low self-esteem.

- **Projection:** this term is used in psychotherapy. Predators who use this technique will look for victims to use as scapegoats. When the manipulator does something wrong and is confronted, he or she will "project" the guilt onto the victim in an effort to make the victim look like the responsible party.

- **Feigning innocence:** this technique can be used as part of a strategy of denial. Under questioning, the manipulator will "play innocent" by pretending that any violation was unintentional or that they were not the party who committed the violation. A skilled manipulator who lacks morality and empathy can be very successful at planting the seed of doubt.

- **Feigning confusion:** this technique can also be used as part of a strategy of denial. Under questioning, the manipulator will "play dumb" or pretend to be confused about the central point of the conflict or dispute. By creating confusion, the manipulator hopes to damage the confidence of their victims.

- **Peer pressure**: by using claims, whether true or not, that the victim's friends, associates, or "everyone else" is doing something, the manipulator will put pressure on his victim to change their behaviors or attitudes.

CHAPTER 14:

Psychological Manipulation Techniques

All effective actions have the same structure—a sequence of stages—the absence of any of which dramatically (sometimes to zero) reduces the likelihood of success.

The impact, built clearly on this structure, is triggered with the greatest possible probability—true, not one hundred percent.

The impact, I repeat, refers to any and in any field—in politics, in business, in personal relationships, in sports, in war, in religion. If the effect worked, you are very likely to find a familiar structure in it.

This miracle is called a single impact structure. A single impact structure can be described in two languages, each of which is useful:

- Background lines

- Stages of exposure

Background Lines

So, whatever our goals, if we want to influence another person (or group of people) successfully, we must build three lines of communication:

- Contact line

- Line of distraction

- Line of exposure

Contact Line

Contact is an opportunity for mutual exchange of information. Contact is a desire to perceive each other. Contact is the assumption that communication is more beneficial than ignoring. If there's no contact, nothing—therefore, the mainline is the line of contact. It begins earlier than all; it ends later than all.

Since it is precisely we who are interested in establishing contact, we are doing everything to make it appear and be present throughout the communication. We find time for a meeting, we call up, we try to be noticed, and we dress and talk so that we are agreed to be distinguished from the general background—and even when a person "escapes" from communication, he thinks, "Is it not that I run too fast?"

Any advertisement should contain "contact information," the one on which the proposed product or service can be found—at least, with the help of a search engine.

If the advertisement is new-fangled and contact information has not yet been offered, it means that the seller prefers to keep in touch with you through his advertising media. A telephone and address will be offered later. This also corresponds to the structure.

Conversely, when a person is afraid that the impact of the other side will be more effective than his, he can just break the contact—so debtors avoid meeting with creditors, so passers-by try to get around street vendors and gypsies, so many business people refuse to watch TV, so children run away from home to not be invited to dinner, so weak fighters try to escape from the enemy, running around the edge of the tatami.

However, contact is not only important for this. Through the contact line, we receive information about the interlocutor's reaction to our influences: feedback. And based on this information, we correct our behavior. This is one of the main differences between a literate communicator and an ordinary communicator—a literate one notices when he is mistaken and quickly fixes what needs to be fixed.

What the interlocutor likes, what he agrees with, what worries him, what he hides—he will tell us everything—not a word, so a body. Generally speaking, our line of contact pertains to the line of influence of the interlocutor on us. It depends on him what we will do next. The words of the interlocutor give us the key to how to communicate with him—appearance, emotional reactions, the appearance or disappearance of signs of trance, changes in his posture and breathing—open only your eyes and ears!

Distraction Line

A man is designed so that his first involuntary reaction to a direct offer or request is a refusal—anyway, any new information. Outwardly, he may not look, but he is internally tense. (Track, by the way, your reaction to these allegations. Did you agree at once?) Then, after thinking and weighing the pros and cons, he can make a positive decision—but inexperienced communicators by this time may already leave upset.

We all unconsciously strive for the same thing—to maintain the status quo, so that nothing changes, to make everything familiar, and so that there were guarantees that tomorrow would be like yesterday—because we are already used to what we have. Let us live in a swamp, but it is ours and is familiar to the last bump. Here, we can easily get rid of any enemy—but we won't fight back, so we'll hide in a pre-prepared assortment. Therefore, the reaction to change is appropriate—wary.

And all this goes by the mind—involuntarily—that is, quite reasonable, logical, profitable ideas and suggestions pass by. In the sense of being eliminated, it is rejected at distant approaches. And few are able, having thought it all over again, to return to what he had sifted out. Therefore, even when we offer a person a truly valuable transaction, point of view, or information, we have to introduce a line of distraction.

Line of Exposure

When there is contact or when the interlocutor's consciousness is reliably distracted, a line of influence may appear—fragmentarily, imperceptibly, and always ready to hide even more reliably. On this line, we inspire—throw ideas, form the necessary attitude, suggest suitable interpretations, motivate, awaken desires—the main work is ongoing.

It is clear that the vast majority of suggestions are indirect. Yes, we are not impudent. We act just where we are not resisted. We do not suggest, "Give us all the money." We explain, "It's not just a cactus but a big-money cactus," and therefore, this cactus costs "only five thousand American dollars." We are not saying that the person needs to obey everything; we only make it clear that in the prevailing— terrible!

And I remind you: the line of action is fragmented. Most of our words are either reliable or unverifiable in the current conditions. However, our suggestions are forwarded: there is a not quite logical combination, and there is not a completely substantiated statement. Here, we say "possible," and after a couple of sentences, "only possible." Here, the word in one sense; there, in another. Likewise, for example, you can create a mood with one story, and then transfer it (there are special methods) to another— and all this briefly, forwarding, no pauses, continuing to speak, without stopping the speech flow, taking attention away from "slippery places."

The second feature—all forwarding work for the same purpose, inspire the same thoughts—let the wording be different, but their essence is one. Thus, an outwardly ordinary conversation with all the usual paraphernalia turns out to be filled with a dense stream of suggestions that work for a given purpose.

At this moment, all three lines are simultaneously involved: impact, distraction, and contact—but that is the essence of a single impact structure.

Stages of Exposure

If you need to know about the three lines of communication necessary for success in order to understand the essence of a single impact structure, for practical use, it is useful to consider it as a sequence of stages, each of which is necessary and sufficient in its place.

How to move from lines to stages? It's very simple. If you project the background lines on top of each other, it turns out that there are five key segments in a single impact structure:

- Fixation of attention

- Depotentialization of control

- Intervention

- Latent period

- Synchronization

The presence of each of them is mandatory. The absence of any of them can ruin the effect on the root—and it is clear that, without finishing the previous one, it is impossible to move on to the next. However, now, the difficult task of holding two or three background lines at the same time turns into a clear step-by-step scheme, from which it is clear what to do and why.

Fixation of Attention

Attraction and retention of attention—without it, no impact on a person is possible. For if you did not attract his attention, you, for him, are not—and nothing can affect. Therefore, the first active step in any manipulation algorithm is to fix attention.

Hence, the goal of the stage is to attract and capture the attention of a potential interlocutor so that it turns from potential into reality. To begin with, you provide yourself with the opportunity to be seen and heard. In order to do this, you can:

- Be in plain sight;

- Appear in a personal area (approximately 1.5 meters from the body);

- Say hello;

- Contact by name;

- Offer to talk;

- Offer to look at what you show;

- Ask for a moment of attention;

- Sometimes, touch;

- And so on.

However, it is not enough to attract attention—it is also necessary to keep it.

The attraction of attention is similar to wrestling capture—after it, reception is possible—and experienced fighters, by the way, are fighting precisely for the seizure, as the rest is a matter of technology.

Then, you can make a trance, "powder your brain," and offer the interpretations we need. There is attention; they listen to you.

Attention must be attracted—and attracted attention must be retained (and in case of distraction, returned).

In other words, to be effective, you must be able to attract attention constantly, over a given period of time, and then let go, and become invisible—you need to be able to do this, too.

Depotentialization of Control

I used to talk about this stage as a distraction of consciousness. The practice has shown that this is not entirely true. The fact is that if you work honestly (i.e., you suggest that for which a person will then be grateful to you), it will not be conscious resistance that will hinder you at all but the dullness of his unconscious. Prejudice, beliefs, inertia of thinking, instinctive resistance to the new, stereotypes learned decades ago, and banal laziness—all this forms a fairly rigid network of control that does not allow almost anything to human consciousness.

So a direct appeal to a reasonable and conscious part of the interlocutor is often our goal. Further, the man himself will "understand his happiness." Well, if for some reason you want to create something that is more advantageous to you than him, then you will have to depotentialize (lower the resistance potential) not only unconscious resistance but also the possibilities of his consciousness.

Hence, the goal of this stage is to enter into trust and cause a trance state of the interlocutor. That is the very state in which he cannot or does not want to resist our influences. How to do this is further written. Here are techniques for tuning, techniques for causing confusion, conversational trance and the use of decor. In a word, humanity has developed a huge potential for depotentialization. Potentially, you can use it.

Intervention

The purpose of the stage is to quietly forward the necessary suggestions, weaving them into the context of communication. At the same time, I remind you, while maintaining the capture of attention and depotentialization of control! A particular art here is the selection of goals for suggestions.

CHAPTER 15:

Dark Manipulation

Manipulation can feel overwhelming and leave you with doubts about your abilities. Being continually manipulated can leave you angry, demoralized and despondent. You're wondering how you didn't see it coming. Nevertheless, might you have stopped it, if you knew how to identify the indications that mean that someone may not be good?

Manipulators exercise their power to manipulate and reap benefits from you by manipulating your feelings and distorting your mental beliefs. They are preying on your vulnerabilities and taking advantage of you by communication tactics designed to confuse you so that before it's too late you don't see what they are. Identifying whether you are being manipulated to shield yourself from being abused is critical, and promoting a healthy balance of power in relationships. And it begins with learning how to evaluate the men.

Another way of knowing whether you're being fooled is by body language. The strong, non-speakable and subtle signs that speak volumes when you know what to look for. Through observing the transmitted movements, postures and facial expressions, one can recognize and understand the full meaning of what someone is trying to say or not.

Learning how to evaluate someone will provide some interesting discoveries, and more importantly, open your eyes to the signs that you might be taking advantage of so that you can take action to avoid or fully stop the advances.

The Behaviors of Manipulative People

- **Passive-aggressive behavior:** turning off mood to make someone accept your biddings. The person may see it as "for peace to reign" while the manipulator has another motive.

- **Implicit threats:** threat is an implicit behavior used to coerce someone into doing what he naturally wouldn't do. Though the threat can be implicit or explicit, implied threats have proved to be more effective.

- **Dishonesty:** lies and hoardings of truth make a victim unaware of exactly what he is doing or its implications.

- **Withholding information:** by withholding information, a manipulator can influence one's decision or act because he would remove some information that would give him in.

- **Isolating a person from loved ones:** once you are isolated from your friends and family, you would easily comply with any demand put up by someone. The isolation can be in form of physical kidnap or using words to make you feel not loved anymore or being left alone.

- **Gaslighting:** is an act of messing with someone's psychological state by creating doubt about themselves and questioning their sanity. The manipulator would brainwash the victim into believing that something is wrong with them.

- **Verbal abuse:** abusing people or their victims verbally is another manipulative act. They call them names or use foul languages to make them reconsider their stance. If a woman asks her husband to confront a particular person and receives a negative reply from her husband, she may resort to calling him names like "coward" and reminding him every minute (using words) how a coward he is.

- **Use of sex to achieve goals:** is one of the most common manipulative acts especially in intimate relationships. The manipulator amongst the couple uses sex to make the other person subject to him or her.

- **Flattery:** some people are easily ticked with flattery. It is very easy to make them do anything by praising them.

- **False intimacy:** people feign to be your friend just to get you to do one thing or the other for them. You would see them as your friends and because of "what are friends for," you would easily become their prey.

- **Favor or gift:** accepting favor from people makes you indebted to them and similarly by gifts as well. The manipulators know this and they throw the gate open by giving you gifts or doing you favors. Any time you want to go against their will, you hear yourself saying "I am doing this because of ...." Then, you become their pawn.

- **Over asking:** is another manipulative act where the manipulator starts by asking for something that looks big and offers the one, he wants—which is smaller than the former as a humble suggestion. Without your knowledge, you would fall into the trap.

- **Guilt trip/shaming:** this manipulative act involves the manipulator using different forms of verbal and non-verbal cues to induce a feeling of guilt in a target to control their behavior. The guilt created in the target makes it difficult for him to say no.

- **Test intention:** involves the manipulator telling their target stories related to what he has in mind to achieve with them and watching their reactions.

- **Punishment:** a manipulator can punish his target if he is not getting what he wants or to get a better result. It can be physical (which can be in form of beating or starving) or mental punishment (ignoring the person or rejecting their offers).

- **Faking normal:** making someone feel that doing something especially a bad thing is normal is manipulative. A prostitute tells her friend she wants to bring into the game that "everyone does it."

- **Playing the victim:** this is also called self-victimization. By playing the victim, a manipulator can make his target submissive to his selfish desires.

CHAPTER 16:

The Qualities of a Manipulative person

Manipulation is beyond telling someone to do something and they would do it. There is chemistry behind manipulation. For someone to be able to manipulate people successfully, the person must be flexible, pay attention to details and above all be able to read minds.

Flexibility: for someone to be a good manipulator, you must be flexible. This flexibility allows you to fit into any context. You can easily adapt to the lifestyle of your victim to prove that you two are alike just to draw him closer to you. If the victim likes hip hop, you must have the tendency to like hip hop too so that both of you can operate on the same level. At the same time, if there is a need to give the victim the opposite of the personality, he portrays to get to him, your flexibility should allow you to flip in a second to that character he needs regardless of the kind of person you are.

Pay attention to details: a good manipulator must be able to pay attention to minute details. This ability makes it possible for him to know the kind of person their victim is and know which role to play for them. If you are not paying attention, you may get the wrong information and act with that knowledge and you would be ejected.

Ability to read minds: this is the most important of all. Manipulation is a mind game, so for someone to gain mastery of it, the person must be able to read minds. Reading minds is the hallmark of manipulation. This enables you to know what to say, how to say it and when to say it to please the victim.

How Do We Read Minds?

Reading minds is an art that many people would learn if they have the opportunity. You would not just manipulate people by learning this art, but you would easily detect a manipulator as well. Reading minds is not simple like making eye contact or observing body posture, it goes beyond what the naked eyes see or what the ears hear.

If you want to learn how to successfully control, influence, persuade or even manipulate people, you must master the following six skills:

1. Sub-textual Communication

To be able to read minds, your mind's perception must not be blunt. It must be sharp. You should be able to give implicit and explicit meanings to people's words and actions. Communication is more than mere fusion of words: find the difference between what the person said and what the person means and conclude. If you ask me "how are you?" and I say "I am fine," you should be able to understand if I am lying to be fine, I don't want to talk to you, I am scared of you, I am truly fine, I am expecting more questions from you or I am truly fine from my response.

To learn this act, be more observant, look closely around you and watch the people you see. You can use any member of your family or friend as a specimen. Observe them when they talk: note their choice of words but pay more attention to their facial reaction and body movement. You can analyze these to know what exactly they mean to say when they say another. Find out their drive and values then try to predict their next move.

A good example is a game of cards where a player studies the other players to know how they play, what their major weapon is, whether they are playing to win or to stall the game to continue for a while, and how they think. A few minutes after studying the player, the one doing the study can predict the moves of other players and predict their moves accurately.

The same applies to reading minds. If possible, write down what you have learned of your target and what drives them. An extrovert may like someone who is reserved, who can listen to him while he does the talking or in simple words, not another extrovert like him who would also want his voice to be heard. A manipulator would want a calm and easygoing person whom he can easily cow to do something for him and not another like him. A religious person would want someone of the same faith with him so they can share ideas and strengthen their beliefs.

When you identify what makes people move, you can easily manipulate them. When you know that a lady loves flowers and getting her flowers can make her fall head over heels with you, you can easily manipulate her by getting her the gift of her heart—flowers and ask her for a favor in return. There is a saying that unlike poles attract. Most of the time, people crave to associate with people who have things they do not have. Although on a few occasions, things may come out to be the opposite. You have to be very observant to know the needs of the victim.

Note that the power of observation is inherent in men, but in a passive way. It can only be groomed and heightened. Noticeable powers of observation threaten the people around you. It may not be your intention to scare or threaten the people around, but if they are aware of your strong power of observation, they may run away from you, be afraid of you or find it difficult to trust you. They may also be scared that you could expose them. To prevent such situation, it is safer to appear, naïve and/ or unintelligent to conceal what you know.

2.   Learn how to think with Logic Instead of Emotion

If you must learn how to read and manipulate minds, you must have a high degree of self-control. You must not become emotional easily. You must learn how to think with reasoning, deductions, logic, facts, figures and not easily be drawn to believe opinions. If you easily think with "face" opinions, then you are liable to pass wrong judgment or prone to being easily manipulated. Those people who think by analyzing facts and figures are good manipulators and cannot be easily manipulated.

Master your emotions and put them in check so that it doesn't displace your reasoning. Even if you are angry at a person on an outcome, you do not need to react impulsively. Instead of reacting instantly, take your time and think about it before taking a step. It may not be as easy as it sounds but it requires constant practice, and with time, it would get better. It is important to understand that emotional reasoning breeds incorrect deductions and poor judgment.

You can engage in a conversation with the victim and they will start telling you stories of their ugly encounter. If you do not control your emotions, you may make a rash decision that you would regret later.

3.   A Manipulator Must Develop Wit

People test another through the use of tests and psychological ambushes. For becoming a good mind reader and a manipulator, you must develop your intellectual ability - faculty of thinking and reasoning. You must be clever enough to know the proper reaction for a particular action. Celebrities and politicians are also often interviewed to test their wit. If you have successfully developed your wit, you would know the right words to use when your wit is tested. You would rather turn the situation around to your advantage like boosting your social worth. In other to get better and get used to this, you can get involved with arguments and debates or word banter with your acquaintances.

4.   Emotional Intelligence

To be able to read minds, you need to develop empathy. In other to know or fully understand what is going on in some one's head, you must be able to see what the person sees and think about how the person thinks. You can only achieve this by putting yourself in the person's shoes and becoming that person in a twinkle of an eye. Then, you would be able to feel what that person feels and understand from the person's perception. People with low empathy would find it difficult to do this because they can only see from their viewpoint. If you can consciously melt into their world like this, you can know their next line of action or what they can possibly have in their mind at a point of time. A teacher talking to a child who has been trying to pick up academically can use words like "I know you may be thinking that going to school is not your calling but know that you are what you believe of yourself" you may be considering dropping out of school, but I am assuring you that it is not the best for you" and so on.

5. A Mind-reader must Learn Cold Reading

Someone who wants to read minds must develop the ability to do a cold reading. By cold reading, I mean studying a person over time and making a theory based on your findings. You can practice cold reading by gathering data of a particular person and making a theory depending on what you have rationalized. To further substantiate your findings, you can then find out by asking the person or people close to him if your theory is right or wrong.

CHAPTER 17:

Types of Manipulation

Indifferent

First up is the indifferent manipulator, which is the one that acts like they don't care. These manipulators often seem indifferent towards anything you are doing or saying. This indifference is not just about your actions, but any circumstances in your life, including difficulties or even celebrations.

In acting indifferent, these individuals have caught your attention. You spend time and energy attempting to achieve that breakthrough to capture their attention, thus hoping to achieve a deeper connection. However, they have already singled you out for some specific reason, so they will provide just enough interest to keep you hooked without really breaking out of the indifferent cycle.

The more indifferent they act, the more questions you are going to ask because you genuinely care. However, when you start asking questions that is when the manipulation starts earnestly because now a manipulator can use that they have information provided through those conversations to dig their hooks in ever deeper. Without them having to do or say anything directly, they have begun to play on your heart-strings, thus achieving the goal of your emotional investment into their lives.

As the victim, you are now in a position that allows them to use your sympathy to "make them feel better," but in reality, the manipulator is now just starting their sting to take from their victims whatever they want, from the emotional to the material. But when the victim has nothing left, then the manipulator moves on to their next victim, typically without any real remorse.

Poor Me

This manipulator may be the easiest to spot, but in combination with other traits, makes them easy to fall for over and over again. So, what do the poor me manipulators do so effectively when dealing with their victims?

The poor me manipulators use sympathy and guilt, appealing to their victims' need to try to help another human being in trouble or assist someone out of a sense of charity or faith. Appealing to their victim's better nature is one consistent way that a manipulator will attempt to get into someone's head. Often it is this goodness that a manipulator can turn on their victim.

It is simply part of our human nature to feel for people who are struggling through something or who are facing various challenges different from the ones that we are facing. We react by doing what we can to help them out, so we tend to cater to their demands without realizing we are being manipulated.

The demands can at first appear reasonable, but over time, will simply grow in complexity. These requests quickly turn into commands and ones that often prove to be real-time suckers. Thus, your whole world suddenly becomes completely focused on the manipulator. So the isolation can begin, making it harder for you or loved ones to observe the manipulation and point it out to you.

Critic

As with other manipulators, this type is a bit more aggressive than the first two types. They will actively focus on their victim's habits and emotional cues. After finding areas of sensitivity or weakness, the manipulator will begin to focus on them, subtlety at first, and then gradually growing bolder over time.

While it might be easy to spot what a manipulator is doing, many of us who fall victim to manipulators are helpless to stop it, unless we work on improving our mindset. Other ways to help avoid being a victim or getting out of a manipulative situation involve using anti-manipulation techniques.

The critic uses criticism to get what they want because the victim is trying to please, although the critical manipulator will set a bar for their standards, which the victim will find impossible to meet. The constant criticism for their victim contributes to neither making them feel like they are not good enough nor will they ever be good enough. Through manipulation the critic makes you feel like you are worthless, and they are better than you.

Thus, to achieve a better sense of self-worth, the victim will attempt to be more like the critic or to do things just the way the critic prefers them. Personality changes may also occur because the victim just wants to gain the affection and praise of the critic. However, the victim does not know this goal is simply unachievable.

Intimidators

When this manipulator comes into play, the victim can be in a very dangerous place. These manipulators are the worst of the worst; they are even more aggressive than the critic. The intimidator is not just critical, but they use fear and violence to make their victims cower.

These manipulators are more familiar with the stick than using a more carrot-like approach. Once their victim is afraid, these manipulators can easily have their demands met. In abusive relationships with intimidators, the tactic of using anger comes out frequently, along with the need to punish. Both tactics play into the fear aspect of the intimidator.

Let's face it, when we are afraid of someone, as individuals we tend to give in much quicker than if we felt in a position of power or a defendable position. These manipulators are all about stripping away any sense of being able to defend yourself, physically or psychologically.

Nobody dares stand up to a person who uses fear to manipulate them because they are afraid of what that person might physically do.

This is where the manipulator uses violence or the threat of violence to complete their hold on the victim. Abusive spousal relationships often demonstrate this type of intimidation manipulation with a mix of violence all too well.

So now that we have a greater understanding of the manipulator, their types and tactics, it's time to get a better understanding of the victim. However, you might be the one displaying those traits. Let's see how those traits play into a manipulator's hands and then later, we will explore ways that you can defend against a manipulator or make the right moves to remove yourself from their grasp.

So, what specifically about your personality or way of carrying yourself is sending up flags for a manipulator to zero in on?

CHAPTER 18:

Manipulation Techniques, Manipulation Tactics and Schemes

There are a lot of techniques that are used by manipulators to gain absolute or a substantial level of control on their victims. Most times, manipulators lookout for some types of personalities to prey on. The reason for this is that they feel the need to manipulate their victims easily. They lookout for the vulnerable parts of others and use it against them.

Most of the time, their preys are either naïve, empathetic, those with low self-esteem, or with a lack of confidence. Below are some common techniques used by manipulators:

Gaslighting

This is a style of manipulation that makes use of three different phrases: "it didn't happen," "you are out of your mind," "it's your imagination." Some experts believe that this may be one of the most dangerous manipulative techniques there is as it aims as disorganizing and killing the victim's sense of reality.

When a person is manipulated with this technique, he loses touch with his reality and is no longer able to trust himself. What is worse is that the victims of this type of manipulative technique do not feel the need to call out the manipulator for maltreating them.

Projection

In this type of manipulation, the manipulator finds someone else to blame for everything that goes wrong around them. This is something that is common with most people but is more common amongst narcissists and psychopaths.

Here, the manipulator makes use of a defense tactic, which involves shifting responsibility from his/herself for wrongdoings and negative attitudes and blames everything on another person asides himself.

Generalizations

This happens in cases where a person chooses to misunderstand another for ulterior motives intentionally.

Have you ever found yourself in a case where a sibling, for instance, refuses to think about the long-term effects of his actions or that of your parents? Though you haven't said anything as such, this sibling goes about telling everyone who cares to listen that you called your parents "wicked" just because you stated that you were not comfortable with a certain major decision, they are making for you.

In cases like this, you find yourself wondering what is really happening and start to believe that maybe your sibling didn't understand what you said. The truth is that this type of person understands their victims clearly, but they choose to run with an entirely different story.

This is very common with narcissists who aren't very good at making very sound intellectual decisions because they are plain lazy when it comes to using their brains, so they would rather make hasty generalization of whatever a person says than to make a critical assessment of the word of another person.

They usually make conclusions and statements that are not in line with the thoughts and words of their victims, and they do not try to look at things from a different perspective to see where their victim is coming from or consider the reasons why they said what they said.

Moving the Goalposts

There is a common logical fallacy known as moving the goalposts, and sociopaths and abusive narcissists make good use of it all the time. In this case, the manipulator makes sure that they always have a cause to complain about their victims, because they find reasons to, and not because they are actually not pleased with the actions or words of their victims.

Even in cases where the victim has found every possible reason to justify their actions or validate their words or even done things to meet their demand, they remain adamantly dissatisfied. In most cases, they simply set higher expectations or change their terms, or they simply ask that you give more proof.

Changing the Topic

This may seem like an innocent action, but it is not. Changing subjects in conversations is one of the techniques used by manipulators. With is a way to run away from being held accountable for their words or actions.

This is also common with narcissists as they do not wish to ever dwell on a topic that will demand that they should be responsible for anything at all. To avoid this, they simply find ways to change topics to favor themselves.

This type of manipulation will go on for as long as possible if the victim keeps letting it happen. In cases like this, it becomes difficult to have relevant discussions whenever the manipulator is around.

Name-Calling

This is a technique that involves attacking the victim's personality by calling him derogatory names. Most victims may think this is normal because they have become used to it from bullies in school, to parents, friends, or partners who call them names, but it is not, and it is as destructive as other manipulative techniques. This type of manipulation is found in all areas of life, and it goes as far as presidential politics.

Devaluation

This is common with friends or colleagues who tend to show love to you while they always have bad or terrible things to say about the last person that was in your place.

Narcissistic abusers always do this. When it comes it intimate relationships, they have very terrible things to say about their exes, but eventually, the new partner is going to find out the reason why the ex was such a "terrible partner" because the narcissist will eventually mate the same treatment that he gave to the ex, on the current partner.

This type of person can also be found in a professional setting as much as it can be found in personal settings.

Common Manipulation Techniques

There are some manipulation techniques used that are not so common but have been proven to be effective when used. Let's take a look at some of those:

Home Advantage

When a person wants to manipulate you, he may insist that you both meet in a place where it will be easy for him to exert his dominance over you and control you.

What they do is simply take you to their homes, office, car, or any other place where it will be easy for them to maintain their ownership or familiarity because you simply do not have such an advantage.

Rather than having you call them; they will prefer to do the calling in a phone conversation. Since they are the ones paying the bills, they are able to maintain their dominance or ownership, and if for any reason you choose to hang upon them, you are tagged rude and manner-less for not observing phone ethics.

Speak First to Determine Your Strong and Weak Points

This is a technique that is common with marketers when they are trying to pitch their sales to you. They come at you by asking general probing questions, which will give you room to speak for a while. This way, they can determine your personality, thought pattern, and attitude.

It is with these findings that they are also able to know your strengths and weaknesses.

Certainly, their questions come with ulterior motives, and they are going to use your answer against you later. This type of manipulation can manifest in your office or your relationships.

Manipulation of Facts

Lies and excuses are a common part of this technique. These types of manipulators are two-faced people. They find ways of blaming the victim for getting victimized. To do this, they alter the truth or choose the information that they are willing to let out. They may also choose not to give very vital information.

This type of manipulators exaggerates, they are biased and may also be prone to understating issues to have things go in their favor.

Presents Overwhelming Facts and Statistics

This is a form of "intellectual bullying," and some people like to engage in it. This is done by assuming that they are experts in certain fields or areas of discussion. They present themselves as though they know the most about some particular areas.

They, however, manipulate people by giving false facts, statistics, or other data because they know that their victims do not know so much about the topic. This is a common strategy in sales and the world of finance. It is also common in professional terrains and negotiations. People usually make use of this technique in social gatherings and other arguments.

By placing themselves as experts, they wield the power that comes with the position, so they try to push through with their real motif in a more convincing manner. Some people do not have any other reason for using this technique, aside from the need to feel a sense of intelligence.

CHAPTER 19:

Body language and How it works with Manipulation

Another very important way that people will often use to communicate with other people, sometimes even subconsciously, without realizing that they are sending a message, is referred to commonly as "body language." Body language, or nonverbal communication, can be incredibly helpful to learn how to read for people who are practicing nonviolent communication, and even for any person who spends any amount of time interacting with other people in any context. There are a lot of different things that people will do that can communicate their needs, especially needs that are not being met or that need to be met in that moment.

A lot of people say that somewhere near 60 percent of all communication that people use is made up of nonverbal cues, or "body language" This includes things like crossing your arms to looking in certain directions. A lot of people will tend to look in certain directions when they are performing certain tasks. For example, they might look up and to the left if they are trying to remember something or solve some sort of problem, or straight up when they are processing a scent or a flavor. One of the most popular tips that people will mention when giving romantic advice is to pay attention to a person's eyes. If someone's pupils are dilated, it means that they are becoming aroused or stimulated. It is often said that the eyes are the windows to the soul, and this is why; the eyes can tell you a lot about what a person is thinking or feeling, and learning how to read a person's eyes can be a very important skill to master. This can even sometimes include the direction that a person points their feet, as well.

I will be explaining the different kinds of nonverbal communication and how to "read" and understand that body language to be able to understand people and connect with them on a deeper level, and ultimately increasing the quality of your communication and your relationship with that person as well.

The eyes are very important to understand how to read to master effective and meaningful communication. The first thing that you might pay attention to is the direction of a person's eyes and their focus when you are talking with them. Are they making direct eye contact with you or are they looking away? Often, a lot of people will make direct eye contact with the people who they are talking with if they are invested in and paying attention to the conversation, but this is not always the case. Of course, a lot of autistic people might tend not to make eye contact with the people that they are talking to, or they might actively avoid it for many different reasons.

This does not mean that they are not paying attention, it just means that the way that they communicate is slightly different from the way that you might prefer. In these cases, you should try to adjust instead of expecting this person to make eye contact with you while you are making a conversation. However, it is also important to understand that a lot of people will not make eye contact if they are disinterested in the conversation or if they are focusing primarily on another thing. This is important to look out for, and even more important is to be able to understand the differences between these two reasons as well as other reasons for a person potentially not making eye contact with you while you are talking to them and understanding how to handle that situation effectively. Some people will look away—especially off to the side as if they are distracted- when they are lying, or some people might tend to look downward if they are nervous or anxious in the conversation. Of course, the pupil trick is also a useful tool for being able to understand how a person might be feeling. If a person's pupils are dilated, then this might indicate that they are expending more cognitive effort—for example, if they aroused or stimulated by the conversation. This usually indicates a positive response and that this person is interested in the conversation. However, this can also indicate irritation in some cases.

The dilation of the pupils simply indicates a heightened level of stimulation or arousal, which can also mean that that person if feeling irritated or uncomfortable as well. However, if this is the case, there will also usually be other signs that they are feeling uncomfortable, so it is important to look for those signs if you suspect that this might be the case. For example, if someone is feeling anxious or stressed, they might begin to blink a little bit more frequently as well. A quickened rate of blinking is often used as an indicator of whether a person is lying, in some cases, especially when combined with "defensive" positions, such as crossing their arms or covering their face a lot. If they are hiding a physical object, then they might also periodically be tempted to glance toward the location of that object, as well, out of a sense of anxiety and desire to retrieve the object. They might even simply glance over at something they want even if they are not hiding something or attempting to deceive in some way as well. A lot of people might tend to look toward a door a lot if they are wanting to leave the room or location that they are in, or at another person if they want to go talk to that person. Another very helpful kind of body language to learn how to read is in the face. This will often include things like facial expressions, or even the meanings behind things like a person frequently touching their face or hiding their mouth.

A lot of people learn to control their facial expressions when they are in social situations, to some degree, which can make it a little bit more difficult to decipher them and their emotional or mental states based on their facial expressions alone, you can often still use them to allow yourself to understand what they might be thinking or feeling in a given moment by paying attention to these important clues and behaviors, once you know what to look for. Of course, the eyes are a very important thing to pay attention to, as has been mentioned, but the mouth can also be a helpful indicator of how a person might be feeling in a particular situation.

One simple thing that you can look out for is whether a person is smiling or not, or if they are frowning. Most people will be aware of the things that these expressions mean- if a person is smiling, they are probably happy, and if they are frowning then they might be unhappy in some way. However, there are also different kinds of smiles that might indicate more specific emotions as well. A lot of people might smile in social situations by default, or even continue to smile when they are uncomfortable and do not want to hurt the feelings of the person who they are talking to. A lot of people will usually tell the difference between these kinds of smiles based on how "warm" they are. Some people will say things like "their smile doesn't reach their eyes," or "their smile is empty." This is because "real" or genuine smiles will often include the whole face, or larger portions of the face, as opposed to just the mouth. Of course, a genuine smile is called so because it is considered to be a "real" smile and an indicator of positive emotions such as happiness or that a person is enjoying your company or the conversation that they are engaged in. However, a "fake" smile often indicates that the person in question is actively attempting to portray enthusiasm or happiness, while they are experiencing some sort of discomfort or unease. Things like pursed lips or if a person does not "smile with their teeth" can indicate very similar things as well.

Another good indicator that a person might be masking their "true" feelings behind a fake smile is whether that person does a quick grimace or some other kind of expression before they quickly correct and smile instead. This is often referred to as a "microexpression," and can be used to decipher the true feelings that a person might be experiencing and that they are disguising with a fake smile. Somewhere between these two is what is commonly referred to as a "half-smile." Half smiles usually only incorporate one side of the mouth while the other half is still relaxed. These half-smiles are usually interpreted to represent some kind of sarcasm or uncertainty. Another helpful kind of nonverbal communication that a lot of people will use to subconsciously communicate with another person is the proximity that they keep to the person that they are talking to. If you are talking to someone and they are standing or sitting close to you, then this might indicate that they are actively listening and are present in the conversation that you are having. However, if that person is backing away from you or if they are keeping their distance, especially when you step forward, then this might let you know that they are uncomfortable or that they would rather be somewhere else.

CHAPTER 20:

Neuro-Linguistic Programming and Manipulation

What is NLP and How does NLP work

Everybody's conceived with similar essential neurology. Our capacity to do anything in life, whether it's swimming the length of a pool, cooking a feast, or writing a book relies upon how we control our sensory system. Along these lines, quite a bit of Neuro-Linguistic Programming (NLP) is dedicated to figuring out how to think more effectively and communicate more adequately with yourself as well as other people. But what does NLP really mean?

"Neuro" is about your neurological framework. NLP depends on the fact that we encounter the world through our five basic senses and interpret that sensory data (sight, sound, taste, touch, and smell) into manners of thinking, both conscious and unconscious. Perspectives trigger the neurological framework, which influences physiology, feelings, and conduct.

"Linguistic" alludes to the way individuals utilize language to understand the world, and then convey that experience to others. In NLP, linguistics is the investigation of how the words you speak impact your experience.

"Programming" draws intensely from learning hypotheses and determines how we code, or rationally perceive and understand, our experience.

Your own programming comprises the inner procedures and methodologies (thinking designs) that you use to make decisions, fix problems, learn, analyze, and achieve desired outcomes.

The NLP Communication Model

The NLP communication model, produced by Richard Bandler and John Grinder, depends on psychological brain research.

As indicated by the NLP correspondence display, when somebody acts intentionally (their external behavior), a response is created inside you (your internal, i.e. mental or emotional, reaction), which makes you react intentionally (your external behavior), which then makes a chain response inside the other individual (their internal reaction) and the cycle proceeds.

The internal reaction is comprised of a person's thought processes and the nature of their mental state.

The thought processes comprise self-talk, pictures, and sounds, and the mental state is the sentiments that are experienced.

History of NFP

Neuro-Linguistic Programming (NLP) was created in the 1970s by founders R. Bandler and J. Grinder of the United States and is a semi-scientific approach to interaction, self-development, and counseling. The founders stated that neurological processes (neuro), language (linguistic), and behavioral patterns that have been learned from experience (programming) are interconnected and can be adapted to specific purposes in life. Bandler and Grinder suggested that NLP techniques can "design" the capacities of people so that everyone can improve their abilities.

NLP can deal with psychological issues like phobias, anxiety, tic disorders, mental illness, vision problems, asthma, common cold, and learning disabilities. It is also used to treat emotional and behavioral problems. NLP opponents argue the concept is not scientifically proven and is not even regarded as entirely scientific. Science-based reviews assert that NLP has been founded on inaccurate analogies of the mechanisms of the mind that are incongruent with existing cognitive theory, and therefore encompasses many factual inaccuracies.

Reviews have maintained that studies on NLP work presented major critical flaws, and have struggled to prove Bandler's, Grinder's, and other researchers' "extraordinary assertions" to be faulty. Nevertheless, NLP has already been embraced as a tool of management training by authorities, counselors, and mentors in companies that conduct seminars.

How to Manipulate Using NLP

Controlling thoughts

The way our brain works can be seen remotely through an electroencephalograph (EEG), and it measures the condition of one's awareness, the force of thought waves, sharpness, and action of the psyche. Science has identified four different brainwave states: Beta, Alpha, Theta, and Delta.

Beta is the conscious state we experience every day, for example, when walking around, with brainwaves in the 14-30 Hz range. We generate Beta brainwaves by moving around and thinking. In this state, the brain is constantly active, and you may experience a lot of thoughts going on in your mind: that's the typical situation of a stressed-out, 21st-century person.

Alpha is a lightly relaxed, drowsy state. The brain is operating in the 7-14 Hz range, and this is where a state of hypnosis and visualization can occur. This is the typical state that you experience when you start a meditation session.

Theta is the light sleep state or deep meditative state, and it's also the lucid dreaming state. The brain operates in the 3-7 Hz range. This state is easy to access through guided meditations or by just going to sleep.

Finally, Delta is a deep sleep healing state, which generates brainwaves in the 0.5-3 Hz range.

Why am I telling you this? Well, you're here to learn how to persuade, influence, and manipulate other people's minds. To effectively do that, you can take advantage of the Alpha state. This specific state operates as a bridge between the conscious mind (Beta state) and the subconscious mind (Theta state). The Alpha state allows us conscious access to the unknown material located in our subconscious mind. When you find yourself in a hypnotic state, this "alpha bridge" allows you to reprogram your subconscious mind, because your psyche turns out to be more suggestive to the orders and can be easily customized. You can access this knowledge and information to help you better understand your actions, behaviors, and motivations, and you can also change your habits and belief systems. Of course, anything you can apply to yourself; you could also apply it to others: that's why being able to induce an Alpha state in other people is an invaluable skill to master.

You have to keep in mind, though, brainwave states do not exclude each other. You can be in the Beta state of mind while walking or talking, but still be producing some Alpha waves as well. If you begin to relax a little bit, you can start generating more Alpha waves than Beta waves. The same happens when you close your eyes and take a deep breath: you'll probably enter a deeper Alpha state, even though you'll most likely generate some Theta waves too. Remember that YOU are the one who generates these different electrical signals. And by learning how to manipulate your brainwaves just a little, you can also learn how to generate the mental state necessary to effectively hypnotize yourself or others.

Entering the alpha state

First of all, you need to relax. Close your eyes and take a few deep breaths, and you'll soon be generating some Alpha waves. When someone achieves an Alpha state, their subconscious mind is ready to be manipulated or programmed. At this point, you can use suggestions and visualizations to send effective messages to their subconscious mind to make the desired change happen. Visualizations are especially effective because the subconscious mind works best with symbols, images, and clear visions.

If the person has old belief systems or core issues that are left intact, their minds may be conflicted trying to reconcile the old beliefs systems with the new ones. So it's important to first let go of beliefs or core issues that created the unwanted behavior in the first place, and only then can we influence the subconscious mind to help us create the desired behavior.

Mind perception

Impressions from signals in our surroundings unintentionally impact our thoughts to a specific degree. Up to 99% of our subjective actions might be unconscious.

Along these lines, it is possible to influence someone's psyche by priming the environment—putting a specific object or message near the subject that sidesteps the conscious personality but is picked up instead by the subconscious personality. Most traps of the mentalists work exactly in this way, as they may wear a red tie that will be overlooked by the conscious personality as though unimportant but registered by the unconscious personality of the observer without even knowing it. Presumably, it's done by using the word READ as a part of the discussion, for example, which will trigger the shading RED in the observer's brain.

These ideas are validated in the onlooker with deliberate behaviors that are utilized by very talented NLP experts. The truth of the matter is that the simpler the recommendations, the more the unconscious personality gets affected.

Mind control procedures

There are a few personality control procedures utilized by NLP experts to control others' minds. For example, closely consider the subtle signals of people like eye movements, pupil dilation, apprehensive tics, body flush, non-verbal communication, speed of breathing, and so forth as they can be associated with the feelings of the individual. For example, eye movements can be tracked to decide how one acknowledges and processes data. Let's say you ask someone about the color of his car, which is not nearby. When he answered, his eyes moved toward the upper right corner before his answer was spoken aloud. Essentially, the eyes moving to the upper right corner would be visual recognition that he's attempting to recall the shade of the car.

Real experts have even conveyed their words following the rhythm of the human heart, i.e., 45 to 72 beats per minute so that they could create a condition of suggestibility in the listener.

They often give you an anchor, which makes it simple for them to place you in a specific state just by tapping or touching you. For example, imagine that you're talking about love and you're listening to the personal experiences that an individual is sharing with you. He recalls them, living those feelings a second time.

The intersperse hypnotic technique, a form of behavioral momentum, is largely used in NLP. Science has proven that when tasks include easy responses it increases the probability that less preferred and/or more challenging tasks will be performed. This incognito hypnosis strategy can have an impact on an individual's psyche to a more prominent degree. However, it does not force them to perform an action they are already against: this may require significant programming of the brain.

You don't want anyone to be able to do the same to you without your full consent. Therefore, here are some ways in which you can protect yourself and your loved ones. A wide range of individuals has attempted to use NLP to talk me into buying something or making decisions to their advantage.

CHAPTER 21:

Verbal and Non-Verbal Communication

L anguage is a blunt force tool. What is language supposed to do? It is supposed to convey thoughts, ideas, concepts, and stories to other people accurately. It gives us a way to interact and puts us all on one level of communication so that we can exchange simple messages to each other and get by. However, language is also responsible for transmitting the most important, deep, and abstract concepts. What it comes down to is the complexity of our everyday experience. How would you describe the flow when you're replaying basketball and making every shot? How would you describe that in words to someone and have them know what you were experiencing? What about when you eat a piece of chocolate? Get broken up with? These are things that can't be described in words, and yet we try to describe them. Sometimes it is done in ordinary conversation; sometimes, it is done in art or literature.

Language is what mutes and bottlenecks our experience into what we can convey to other people. Language is so limited in its ability to truly share our knowledge with others, and it is that limitedness that makes it, so that body language is so important. You are often experiencing both at the same time; you are experiencing someone's language simultaneously with their body language. Non-verbal communication is not all just body language, but a huge part of it is body language.

Think about one interaction that you have had in the last few days. It could be anything from buying something at the store, to a wedding—any tiny little interaction that you had. Try to imagine the interaction from the very beginning.

Body language is comprised mostly of a few factors: effect, posture, and motion. The effect refers to a person's facial expression. If a person is smiling, you could say that they have a bright effect. A person's effect is not always congruent with what they're saying and experiencing. You might see this in someone who is talking nervously about something, and they begin to smile. This means that their expression does not fit whatever they are talking about and that there is incongruence in their effect. When a person has a congruent effect, their facial expressions will change and be malleable. A person who has a congruent and secure effect will be expressing whatever they're thinking about or talking about on their face.

Posture is the way that a person holds himself or herself. This comes from their orientation to the world this can be found in the Enneagram of personality that we talked about earlier. These personality types describe an orientation to the world. Some people are rear oriented as warriors; others are oriented as perfectionists. The way that a person's personality is will dictate the way they hold themselves physically. A person who is up in their mind will have the posture of a distracted person. A proud person will lead with their chest. What the chest symbolizes is a place of pride. It is where the heart and lungs are, and a cage of bones protects ties it's a very important part of our bodies, and when we lead with that, we are showing that we are confident.

What would the chest be doing on a person who did not feel confident? If a person is not confident, they will not walk with their chest leading, rather it will be in a collapsing position. Think about a person who is not confident, and how their shoulders move forward, and their posture seems tired or broken. They are the ones without confined because they are trying to protect their heart.

Another aspect of nonverbal communication is art. When we talk about art in this sense, we are talking about the capital "A" Art that includes sculpture, writing, acting, and all creative arts. Even when language is involved, it is not in verbal communication; it is in writing. All of these falls under nonverbal communication. Learning to participate in artistic creation can help you to be a person who is more in touch with this part of communication.

Art can have all kinds of functions. Sometimes its function is to help sell things. This is a form of communication. When you hear something on the radio that is a catchy jingle that makes you feel a certain way about a product that is a deep form of communication. Art can help us to dance, think, feel joy or sadness, help make things clearer, make political action, call to war, call for peace, etc. Music has a variety of functions. It can be used to help us energize or relax. Art is the same way.

Non-verbal communication happens all the time; you just don't notice it. Your gaze has a deep implication on how people perceive you, the way you walk can tell people a whole lot. A person is a private being when they do not show you much with these.

Some people do not have the power of verbal communication. Some people have very advanced dementia or other mental disorders, such as advanced schizophrenia. Others could be people with learning or developmental disabilities like autism or Down syndrome. Can these people still communicate? Absolutely! They can communicate because their lives have revolved around learning ways for them to communicate.

Some ways through which one can easily communicate with people who are non-verbal are touch, music, art, or hand symbols. People who are non-verbal tend to experience it deeply.

Some people have learning or developmental disabilities that prevent them from reading non-verbal cues. People with Autism Spectrum Disorder have a hard time deciphering the cues of behavior and non-verbal communication. ASD is a somewhat mysterious condition, and it is only diagnosed and marked by certain behavioral patterns and a lack of social ability. This makes it a fascinating condition to learn how to help people with ASD to function better. For kids with ASD to be able to function better, they have to be assisted with integration. This means they must learn to use their sensory inputs in concordance with their cognitive abilities to learn what a person is expressing. They will have to learn that when a person has their face all scrunched up, and they are yelping, that a person is angry. They have to learn about the body language of a sad person and how to act around that person.

This is pretty much what we are doing in this guidebook, except we are talking about it on higher-level order. Rather than teaching kids how to learn the basic cues of non-verbal communication, we are trying to encourage you to learn to trust your intuition and be able to analyze behavior patterns on a deeper level.

This means that when you experience a behavior pattern, you are able to surmise what this means for you and what it means for other people around you. Instead of thinking about your feeling and worrying about it, you can either express it or act on it or do whatever wiles they need to do.

This is where intuition comes in. You've got to trust what you are feeling about a person. If you see that a person walks into the room with a smile you've known before, and they act a certain way that you saw a person act, and you can know that they are trying to deceive you, this will make your life a little bit easier, as you will have that knowledge going in.

If you just started attending a church, and at first you like it because of the community, but then you start to feel that it is just not the right place for you, this is intuition. We can use intuition to the behavior patterns of others to know if they will be good partners, good friends, etc.

Let's use the example of dating to try and illustrate what we are talking about when we talk about intuition. A new partner will be a new experience. It will be something that comes to you when you need it. People that we get involved with are generally on the same level of personal development as we are. If they aren't, these will inevitably lead to tension in the relationship. When we get into a romantic relationship with a person, we start to blend our patterns of behavior. This means that you will seek out a person that will tend to increase the behaviors that you want to improve within yourself.

This is a good and bad thing. It is a natural process that lets us select people to get into relationships with so that we function better in our lives. However, if we are not able to see how we aren't functioning well in our lives, then we will just be looking for someone to help us continue the patterns that we already find so easy to do. This is how patterns in relationships are perpetuated.

NLP in Purchase

NLP enhances negotiation skills and selling skills. Clients who use NLP in a business report that their managers are excellent coaches, motivators, and influencers.

NLP multiplies excellence in any field. This is a skill known as the modeling in NLP. It uses the incorporation of all other intermediate skills. This is very useful in a business organization if, for example, business took good employees from each field and brought them together. The work done will be excellent.

NLP helps to improve communication while doing business. During communication, there is the use of verbal and nonverbal cues. By using NLP, one will be able to understand the spoken and unspoken language of customers and prospects.

It helps one to emulate the successful efforts of other businesses easily. NLP teaches one to understand how successful people work and converse. One can then emulate those using NLP strategies to copy those successes to fit their businesses.

NLP gives one sales staff mind-reading abilities. This enables them to understand nonverbal cues and eye movements, hence enabling them to answer customers' questions and provide useful information about the products. They also understand how a client feels about the product in question, which makes it easier for them to close sales.

NLP improves negotiation skills. Negotiation is one big requirement in the business world—negotiation with vendors, employees' marketers, advertising firms, and many more. With NLP negotiation skills, everyone in the business will be more effective and persuasive.

NLP boosts morale. Why wouldn't one's morale be boosted if everyone in the company or office knows how well and effectively you communicate? One is able to make themselves clear as well as able to relate with everyone in the office. This makes the workplace much more fun since there is a better understanding of one another.

NLP is the best customer service tool. NLP helps to understand customers' complaints and suggestions after a sale. One can be able to discern if a customer is complaining because of awful customer service or if he or she is just having a bad day. When one's customer care is able to understand the customer's nonverbal cues, then he will be able to deal with the angry customer and make them happy so that they would come again.

CHAPTER 22:

Hypnosis

Although brainwashing is a very common mind control method that so many people may already be aware of, there is also an important type of mind control that many people may be aware of. This is known as hypnosis and should be given as much importance as the others.

Generally, most of those that know a thing or two about hypnosis get their knowledge from stage plays where the actors perform ridiculous acts. What is seen in plays is also a type of hypnosis, but there is a lot more to it than what is portrayed in these shows.

Hypnosis, according to experts, comes from a state of consciousness dealing with focused attention and the reduction of awareness on the peripheral level, which deals with the ability of the participant to give a response to the suggestions that are given. What this entails is the participant transcending to an entirely different state of mind, making them more susceptible to taking and acting on all the suggestions that the hypnotist makes.

Two different theories attempt to explain what really goes on during the period of hypnosis. The first is known as the altered-state theory. Those that belong to this school of thought believe that hypnosis is like a trance or a state of the mind where the target discovers that their state of awareness is different from what they would ordinarily notice when they are conscious. The second theory is the non-state theory, which is of the opinion that people who are hypnotized do not necessarily have to go into another state of consciousness. Those that belong to this school of thought believe that the hypnotist works with the target to enact an imaginative role.

When a person is hypnotized, he learns to gain more concentration and focus that is combined with a newly learned ability to concentrate a great deal on a certain memory or thought. When they are in this state, the participant will be able to filter through and block any source of distraction. Those that are hypnotized are thought to be able to exhibit a high ability to respond to all the suggestions they receive, especially when the hypnotist is the source of that suggestion.

History of Hypnosis

It is not clear exactly who discovered the possibility of hypnosis or when, but one thing about it is clear. It has been in action for quite a long time. Its earliest developments, however, is credited to Franz A. Mesmer in the eighteenth century. Long before the discovery of anesthesia as early as the mid-nineteenth century, hypnosis was used as a pain reliever during surgeries with significant success. James Esdaile, a surgeon from Scotland, used hypnosis in the 1840s in India to perform multiple surgeries with tremendous success. Prior to its use, close to half of all surgeries conducted were fatal due to extreme pain leading to shock. Hypnosis came as a saving grace to this situation with tremendous success. For the multiple surgeries (Over three thousand), conducted by James Esdaile using Hypnosis as a pain reliever, the total mortality rate due to pain shock fell below five percent.

The Process of Hypnosis

From the American Psychological Association of Hypnosis, it must be mutual. This implies that one cannot be hypnotized without their consent or knowledge. The reason for this is because it is an 'interactive association' that requires input from both parties involved. Having stated this, it is now prudent to describe some of the steps followed and the results of these steps, when doing hypnosis. To do this, we shall use an example where hypnotherapy is to be applied as a pain reliever for someone who has a migraine.

The first step that is required for the process to be effective is to find a peaceful and calm place. Hypnosis has a greater chance of success in locations where there are minimal distractions from the environment. This is so as to enable the person to be hypnotized to concentrate and to better picture the suggestions being fed to him by the hypnotist. Of great importance is that the selected location must be where the patient feels secure. One will never be hypnotized if they are in a place where they feel that their security is at risk. For this step, given these conditions, an ideal place may be the home of the person to be hypnotized as this is likely to be the place, he would feel most calm and secure.

The next step is the preparation phase. Here, both parties will discuss issues surrounding the process and the desired outcome. Having said that, hypnosis is somewhat a guided imaginative process, the hypnotist has to know what the patient wishes to get out of the process. In our case, the patient will tell the hypnotist that he wishes to be relieved of the intense headache he or she feels. This exchange of information is important as it is what will form the basis of the suggestions issued by the hypnotist. It may be compared to a medical examination where the doctor endeavors to find out the problem ailing the patient. It is clear from this analogy that the success of the whole process is pegged upon this stage.

The hypnotist then gives the patient some instructions regarding the process, some of the things to expect, how to react to them, what to do to relax and get into the zone, among others. This is important so that nothing comes as a surprise to the patient, thereby enabling the process to go on smoothly. Having prepared well, it is now time for the process to begin.

The hypnotist's first task is to get the patient into a complete relaxed state. This is done by giving a series of instructions to the patient. This stage of hypnosis is referred to as the induction state of hypnosis. The patient is expected to vividly imagine these suggestions. An example of a suggestion at this point may be, "Imagine that you are in a place that you like, a place that smells very good, surrounded by nothing but nature." the patient should respond to this suggestion by trying their best to picture themselves in the said place. In addition to these suggestions, the patient is often encouraged during the induction phase to control their breathing patterns. This is an elaborate trick to shift the patient's focus from the conscious mind to the subconscious, which is what is tapped into during hypnosis. The more that this goes on, with due cooperation from both parties, the more the patient sinks into a trance.

Hypnotherapy

Hypnosis is a human condition including focused attention, lowered outer awareness, as well as an enhanced capacity to respond to the pointer.

There are completing concepts clarifying hypnosis and also related sensations. Altered state concepts see hypnosis as a modified mindset or trance, marked by a degree of understanding different from the normal state of consciousness. In comparison, nonstate theories see hypnotherapy as, otherwise, a kind of placebo result, and a redefinition of a communication with a specialist or form of imaginative function implementation.

Throughout hypnosis, an individual is stated to have enhanced focus and concentration. Hypnotized topics are reported to show an enhanced reaction to suggestions. Anesthesia usually begins with a hypnotic induction involving a series of initial guidelines as well as recommendations. Making use of hypnotherapy for therapeutic purposes is described as "hypnotherapy," while its method as a kind of home entertainment for an audience is called "stage hypnosis." Phase hypnosis is often executed by mind readers exercising the art kind of mentalism.

Hypnotherapy for pain management "is likely to lower acute as well as persistent pain in most individuals." Making use of hypnosis in other contexts, such as a kind of therapy to get and also incorporate early injury, is questionable within the clinical or psychological mainstream. The study suggests that hypnotizing an individual may help the formation of false memories and that hypnotherapy "does not help individuals recall occasions a lot more accurately.

Hypnotherapy is a frame of mind of extremely focused focus, diminished peripheral recognition, as well as heightened suggestibility. There are numerous strategies that experts utilize for causing such a state. Capitalizing on the power of suggestion, hypnosis is usually used to aid individuals to relax, to reduce the feeling of pain, or to help with some preferred behavioral modification.

Therapists cause hypnosis (additionally described as hypnosis or hypnotic idea) with the help of mental imagery as well as relaxing spoken repeating that alleviate the individual into a trance-like state. When loosened up, patients' minds are more open to transformative messages.

Hypnosis, additionally referred to as hypnosis or hypnotic idea, is a trance-like state in which you have increased focus and concentration. Hypnotherapy is typically finished with the aid of a specialist using verbal rep and also mental images. When you're under hypnotherapy, you generally really feel tranquil as well as loosened up, and also are much more open up to recommendations.

Hypnosis can be made use of to aid you in gaining control over undesired habits or to help you deal much better with stress and anxiety or pain. It's important to understand that although you're much more available to idea throughout hypnotherapy, you don't blow up over your actions.

Stages of Hypnosis

As mentioned earlier, there are different levels of hypnotic trance. Given that hypnotic capacity varies from one person to the next, some people will be able to achieve the highest level of hypnosis where they will go into a deep trance. On the other hand, others will only go into a light trance and fail to progress from there. Generally, there are three main stages of hypnotic trances, although you may find that in some areas, they are classified into more stages. The following are the three main ones.

Hypnoidal State

This is the first state of trance that a person under hypnosis attains. It is essentially the state that the induction stage of induction aims to achieve. Most people are able to attain this state of light or mild trance with guidance from a skilled hypnotist and some initiative on their part. There are signs to watch out for to determine that a person is in a hypnoidal state. The main one is the fluttering of the hypnotized eyelids in rapid succession. During this light trance, the patient is in a fairly relaxed state and is receptive to suggestions, albeit not all of them.

Cataleptic State

Beyond the light trance, up the ladder of hypnotic states, is the cataleptic state. At this stage, the altered mental state that was achieved during the induction state is significantly deepened. The patient at this stage is very receptive to suggestions and is in a somewhat deep trance. At this point, the patient may still be conscious of their surroundings. In most patients, this state is characterized by the side to side movements of the eyeballs.

Somnambulistic State

This is the deepest state of hypnotic trance that a person can achieve. You may, however, find in other classifications some other subdivisions within this state. It is important to note at this point that this is a generalized classification and other specific ones with more classifications may still be accurate.

CHAPTER 23:

Brainwashing

Brainwashing is a concept of so-called psychological manipulation. In this process, tactics of mental reprogramming attack the self-confidence and their judgment of the target person to destabilize their basic attitudes and perceptions of reality and then to replace them with new attitudes. Older brainwashing methods attempted to break the psychological resistance with physical violence. Theories of brainwashing initially arose in connection with totalitarian states.

Brainwashing and Mind control

There is a very clear distinction between mind control and brainwashing. Brainwashing begins with the victim understanding that the other person is an enemy. The person is aware that the other person does not like them and does not have their best interests at heart. Over time, however, in brainwashing, an individual comes to change their belief system into one that is more conducive to staying alive. Instead of hating the enemy, they adapt and give up on some of their own values to show that they would do something that the enemy approves of to make the abuse stop and to stay alive. Often, the person brainwashing is very violent physically, and the person has no choice but to conform or die. Brainwashing typically fades away as the person is removed from the brainwasher.

On the other hand, mind control is more insidious. It is subtle and the person on the receiving end has no idea that it is happening. Often, the one doing the controlling is a close friend or family member, or someone else in a trusted position for the one being controlled. The victim is not giving in to the other person's values in an attempt to survive or maintain a relationship, but rather, has been slowly spoon-fed information and thoughts that have slowly changed their thought process. The manipulator has slowly but surely managed to take over the other person's thoughts and feelings and does so from the inside out. This means that no harm triggered thoughts and feelings. There were no discernable places where the manipulation happened. The person being mind-controlled does not understand when or how it happened, but suddenly realized one day that the thoughts inside his or her mind were not their own.

Signs of Attempted Mind Control

When you are attempting to identify whether someone is mind-controlling you, there are five key factors to look for:

Isolation

Often, those who are attempting to manipulate someone else, they involve isolation. This is because when someone is isolated away, the only contact that individual his with other people is the manipulator. If your spouse or partner suddenly has a problem with any attempts to go see someone else or to make friends outside of the marriage or relationship, they may be trying to keep you alone. When you are alone with no one else to talk to, you are far more likely to fall for whatever the manipulator is telling you simply because you do not have anyone else available to talk to you. You do not have anyone there to tell you that what is happening makes no sense. You are all alone and vulnerable, which is exactly what the manipulator wants. The manipulator will try to separate you from friends and family members, and may even try to sabotage all of those relationships, along with your workplace relationships simply because he wants you under only his thumb.

Moodiness

Watch your partner when you do not do whatever it is that they are requesting. Do they seem sulky? Do they make you feel bad about what you are doing to the point that you may even concede and change your behaviors to stop a behavior? If you feel as though you are stuck walking on eggshells to please the other person to avoid an argument, you are seeing the first signs that your mind is being controlled and that the other person has been successful. Your behaviors are being changed in response to the other person according to what the other person wants, and that is not healthy or okay in a relationship. You should never be changing who you are in response to someone else, and while communication, compromise, and negotiations are healthy and necessary; sometimes, they do not involve changing your gut reactions to things.

Metacommunication

Metacommunication refers to all of the subtle, typically unnoticed behaviors a person engages in that reveal their mood and set the stage for the interactions. They are small and meant to convey whatever is being felt at the moment. For example, if you ask your partner if they liked a gift you gave them, and they say yes while sighing and not looking at you, you know that you did not actually do a good job in picking out a gift. Often, those who seek to mind control others will use this metacommunication intentionally to add sort of subliminal, unconscious thoughts to the other person's mind.

Controlling behavior

Often, those who are attempting to manipulate you will use controlling behaviors to do so. They will not allow you to do what you want when you want, and they will hold you to strict schedules. They may even start to regulate when you can do things such as eat, sleep, or use the bathroom in an attempt to control your mind and what you are doing. This is unhealthy and inhumane and should not be happening in your relationship. When this is occurring, it is clear that the other person is trying to hijack your mind and has gotten far enough that he is able to influence even your most basic of actions and functions.

CHAPTER 24:

Deception

Deception is another key aspect that comes with dark psychology. Like many other tactics that come with dark psychology, it is sometimes difficult to tell whether one instance of deception is considered dark or not. But before we explore more into this, we need to first understand what deception is all about in our world.

Deception is going to be any word or action that is capable of making someone believe something that is not true. Fraudulently providing evidence for something false, implying falsehood, omitting the truth, and lying are all examples of deception.

Not all types of deception will count as dark psychology. Everyone is going to deceive others to some extent or another they may deceive others because they feel inadequate, because they feel embarrassed, or even as a kindness. For example, some studies have shown that many men are going to lie about their heights. This doesn't mean that they practice dark psychology. In addition, it is common for people to deceive themselves about a range of issues such as their happiness, their ambition, and their health.

Deception is going to become dark any time when it is carried out with an indifferent or negative intention towards the victim. Dark deception is an understanding that the truth is not going to serve the deceptive aims of the deceiver. The deceiver is going to take the truth and either ignore, hide, or change it in favor of a version of events that suits their purpose a little bit better. Those who employ dark deception mean to do it as a way to harm, rather than to help. They want to help out their interests, but they don't care who gets hurt in the process.

Deceptive Tactics

There are many different deceptive tactics that the manipulator is able to use at their disposal. Remember that this deception is the process of hiding information from the victim to reach their overall goals. There are four categories of tactics that fall into deception, and any given deception is likely to involve a blend of each of them, which can make it even harder for the victim to figure out what is going on.

The first deceptive tactic that can be used is lying. This is the first technique that the manipulator is going to choose as soon as they know that the victim is susceptible to lies and has trouble figuring out the truth. This is often because the victim is someone who trusts others. Or the manipulator may have worked on this victim for some time so that they lower their guard. The manipulator is also able to find ways to hide the lies and then explain the discrepancies if the victim starts to notice.

Any deception that occurs with lying is likely to occur in a way that is very subtle and is thought out ahead of time. A deceiver is going to embed their lie into some truthful information. For example, the manipulator would start with a story that is about ninety percent true and ten percent false. Because it sounds legitimate and most of the story can be proven as true, the victim will think the whole story is true.

Implying is another form of deception. Implying is when the manipulator is going to suggest something false is true rather than boldly stating it. If the manipulator wants to deceive a victim about how much money they have, then they could either lie or imply about it. A lie would be something like "Oh I'm a successful guy. I've made a lot of money," even though the manipulator knows this information is not true. But when they simply they are rich, they may say something like "it's so stressful trying to handle things with my accountant. Trying to get my tax bill down takes a lot of my time." The manipulator has acted and spoken in a way that makes the other person think they are wealthy, but they never state it.

Omission is another option for the deceiver. This is a failure to mention something, usually a fact that is pretty important, that is true. Omission doesn't use a falsehood to cover the truth like the other two options. Instead, this one is going to ignore the truth or just leave it out. Often this piece of information is important for the victim to know about to make an informed decision. The manipulator would leave this out to protect themselves and ensure that the victim didn't have all the information.

The Process of Deception

Deception, boiled down, is essentially lying. Whether the truth is only half the truth, or the information is twisted to fit an agenda, it is a lie. But how often do we find ourselves lying? While no one likes to admit that they have lied or lie regularly, is has been found to be a regular part of life.

Bella DePaulo, Ph.D., a psychologist at the University of Virginia, conducted a study in 1996. The study used 147 people ranging between 18 and 71 years of age. Each person was asked to keep a journal of all of the lies that they told during one week. The study had the following findings:

1. Most people lie once to twice a day.

2. Men and Women, equally, lie in a fifth of their social interactions that last more than ten minutes.

3. In one week, both sexes deceive thirty percent of the people they interact with face-to-face.

4. Some relationships attract deception more than others.

While we grow up being taught that lying is bad, and telling the truth is always the best way to go, as adults we don't follow that rule at all. Even some of the most influential professions such as lawyers, accountants, and politicians lie and deceive on a regular, or even daily, basis. Oftentimes, lying keeps you from receiving punishments. For example, if you are late to school, telling them that you overslept will give you detention, but telling there was an accident will usually let you off the hook. For such small insignificant occurrences, we are pressured into lying to not pay unneeded penalties when nothing is changed by our lateness.

DePaulo's study also included breaking down the types of lies, and the types of relationships most affected by them. She found that couples that are dating lie to each other about a third of the time. Most couples lie from the beginning about things like prior relationships and sexual history. Within marriage, the lies go down to about ten percent, and usually about small everyday things. DePaulo stated, "You save your really big lies for the person that you're closest to."

There are other types of lies as well. The small lies we tell others to avoid hurting their feelings. When we tell someone, we like their new haircut or the color of their new magenta shoes. We tell people that they are good people, that their mistakes don't define them, when we know they often do in our society. People with extroverted personalities tend to lie more, especially when under pressure. We also, when facing mental health issues such as depression, we tend to lie to ourselves. Those lies can go either way. We can deceive ourselves into thinking everything is fine, or we can further dwell in our pits of self-loathing, creating lies about ourselves that drag us down further.

Ways to Spot Deceptions

If you really want to know how to be an effective liar, the answers are all over the place. First, sit and think about a time you have been lied to, but the liar was terrible. Think about the things that were dead giveaways to you. It might have been body language, it might have been their inability to repeat the lie, it could have been filled with absolutely ridiculous information that anyone would have known was a lie. Whatever it is, take note of that. Those are things you do not want to make the mistake of doing. Beyond knowing what not to do, there are several things you want to make sure you always have in line before lying.

Reasoning is Everything

By reasoning, we don't mean your motive. Reasoning means, is it worth it? Pathological liars have a mental condition that triggers something in their brains that is almost a reward for telling a lie. Most pathological liars no longer have any idea what they are saying, and whether it is truth or lies. They will lie about anything at any time for no reason. To be good at deception you basically have to be selective. Keep your lies to a minimum. This will not only save you from having to remember all of your lies, but it will also create a persona of trustworthiness, so when you do lie, no one will question it. Pick the best times to lie, the times you will get the most out of it.

Have Your Story All Laid Out

There is nothing worse than telling a lie and then having someone ask questions, especially when you don't have the entire story and all the details laid out ahead of time. Making spur of the moment decisions on your stories can often lead you down a bad path. Things don't line up, timelines are off, and lies don't seem to fit together. On top of that, all of the lies you told spur of the moment now have to become cemented into your mind. You have to remember what story you told. To have a fluid deception, you have to layout your story from the beginning to the end. Look at it from an outside perspective and think about all the questions that could be asked. Integrate that information into your mind and then test it for inaccuracies. Compare it to any proof that might be brought forward.

Create a Lie That Is Not Completely a Lie

There are always some truths to lies. One way to get around getting caught in a lie is to tell the truth but leave it short storied. Allow the other person to draw conclusions based on how your lie is told. Give a false impression when you tell your truth, one that pushes the other person in the direction that you want to see them go. Creating a lie from truth will also help to avoid questions, which can significantly increase your ability to successfully carry out your venture.

Really Know the Person You Are Lying To

As is with manipulation, deception works so much better if you are able to tell your lie to a person that you know well. You can incorporate a personal touch that uses emotions, experiences, and thoughts that you are aware that a person has. This will automatically help the other person take your statement as truth without overthinking it. When it is something foreign to the person, they will oftentimes begin to question things, search for answers, and ask a lot of questions. All of these things can lead to your lie being found out.

CHAPTER 25:

Reverse Psychology

This is a strategy that is used by people to get what they want by asking or demanding what they do not want. Scientists use another term: self-anti-conformity because your demand goes against what you want.

Another way that psychologists explain reverse psychology is through the term reactance. It is referring to the uncomfortable feeling that people get when they feel that their freedom has been threatened. The normal way to respond to that threat is to the opposite of what has been demanded of you. It's the going against authority aspect.

Reverse Psychology

Reverse psychology is prevalent in many different types of professions because it can help people get what they want, and it can be productive, as well as successful if executed right. For instance, some techniques in sales are based on this very principle, such as the Door in the Face technique. We have all fallen victim to this. Let's say that you are in a used car lot trying to buy a car. The salesman gives you this outlandish price that you would never consider paying. You want to buy the car, but you do not want to pay that much. So, you make a counteroffer for less. This is exactly what the salesman wants. You get the smaller price and the salesman makes the sale, which was his goal in the first place - putting you in a car.

The tactic can also be used in marketing. Here is an example of a store that sells high-quality merchandise. Most of the time, when we go shopping, we see advertisements and the name of the store on the outside of the store. We know where we are going. Well, what if the high-end store has no signs or ads on the outside of the store. It just looks like a regular building. You would have to know where the store was or have been there before to know that they did sell clothes. We all know that this indicates that the retailer is not trying to sell to just anyone. This enhances the mystery of the place and it makes it an exclusive venue. Those who do not want to be excluded or those who are comfortable with the exclusivity will want to buy from the store.

This is a tactic that can be used for good as well. For instance, a parent might use it to get their kid to eat their broccoli. We all know the story; the parent tells the kid to eat their vegetables because they are good for them. But the kid doesn't like them and won't eat them. It is like a constant battle. So, what does the parent do? They use this tactic by getting the kid to want to eat them. How do you they do that? Haven't you ever bought some sweets that you didn't want the kids to eat? You put them in the fridge and tell the kids that those belong to you and not to touch them? What happens? The kid finds a way to eat sweets because they can't have them. They're yours. Why not try that tactic with the broccoli? See how fast the kid jumps on those because they can't have them. We always want what we can't have.

So, does reverse psychology work? That depends on the people involved. First, the victim has to believe that the culprit wants them to do something before they react to their demands and do quite the opposite. And, if they are aware that you are using this tactic on them, then it is never going to work. But just like persuasion, manipulation, and deception, some people are more susceptible to reverse psychology than others.

Who are Victims of Reverse Psychology?

Anyone can fall for any of these tactics because no one is safe from those who will do whatever it takes to get what they want from others. With this being said, those personalities who are more relaxed and laid back don't usually fall for reverse psychology techniques.

So, who does fall more easily for reverse psychology tactics?

Those personalities that are more irritable, stubborn, and overly emotional will find that they fall for these tactics easier than others. Children are more susceptible as well because the cognitive parts of their brains have not fully developed yet. They might not perceive social cues that others can because they are less aware of what is going on. As they get older into their teen years, they might be able to sense what is going on, but they are also at the time in their lives where they are trying to be more independent. However, they do still have a strong urge to fight against authority and might do the opposite of what is asked of them just despite of that.

How to Use Reverse Psychology

It might sound simple, demand the opposite of what you want. However, here are some steps for you, just in case.

Your victim needs to have at least heard of both options.

Argue against the option that you want

Use nonverbal communication to back up what you are saying because it will make your case stronger.

Reverse psychology can be dangerous—especially if the victim finds out what you are doing, and if the motives behind it are wrong. With that being said, it can be used for good—as shown above in the parent example. If you decide that you are going to use it, you should be careful and now what you are doing first, as well as knowing the consequences of using the strategy. Sometimes a more clear, concise and direct approach could be better.

You probably have a passing understanding of reverse psychology, namely that it is telling a person to do one thing, so they do another. Well, it does run deeper than that, which seems to imply that people make decisions on a binary. This is not the case normally. One of the most brilliant things about reverse psychology is that, when deployed correctly, it is, itself, the impetus for limiting another's thought to a "yes or no" question. Say a skilled dark psychology practitioner decides he or she wants his or her friend to come along to the beach, but he or she knows that that friend hates going outside. To make that friend come along, he or she says, as if a normal statement, "You probably don't want to go. You're not really into fun like that." In that scenario, the dark psychologist is using reverse psychology, clearly, but what he or she is also doing is turning the question of whether or not to go to the beach into a question of whether or not that friend is fun. So, of course, the friend decides to go to the beach! Hopefully, you're starting to get a picture of the varieties and permutations of manipulation as they function on people in the world. From the above, you should also get the idea that, while there are distinct words for different kinds of manipulation, ultimately, they blend and can be used in tandem with one another. There is no reason why an attempt at semantic manipulation can't be employed along with reverse psychology, perhaps as a means of framing the yes/no dichotomy through which the target of the manipulation is meant to think. Likewise, it is impossible to imagine Machiavellianism without covert-aggression, and fairly difficult to imagine the reverse. Taken in reality, in their actual use, these concepts all blend together.

Mind Tricks

You have heard of mind games. You had surely played them before and had them played on you. You can use mind games as an effective persuasion tool when you know what to do and when. Numerous techniques are effective, and they are not that difficult to learn. This means that once you know what they are, you can start utilizing mind games right away to start getting what you want.

Kick Me

This likely reminded you of that game when you were a kid where you put a sign on someone's back that read "kick me." This is similar. You want to make yourself look like someone that deserves pity. Once you get pity from someone, it is easier to get them to do what you want. You can use this for just about anything in life from getting someone to allow you to apologize to getting a boss to give you a promotion once you get really good at it.

Now That I've Got You

This is a game that you will use when you want to show a person you are winning and better. You can also use it when you are angry and want to justify it. For example, your friend had a party, but he neglected to invite you. So, you decide to host a party the following weekend with the intent to just not invite him. This game basically has you working to one-up another person to get them to give in and give you what you want.

You Made Me Do It

This is another one you used during childhood and you likely did not even realize at the time that it was a type of mind game. This is a game that works to make another person feel guilty while simultaneously absolving you of any responsibility for your actions. For example, you want to be left alone. However, someone comes into the room to ask you a question. As a result, you are startled and drop your beverage. You tell that person that they made you drop your beverage.

CHAPTER 26:

Mind Control and Mind Games

Mind Control

The concept of mind control has existed for as long as psychology has been studied. You have probably overheard a person express their fascination or fear concerning what would happen if there was ever a chance that someone was able to control the minds of others and make them follow his or her commands. Similarly, there have been multiple conspiracy theories about influential people or authorities utilizing their positions to force small groups of people to do certain things. There have even been court cases where the accused people blame "brainwashing" for causing them to commit their crimes. Collectively, these three examples tell us that people understand that mind control is real.

However, the form of mind controls that people seem to define is that which has been portrayed by the movies and media, which unfortunately, is just but the tip of the iceberg. Mind control exists in many forms, and people appear to understand very little about it. It pushes the need for an accurate understanding and description of what exactly is mind control. If we take the words of psychologist Philip Zimbardo, mind control is defined as a process whereby the freedom of action and choice of an individual or a group is compromised by agencies or agents that distort or modify motivation, perception, behavioral and cognitive outcomes. In summary, mind control is a system that disrupts a person or group at their core, that is, the level of their identity (which includes behaviors, decisions, preferences, beliefs, and relationships, to mention but a few) and creates a pseudo personality or pseudo-identity.

Mind Games

One modern incarnation of the mind game is the type used by Jedi's inside of the Star Wars franchise. A Jedi mind trick in the franchise is when an experience Jedi warrior can use the power of the Force to implant suggestions in the minds of weaker willed individuals. As it plays out, the Jedi mind trick looks more like a form of coercive control.

Here too, the dark manipulators of the world would be salivating at the thought of gaining such power. It is not merely because of how effective it is in the franchise, but because such ability implies that the attacker is in a way superior, or more intelligent than the person they are "tricking."

Mind games in real-life work a little different. A mind trick may be a simple stab at the other person where it hurts to get "under their skin" or to strike a nerve with them. The purpose of the mind trick is not to control outright—as in the case with the powers of the Jedi—but to divert frustration, as well as a wide range of other emotions inside the target.

The role that mind games play in dark psychology is more akin to an auxiliary tool for manipulation. A successfully deployed mind trick may soften up an individual for additional attacks. It can also be used to evoke certain behaviors, much like someone poking a pull with a stick to get it inside of its pen. Finally, it can be used as smoke and mirrors to divert attention from the attacker.

Defining the Mind Trick

A Jedi master can beam a supernatural manifestation of the Force into their victims and implant a thought. A dark manipulator has no such recourse. Instead, they need to do it through language. Spoken and written (or texted) word is the primary attack vector of the mind trick, but it can also come in the form of actions taken against the target.

Another term that could easily be used to describe a mind trick is a mind game. Both can be used interchangeably, but the mind game most commonly refers to a more massive campaign or goal that is being carried out through using mind tricks. The mind game becomes the overall strategy, with each mind trick being individual tactics.

A mind trick can be a spoken sentence or command, but it can also be an action. This opens up the possibility of unilateral attacks that don't rely so much on language. Activities like eating someone's lunch at work, giving them a gift for no reason, and using the silent treatment are all examples of mind tricks that don't require an attacker to utter words.

Mind Tricks in Human Relations

People play mind tricks on each other all the time. It has come to be expected in relationships, at least to some degree. Usually, they result in mind tricks because there is some issue in the relationship that they are too squeamish about addressing and instead prefer to use side-channel attacks.

Mind tricks are also used offensively to break an opponent from afar. Mind tricks take the form of harassment if the objective is to disorient someone or to push them "off their game." Any competitive pursuit will have a specific element of mind trickery going on. This is evident at just about any significant televised fight weigh-in or briefing. The two fighters or boxers are already at each other's throats without even being in the ring.

A mind trick directed at someone else can either be aggressive or passive-aggressive. Both have their unique set of applications, their strengths, and their weaknesses. Overt aggression can be used in fear-based tactics to get someone to back down. Passive-aggression can be used to annoy somebody, often without them being able to retaliate.

The effectiveness of the mind trick will vary in the context of the situation. And it applies as well in the psychological makeup of the target. If the objective is stalwart in all aspects of their psychology, starting a mind game campaign against them might not be wise. On the other hand, someone who is easily excitable, emotional, or hot-heated is more susceptible to mind trickery.

In the Workplace

Office politics is the primary area where mind tricks are used on a near-daily basis. Here, there are protections in a place where one couldn't just muscle their way to the top. Instead, the battle is fought through wits. Even if one has no desire to climb the social ladder, they might want to defend themselves from being mistreated by others.

Be wary of the overly friendly coworker who is suitable to you, but who openly talks smack of other workers behind their back. This is a manipulation technique used by psychopaths and less scrupulous workers to gain your trust. Before long, this trust relationship is elevated, and it will be target who dishes out the dirty work of their manipulator. This is a type of aggressive mind trick.

Spreading rumors and badmouthing others are some of the basics of mind games in office politics. A single person spreading discord from inside the organization can take down entire teams one by one. There will almost always be at least one bad apple in a large workplace.

Reverse badmouthing is just as bad. This is what happens when a coworker approaches you and indirectly convinces you to badmouth someone. Usually, by saying something like, "Don't you think X is terrible at making reports?" If you agree with them, they can then go up to X and tell them that you think they are bad at making reports. These people are generally very persuasive, so they are best kept at a distance.

Very often, the terms "office politics" have nothing to do with actual political like behavior. A lot of it means drama in the workplace, in the form of badmouthing and spreading rumors. Those who are targeted may be skipped when it comes to hand out promotions, given that their attackers were successful in their efforts to discredit them.

Passive Aggression and Sabotage in the Workplace

Remember that the goal of office politics is to gain promotions and pay raises while at the same time excluding others from getting them. They may also determine who gets to work on what and gets to offload their "dirty" or undesirable work to another employee. Like general managers and bosses, the people who make decisions are never to be treated as friends.

Passive-aggression can be "accidentally" misplacing employees' work orders, causing them to have to resubmit it and fall behind everyone else. Very rarely will passive-aggression come in the form of purposeful inefficiency unless it is coming from the top. A company's seniority can afford to slack off during work purposely, but if the lower employees do it, they can be fired in time.

Sabotage is pretty straight forward and is a risky option because if caught, the consequences are severe. But if executed well (perhaps with help from an underling or a "minion" who the attacker has manipulating into doing their bidding) then the sabotage can get employees fired, or even seriously injured. The most common targets for destruction are machinery and computer systems.

Aggression in the Workplace

Aggression ins office politics most commonly comes in the form of badmouthing, but may also be through one-upmanship, or continually being in a competitive state where one must be superior to the other. One-upmanship is interesting because it doesn't always reflect some political goal. It may only be a projection of insecurity.

An attacker who uses one-upmanship is trying to get into the head of their target. The goal may be to affect their self-esteem or to belittle their achievements. An attacker can also lure someone into a game of one-upmanship to exploit insecurity. For example, a coworker continually finds the need to be better than others may be projecting, while the coworker who does it selectively is looking to fulfill an objective.

Mind Games in Interpersonal Relationships

Sometimes in romantic and platonic relationships alike, there is the tendency to play similar games. When it comes to romance, an attacker may exhibit pettiness or overly controlling behavior to get a reaction from their partner. Most of the time, this comes under the context of emotional manipulation and abuse.

For example, an attacker may try to wage a jealousy campaign by purposely flirting with other people while in the earshot of their partner. They might have zero intentions of getting involved with someone else, but they want to see how the partner behaves in response. There is a power relationship here where the attacker is clearly in control of the other.

Other manipulations may be gaslighting based, again, for emotional manipulation. Something common in romantic relationships and familiar ones is the charge of not receiving enough emotional support. Commonly found in single parents, or parents with partners that work away from home, emotional support may be used to gaslight children of narcissistic parents.

Emotional incest happens when a parent demands that their children give them the same sort of emotional support one would typically expect from a spouse. It can be particularly damaging to the child's self-esteem and lead to behavioral problems down the road, just like common incest might do.

A lack of emotional support (or a perceived lack) in romantic relationships opens up the floodgates for a particularly nasty breed of gaslighting where the targeted partner is made to feel that they are not good enough.

CHAPTER 27:

Character Traits of Manipulators

Being able to tell if someone is taking advantage of you or manipulating you is one of the most important survival skills that you need today. Everyone around you has their interests and agendas, but it's crucial to be able to tell when those agendas are malicious or likely to cause you unintended harm.

Manipulators have many identifiable behavioral and character traits. With the information you learn here, you will be able to tell whether or not a person is a manipulator, whether or not his/her brand of manipulation is meant to cause you harm, and what kind of manipulator he/she is.

Here are the character and behavioral traits that you ought to look out for if you suspect that someone is a manipulator.

Lying by the commission and lying by omission

A lie of commission is what's called a "classic lie." When someone says something that they know is not factual, then that is a lie of commission. In other words, a lie of commission is something that is simply untrue. It involves purposefully telling someone something with the intention of deceiving them. It is extremely deliberate, and its main purpose is to gain a personal advantage in a given situation.

Lying by the commission isn't always done with malicious intent, but people who are more comfortable telling outright lies are more likely to be manipulators. Everyone lies. Even seemingly innocent young children will tell a lie of commission to get out of trouble; a child with jam on his face will deny touching it because he is trying to evade the consequences of telling the truth, not because he is malicious.

Denial

When you say that someone is in denial, it often means that they are having a difficult time accepting reality. However, denial takes on a whole deferent meaning where manipulators are concerned. Manipulators use denial to feign innocence when they know full well that they have done something wrong.

Manipulators use denial to control other people's impressions of who they are and interpretations of the things they did. Some manipulators are so good when it comes to using denial that they are able to get people to start second-guessing themselves. Denial is a crucial behavioral trait in predicting whether or not a person is likely to gaslight you. If in the early stages of a relationship, your partner blatantly denies something you both know to be true, you can rest assured that he is the kind of person who will be gaslighting you for years to come.

Rationalization

Rationalization is similar to making excuses. Manipulative people are very skilled when it comes to concocting narratives that justify the way they treat other people. When you confront a manipulator, even with the most damning accusation, he will come up with a well-thought-out and rather convincing explanation for his actions. When ordinary people rationalize or make excuses for their actions, you get the sense that even though they are trying to assuage their conscience, they feel guilty and they are even apologetic about what they have done. However, when manipulators rationalize their actions, they are trying to manage the way you perceive them, and they feel justified in their actions.

Minimization

Minimization involves trivializing a person's emotions or actions for manipulation. It often combines elements of denial and rationalization; it's somewhere in between those two characteristics. When a manipulative person can't completely deny something, and he can't completely rationalize it either, he will settle for minimizing it.

Manipulators downplay the significance of certain events or emotions all the time. The emotions or actions that they downplay could either be yours, theirs, or those of a third party, as long as it serves their purposes.

If you have accomplished something significant, a manipulative person may try to belittle or to discount that achievement. A narcissistic person may try to make your contribution to a team effort seem like its "no big deal," even if it was pivotal to the success of a project you are working on together.

In a relationship, your partner may trivialize your emotions and make them seem insignificant. If you react emotionally to something they have done or said, they may say that you are too sensitive, and you are making a big deal out of nothing, or that you are immature. Both male and female manipulators can have this character trait. A man could say that a woman is a "drama queen" for "overreacting" and a woman could accuse a man of being "unmanly" for expressing strong emotions.

Minimization often works on people because it makes them feel self-conscious. If someone accuses you of blowing things out of proportion, you are likely to take a step back to see if you are overreacting.

Diversion and Evasion

Evasion and diversion are used by manipulators to keep the spotlight away from their manipulative behavior. These tactics also help them to avoid being exposed for who they are, and they keep them from having to take responsibility for what they are doing.

Evasion involves providing rambling or irrelevant feedback in a situation that demands direct responses. When manipulative people are asked direct questions, they start talking about vaguely related things that aren't even relevant to the conversation.

A person who uses evasion will try to avoid giving a straight answer to a question that you have asked them. On the other hand, a person who uses diversion will change the topic or steer the conversation in a whole other direction. Diversion involves avoiding a topic by bringing up a different topic, especially one that is likely to spark outrage.

Covert intimidation and guilt-tripping

Covert intimidation and guilt-tripping use the same underlying principle; they prey on a person's emotions. Covert intimidation preys on fear, while guilt-tripping preys on compassion. People who use these techniques have what psychologists refer to as covert-aggressive personalities. They are "wolves in sheep's clothing." They present one face to the world, while deep within, they are very malicious people.

Covert intimidation involves threatening victims in subtle ways. It can be used by people who are close to you if they understand your fears or desires. Your boss could use covert intimidation to get you to do his bidding at work. If he knows that you are working towards a promotion, he could ask you to do him certain favors, and then imply that your promotion is dependent on that favor. He may not say it directly, but it's all going to be in the subtext.

Shaming

Shame refers to the uncomfortable feeling of distress or humiliation, which results when we are conscious of certain behavior that we consider to be wrong or foolish. The thing to understand about shame is that it's a social construct, and it's highly subjective.

You'd feel shame if the wind blew up your skirt in a public place, but there are remote tribes of people and even communes in Western societies where people walk around naked. The point is that most shameful things are only shameful because we perceive them as such. Manipulators can use shame against you by either convincing you to be ashamed of something that you weren't, or by revealing (or threatening to reveal) your secrets to people who revere you.

Vilifying the Victim

Manipulators, especially Machiavellians, tend to be smart and devious, so they can easily find ways to vilify their victims. There are two ways that this can happen; they can either convince other people that the victim is the real aggressor, or they can convince the victim that he/she is the one who did something wrong. Vilifying the victim involves using several tactics, including rationalizing, and gaslighting.

People who vilify victims try to justify their actions by making it seem as though the victims are the "bad guys." For example, someone who cheats on his spouse may explain his behavior away by telling people that his spouse is a "bitch," or she is "frigid" and "controlling." The manipulator is trying to rationalize his actions here by creating the impression that whatever he may have done, the person he did it too, had it coming, and she probably deserved worse.

Seduction

Seduction is an integral part of romance and courtship, but it can also be a very effective manipulation tactic if a person has malicious intentions. We all want to be liked and to be valued, so when someone says flattering things about us, we are likely to believe them. Seduction is one of the first manipulation techniques that most manipulators will deploy when they meet you for the first time. As we have mentioned several times already, manipulation techniques tend to be more effective when the manipulator and the victim have some sort of emotional connection; seduction is the first step towards establishing that connection.

STEVE BROOKS

CHAPTER 28:

The Signs of a Manipulative Person and How to Spot Them.

1) They would try to cripple your self-confidence: These kinds of people would try and lower your self-confidence so that it becomes easier for them to have more power on you, which would make it easier for them to take advantage of you. They would always strive to make you feel that they have many more qualities than you so that you feel inferior to them. They would always try to find things that you are not confident about or you are not that great at so that they can comment on it and make you feel demotivated. These people might be your friend, family member, office colleague or your partner. All these things can make you sad and negative about yourself. So, in the future, when you come across anyone like this, make sure that you stay away from them and eradicate negative vibes from your life.

2) Pass the Blame: This is another thing which they are very good at—passing the blame on you. It might not be your fault and you would have done nothing but they would try to make you realize that it was your fault and make you feel guilty and bad about the situation. Another thing which they do is make you feel guilty about you performing better than them or leading a better life than them, which you have no control on. It might also create a situation when you start doubting yourself but beware and confident and start being ignorant towards such people.

3) Do not accept blame: What they do is not accepting their fault, which means do not take the blame on them. Even when it would not be your fault, they would look upon you as a defaulter and would not accept their fault. They would try to convince you that it was your fault so that you become weak and they can take advantage of the situation. Especially in a relationship, few partners would always

try to prove that it is your fault, not theirs. This might put you in stress as the other person always wants to be in a winning situation. If you feel stressed and anxious then you should always try to talk or come out of the relationship or the workplace.

4) Try to change the topic: This is another imperative thing to remember. A manipulative person would try to change the subject where he thinks that he/she is wrong. They only care about themselves and would try to avoid such topics to have the power on you. When they get to know that they will have to answer a lot of questions or to hide the truth they will change the topic and start discussing points where it is your fault, just to take charge of the discussion. You might feel bad and helpless about it but remember and learn to stick to your point and make them realize that you are not weak and know how to prove your point.

5) Rationalizing their behavior: They very well know how to act in a different kind of situation and take charge of it. Even when their behavior was rude and unacceptable, they would make you realize that it was fine and need of the hour. They know how to justify their behavior and insist you to realize that it was fine. They know how to prove them right in all sorts of instances.

I am pretty much sure that these points must have given you heads on about the characteristics of a manipulator. But this is not enough, there are other signs which you need to be alert of, let's take a glance at them in specific aspect:

1) Criticizing in public: this is a major characteristic of a manipulator, they target the victim in public and criticize them openly. This is the best way according to them to make you feel embarrassed in front of everyone and feel supreme. They would never offer any help to you or provide any solution instead they would always criticize in front of others and remind you of your flaws. They just need to show their importance and want to be in good books of others. To avoid this, you should maintain a distance with them or change the subject if they start talking about you.

2) Make you feel comfortable: these people are smart enough to realize where you can open up and discuss the personal matters or office grudges. They would try and take you to your favorite restaurants, cafes, parks, etc. Where you feel more comfortable and secure so that they can be more dominant on you and influence to take out the thoughts and discuss the issues in a relaxed manner. So, ensure that you meet these kinds of people only in business meetings or in a neutral setting.

3) Push you to be the first one: manipulators know how to start the conversation. They would always want you to share your views, thoughts, and points first so that they know about your drawbacks and strengths first. They always try to assess you so that they can dominate you or make you feel low when the time comes. This is the easiest method for them as you tell them about your weakness, which becomes their strength. If people like this ask your views, always talk to them in a general context and do not share your points, till the time they tell their points.

4) Administrative Hindrances: being manipulators, they very well know how to influence people and use them against you. They would try to exploit administrative hindrances just to make your work slow so that you do not complete your project on time. Not only this, but they would also try to hide essential facts and findings from you so that you may not use it. In cases like this, you should always try to find different ways of taking out the important information.

5) Misinterpreting the truth: lying is the easiest thing for a manipulator, but they are even smarter. They would not lie to you; instead, they would misinterpret the truth by not giving you the complete information, exaggerating or intentionally not telling you the essential facts. So, whenever you have any doubts about information, you should always double-check so that you have the correct data and facts.

CHAPTER 29:

Favorite Victims of Manipulation

There are situations where any one of us could find ourselves being easily persuaded. Every day we are bombarded with advertisements, all urging us to buy their wares. Extolling the virtues of one product over another. Building a discourse where not buying certain goods is almost seen as unthinkable, out of sync with the zeitgeist.

1. Sales Tactics

This is the obvious example of such a situation. It seems to be the acceptable face of social manipulation. Commercial products always seem to carry some type of manipulative tactic. All in aid of getting the public to buy the goods. The worse of it is that we are aware of the scheming maneuvers, and yet we still fall prey to them.

When marketing is done well, it works. That's why advertising is a multi-million-dollar enterprise. Companies do not have huge advertising budgets for no reason. For example, how often do we succumb to their, "Buy One Get One Free" offers or half-price sales? (5a). They seem like a real bargain, saving our hard-earned bucks. Often, we are coerced into buying products we might not even need or ever wanted in the first place. The offer tempts us with generous words, such as "Free" or "Reduced." Yet, it is a marketing ploy to manipulate customers to empty their purses and wallets. It even has its acronym, known as BOGOF. Customers are seduced by attractive false pretenses. Are the stores or companies really being kind in giving us free products? How can they afford that? The truth of it is that they are not giving anything away for free.

2. Working Environment

Anyone who is vulnerable is a potential target of a manipulator. It is not always the obvious people that can get ensnared. Already we have learned that such a character will initially behave with impeccable manners. This false front is performed to impress and gain trust. If you do not know this person already, it may be hard to recognize that you have become their target. That is until it is too late. On a personal front, this type of relationship can occur at work, or even in intimate relationships.

Consider your place of work. Do you have a boss that makes your life a misery by demanding work at higher and quicker levels constantly? Browbeating you to meet impossible targets. Warning you of a reduction in your salary or canceling any bonuses. Could even threaten to sack you. At that point, you become trapped. This person knows we all have responsibilities, such as mortgages or rents and families to support. We cannot walk away. In such a situation, any of us could become this vulnerable person. This is the victim of a controlling manipulator.

Here are some typical manipulative tactics of this character. See if any of these sounds familiar in your current work situation. "Careerizma" is a career website that provides useful guidance and resources.

- Fake Praise

The boss said they liked your idea and think you're a great person, but then they go with someone else's idea instead. What was the point of the pretense in the first place? Like many manipulators, they like the feeling of control. By leading you astray, it gives them a sense of power over you. This is about building a person's confidence up with false praise and then crushing them. At this point, they may belittle you or devalue your work. Diving in with the kill to make you feel worthless. Now they have you like a puppet under their control.

- Stealing the credit of your talents

Using you to write up their reports, then taking all the credit for it. This is a classic manipulative strategy. They tell you that you're perfect for the job. Show you how they trust in you as the best person to get the job done. All that encouragement was a complete front for their real plans. Once the job is completed, they claim any praise for themselves. Now you are left on the sideline, feeling well and truly exasperated. Should you question them about it, they'll claim your report was a total mess. It's better now because they spent all morning putting it right.

- Embarrassing you

Putting people down, in front of others, makes these characters feel powerful. Say that you put forward an idea, they may laugh and ridicule the very thought of it. After a while, you no longer believe in it yourself. Were you to confront them about their behavior, they' would come back at you with sarcasm, "Hell, man, can't you take a joke?" Cruel jokes and sarcasm, all will be done at your expense.

- Blame shifting

Whatever has gone wrong is everyone else's fault, but theirs. Never would they admit up to their shortcomings and mistakes. Not only that, but they'll often deny any negative things they might have done. Should you attempt to explain the wrong they did, they would only claim that your version of events is wrong. Typically, they will say, 'I don't normally behave like that, only when I'm around you." This is what Freud called projection. They are projecting their misdemeanors onto someone else.

3. Personal Relationships

This is a terrible situation to find yourself in. Being in a relationship whereby your supposedly loving partner keeps you on a leash. When someone wants to control everything that you do, it can become a dangerous situation to find yourself in. This type of partner might tell you it's for your good. They are keeping you safe, under their protective wing. Yet, being on the other end of such treatment does not feel safe. It is a suffocating experience that comes with other serious problems, such as sexual, physical and mental abuse.

How to Identify Manipulators

It should be noted that manipulation does not work for the manipulators alone and no one, either the victim of manipulation or the manipulator, gets any real profits. Whether you manipulate or get manipulated, the result is a loss. Before getting to know how to identify and resist manipulators, you need to know how manipulation negatively affects the manipulator and the victim.

Powerlessness: it is due to the helplessness feeling that manipulators opt for manipulation. It is due to impotence that a victim gives in to the manipulator's trickery.

Inadequacy: manipulators feel that they lack some qualities possessed by other people and in the pursuit of such characteristics, they manipulate those they believe possess these qualities. Once manipulated, a victim feels stupid and regrets if only they had acted smarter to outwit the manipulator.

Victimization: manipulators believe that life has victimized them by not being fair to them or giving them what they deserve. A manipulation victim also feels victimized when they fail to do what the manipulator demands. Anger and Frustration: manipulators are always frustrated when their targets turn down their demands or requests. The victims also feel bad when doing what the manipulator asks them to do, especially if it is forced manipulation. If you allow yourself to be manipulated, you sacrifice your rights to self-determination, self-esteem, finances, energy, and even your principles. If you manage others as well, you surrender your self-respect and self-reliance when you try to use others to benefit yourself. Either successful or not after manipulating others, there is the emotionally immature feeling that always haunts a manipulator.

How then should you resist a manipulator, persuader or a cult leader?

CHAPTER 30:

How to Protect Yourself Against Emotional Predator

The power of manipulation lies in its hiddenness. One can be manipulating us without us having the least suspicion that something unwanted is going on. Today in our modern western world we are very much aware of the value and benefits of human freedom. Yet, we so easily fall under the influence of manipulators. How come that we so often give up on our rational capacities and our free will? Why we so slow or even incapable of realizing what is going on while our best or vital interests are at stake?

Four Basic Acts

There are four essential acts we should be aware of to protect ourselves from the subtle influences:

1. The power of the touch

A gesture as simple as tapping someone's shoulder or a gentle caress can produce a strong emotional impact on us that will influence our decisions. This influence happens unconsciously. The touch can, in an extremely direct and simple manner, open us to suggestion.

2. The impact of the speed of speech

The received information for which we don't have enough time to process all its significance and consequences can under certain circumstances of pressure make us take rush decisions. By speeding up his speech the manipulator makes an artificial sense of pressure making us more easily choose the first thing that comes to our mind – hopefully, the idea that he suggested. During this subtle process, many of us will think that we were in full possession of our cognitive capacities and of the power of our free will.

3. The influence of the field-of-view

By placing an object of his choice in the center of our field-of-view or by moving it slightly closer to us, the manipulator makes us perceive its importance and remember it. This simple but effective gesture leads us to often choose that precise object. Similarly, we often chose what has first been offered to us.

4. The effect of the precise questions in suggesting ideas

By asking the adequate questions, the manipulator can lead us to make decisions for which we will be convinced that they are our ideas. These could be questions like "What do you think the benefits would be?" or "Why do you consider it a good choice?" or again "Isn't he forbidding you to do everything you like?" Such questions tend to narrow the range of facts we are taking into consideration and to focus only on what has been suggested to us. When we find ourselves in such situation, we either chose to defend opposite ideas, or we opt for the affirmation of what we have been told. In both cases, our mind operates within the limit determined by the manipulator who has posed the question, just as he has intended.

Tactics That Protect Us Against Misuse of Reciprocation

The difficulty with the social rule of reciprocation is in its commonness and the force it exercises upon us when we already feel obliged to reciprocate. The wise thing would, therefore, be simply to prevent it from happening. Easy to say, but very often it is difficult or even impossible not to enter into this game, which dictates its proper set of rules. Many of us will just not know how to refuse a gentle offer of favor or a gift.

The first thing to pay attention to is whether the offer is honest or it is an attempt of using the reciprocity in view of selfish interests. It would not be the most prudent to simply assume the worst. Such negative attitude could become a hindrance in experiencing some of the most beautiful moments of human life: the gestures are made with gratuity. What one could do is to try to be as much as possible realistic in dealing with the offers of other people, and with the processes of the rule of reciprocity they engage us in. During the process, we realize that the person offering us gifts was lacking honesty, there is nothing that obliges us to reciprocate such action. The rule of reciprocity is not meant for the tricks played on us. We are free from the obligation to reciprocate a favor when there is no actual favor to reciprocate for. The reciprocity is an act of justice, and it would be unjust to encourage somebody's injustice. That does not mean either that we become authorized to answer with injustice for injustice. Still, with proper intention, one can use his newly acquired position of power to make the other person taste some of the effects of exploitation he had intended for us.

Practical Tips to Deal with Manipulative People

Being a manipulation expert is as much about spotting manipulation and deception in others as it is about leading others to do what you want them to.

Do you want to safeguard yourself from manipulation daily?

Do you want to prevent people from taking advantage of you for fulfilling their own selfish goals?

Do you want to be able to sniff manipulation from miles away?

Here are 10 brilliant strategies to protect yourself from manipulation.

1. Ignore Their Words and Actions

Manipulators almost always go after shaking people's confidence and making them insecure to get them to do what they (the manipulators) want. They will do their best to plant seeds of apprehension and self-doubt. There is a tendency to make the victim believe that the manipulator's opinion is actually the truth or fact. Rather than wanting to help you, they are more interested in trying to control you.

The best strategy to deal with these negative manipulators is to ignore them rather than trying to argue with them or correct them. This allows them to set an even deeper trap for you. Do not fall for their conflict or confrontation bet. Simply bypass them, without revealing your emotions. Do not let them see the emotions that make you tick. Once they gain a good understanding of your emotional triggers, they will sneakily use it for influencing your thoughts, behavior, and decisions.

Some people are difficult to delete from our lifes immediately. Think—boss, neighbor, family member, etc. Just pretend to listen to what they are saying, agree with it and eventually do exactly what you want.

2. Do not Compromise

Guilt is one of the most insidious tools used by manipulators to get their victims to do what they want. Of course, it can be used positively to influence a person too, but in negative manipulation, its usage can spell disaster for the victim.

Manipulators induce a feeling of guilt in their victims for their past mistakes, choices, and failures. They will make your guilt about being self-assured and self-confident. Each time you experience happiness, they will make you feel bad about it. Their objective is to never make you feel good about yourself or happy.

They'll sow seeds of self-doubt about your true worth, persona, and abilities. Do not get knocked off balance or feel guilty they start blaming you. Do not doubt your self-worth or abilities. Never believe that you do not deserve happiness or to feel wonderful about yourself. Take pride in who you are and your accomplishments. Build a strong sense of self-esteem and confidence. Do not compromise on your happiness or your feelings about yourself.

3. Do not Fit In, Stand Out

It isn't funny how many people make them susceptible to manipulation by trying hard to fit in. Manipulative people count on your desire to want to fit in to push their agenda. They lead you to believe that everyone does what they want you to do and that those who do not conform are abnormal. That is the only way to control your decisions and behavior.

Give up the notion of trying to fit in, and encourage the idea of standing out among the rest. Be different from other folks. Focus on reinventing yourself, laying your own rules (for what is good for you and others) and avoid cowing down to peer pressure.

4. Stop Seeking Permission

We've been conditioned to ask for permission since childhood, right from when we wanted to be fed as a baby to when we wanted to visit the bathroom in school to waiting for our turn to talk in the boardroom. The result of this conditioning is that people seldom do anything without seeking permission.

There is an excessive focus on being polite and making things comfortable for others. Manipulative people want their victims to live by their own self-drafted, imaginary rules or values. The underlying idea is you are not free to take any decision without consultation. Be brave and give up this sense of confinement. You have the power to change your life without the need to live by someone else's self-fulfilling rules.

5. Do not be a Baby

If you are tricked once, it isn't your fault. However, if you are tricked 15 times, there's something wrong with you. Do not let people take advantage of you by being everyone's favorite punching bag. Have the courage to stand up to manipulators and say a firm no when you know they are taking advantage of you. Stop whining about other people are taking advantage of you, and take complete control of your life.

Victims of manipulation almost always complain about how people use them. No one can take advantage of you without your consent. You are indeed responsible for your actions and their outcome. If someone has used sneaky tricks to outwit you, it is your fault. Learn from past blunders and stop trusting slippery people again and again. Move away from them. Focus on surrounding yourself with positive, constructive, inspiring and like-minded folks who make you feel good about yourself.

6. Have a Clear Sense of Purpose

When you do not know what you want, you'll be more prone to do whatever everyone else wants. You'll be easily tricked into doing what other people want you to do without a firm goal or objective in life. People who lack a clear purpose or aim tend to function or go through life more mechanically. There is little logic in their actions or decisions. They will be more prone to experiencing a growing sense of emptiness in them that will craftily be filled by a manipulator.

This lack of objective or constructive activities makes the manipulator feel empowered enough to easily distract you or draw you to their agenda.

Have a higher purpose in life. It can be anything from taking up a cause for the betterment of the community to traveling around the world to rising in your professional life. Do not allow manipulators an opportunity to prey on your sense of purposelessness. When you are clear about where you are headed, it is difficult to stop you or get you to change tracks.

Conclusion

Persuasion, manipulation, naked influence, and the art of reading people's minds are concepts that will aid you in getting the result you want to see. They all have some basic differences between them, but the similarity between them is that they are all a form of human communication. As humans, we are easily changed by what we see and listen to each day. These three concepts all involve getting another person or people to do what you want. In this book, I talked about their meaning, some modern-day examples of how they are used, and techniques you can use to successfully put them in good use.

The power of persuasion is a skill that can be obtained effectively; however, one should be prepared for acing these techniques. The training can again be unmistakable as the sales division of an organization will prepare their workers with such persuasion techniques which are abstract, and its fundamental point would be training the executives to sell the specific item, which is being fabricated by the organization.

The Power of persuasion techniques is outstanding when executed with flawlessness. These are techniques that one can't resist the opportunity to ace it if the person in question is functioning as a sales executive. The persuasion technique training isn't simple training to finish. It requires a great deal of exertion and genuinely refined nature of correspondence skill, which will empower an executive to cooperate openly and thoughtfully with his customers. The power of persuasion can likewise be obtained by another procedure called the natural training process. In this training, the learners are encouraged the craft of perusing the customer's mind simply. When they read the customers' minds with little safety buffer, they will be effectively addressing them with words that they might want to hear and afterward the student would, in the end, influence him to purchase the item. The Power of persuasion techniques must be recognized by each one of those fruitful sales executives who have made it to the title pages of the business magazines. They are there simply because they have a place with the class of those additional normal people who with their instinct, appearance, and correspondence have controlled the mind and basic leadership of thousands of customers. They have effectively utilized their skills to turn the choice of a customer to their benefit and have restored the organization an intensely stacked income box. The mystery equation of the Power of persuasion techniques is taken cover behind the relationship that the sales individual develops with his customer. With relationship comes the condition of trust, and the minute you win the trust of your customer, the activity is done, selling an item is close to a cake stroll from that point on.

The skill that one needs to obtain to hone his Power of persuasion is the delicate skill to banter. It is most imperative to strike a significant discussion before you present yourself or so far as that is concerned about your motivation. It is far and away superior if you keep your aims imperceptible at the earliest reference point. When you see that you are controlling the progression of the discussion, you should affability completely incorporate your motivation and expand upon the item and feature the points of interest the customer may have if he claims one.

The powers of persuasion are the required skills that essentially run the sales division of any corporate foundation. In this manner, the impact of the powers of persuasion technique rises above the customer and the purchaser and in the far end, chooses the fortune of the basic man.